First of the
Summer Wine

First of the Summer Wine

George Hirst, Schofield Haigh,
Wilfred Rhodes and the Gentle
Heart of Yorkshire Cricket

Harry Pearson

**SIMON &
SCHUSTER**

London · New York · Sydney · Toronto · New Delhi

First published in Great Britain by Simon & Schuster UK Ltd, 2022

1 3 5 7 9 10 8 6 4 2

Simon & Schuster UK Ltd
1st Floor
222 Gray's Inn Road
London WC1X 8HB

www.simonandschuster.co.uk
www.simonandschuster.com.au
www.simonandschuster.co.in

Simon & Schuster Australia, Sydney
Simon & Schuster India, New Delhi

A CIP catalogue record for this book
is available from the British Library

Hardback ISBN: 978-1-3985-0152-2
eBook ISBN: 978-1-3985-0153-9

Typeset in Bembo by M Rules
Printed and bound by CPI Group (UK) Ltd, Croydon, CR0 4YY

MIX
Paper from
responsible sources
FSC
www.fsc.org   FSC® C171272

For my father, Tony Pearson,
right-arm tweaker of Windyhill Lane

CONTENTS

Introduction		1
Prelude: The Men in the Postcard		11
1.	The Baby from the Brown Cow	17
2.	The Sunday School Pro	36
3.	The Boy in the Barn	59
4.	The Triumvirate Triumphant	76
5.	Swerve	101
6.	Singles	114
7.	Doubles	143
8.	Titles and Changes	161
9.	Tours and Tragedy	204
10.	Bed and Cricket	215
11.	The Trouble with Mr Toone	228
12.	The Birth of Grim	245
13.	The Fading of the Light	263
14.	On Towards Twilight	274
Statistics		297
Index		325

The North Riding of Yorkshire, 1970

Growing up in a village on the edge of the North Yorkshire Moors in the late '60s and early '70s there were certain sounds that characterised the summer for me. Many will be familiar to you, too: the *pock* of leather on willow, the patter of rain on anoraks, the buzz of wasps round jam sandwiches. Some, though, were unique, not just to the northern fringe of Yorkshire where I lived, but to our household, wedged between the brown and purple hills and the blast furnaces and cooling towers of Teesside. The most common of them were the two snorts that would follow the moment when any radio or TV commentator announced that Garry Sobers was 'the greatest all-rounder in history'. The first snort would come from my father, who would follow it by saying, 'No, he's not . . . Wilfred Rhodes.'

This would be closely followed by the second snort, which emanated from my grandfather, traditionally from beneath the *Daily Express* he had placed over his face following his return from the pub and his routine lunch of three pints of Vaux Samson and a pickled egg. My grandfather's snort was more powerful than my father's, filled with the rich, rolling phlegmyness that comes from a lifetime of working in a chemical plant. He sounded like a sea elephant expelling two sugar beets from its nostrils, a lovesick bull moose imitating Joe Cocker. When my grandad snorted, crowds fell silent. 'Wilfred Rhodes?' my grandad said in a tone that was as close as a working-class bloke from Middlesbrough could get to mimicking Dame Margaret Rutherford saying, 'A handbag?'. 'George Herbert Hirst more bloody like.'

My father did not argue. My grandfather was not a man you debated with. He had grown up in a tough family in a rough part of a rugged town. At the mention of his surname welders and platers flinched; publicans shuttered the windows and policemen whistled for assistance. Reasoned discourse with my grandfather invariably ended in a crunch. As the Leeds United footballer John Giles remarked of his combative team-mate Jack Charlton, 'He wasn't always right, but he was never wrong.'

It was an endless running debate. When asked who the greatest all-rounder in the history of cricket was, the jokey response in Yorkshire was, 'I don't know, but he batted right-handed, bowled left-handed and came from Kirkheaton.' Hirst and Rhodes both answered this description (and doubtless there have been others since who have raised a chuckle in the pub by chirruping, 'Aye that's me, that is'). As to who was the better, well, even Lord Hawke, the captain who nurtured them both when they came into the county side and was generally never short of a forthright opinion, deflected the question with maidenly coyness.

2

The argument erupted fairly often in our house. The occasion I remember most vividly, however, came during the England v the Rest of the World match at Lord's in 1970. Sobers had taken six wickets in England's first innings and then pasted the home attack all day to reach 183. The snorting and the comments were heard in mid-afternoon and shortly afterwards my grandfather announced that he was going out to mow the lawn. He did this with a sergeant-major fervour, trimming the grass brutally short twice a week. Compared to any lawn my grandad tended, the batting strip at Sabina Park looked like an Alpine meadow in June.

Once we'd heard the Suffolk Colt chugging into life my dad began to run through the wonder of Rhodes. He had the wickets (4,204 – 'over 400 more than the next bloke, Tich Freeman') and the runs (39,969 – 12th on the all-time list back then, he's 17th now) off pat, and the rise from being England's number 11 to opening the batting with Jack Hobbs. 'Even when Rhodes went blind in old age he could still tell you more about what was happening on the field than most people who had eyesight,' my dad said in wonder. 'He could tell the style of a shot just by the sound of the ball hitting the bat. "Ooh," he'd say, "what a lovely stroke through the covers that was," and people would look at him astonished because that was exactly what had happened.'

The image of the sightless Rhodes dispensing wisdom to young acolytes struck me with particular force. My favour-ite childhood TV programme was *Kung Fu*. In the US series a neophyte Shaolin monk, Kwai Chang Caine (David Carradine), was trained in the martial arts by the blind Master Po. The two things conflated in my mind. I imagined Rhodes sitting next to a bamboo aviary, speaking in Taoist aphorisms, uttering the words, 'When you can walk across the rice paper without tearing it, Grasshopper, then it will be time for you to leave the Pavilion' to Ray Illingworth or Brian Close.

George Herbert Hirst remained more mysterious. My grandad's sporting passion was, unsurprisingly given his martial spirit, boxing. And while he could talk lyrically about Jack Dempsey, Archie Moore, Kid Gavilan and dozens of other prize fighters, I never heard him say much about cricket at all. His main contribution on the topic – aside from the George Herbert Hirst remark – were insults about a variety of the game's personalities when they appeared on the TV screen. The dapper, pipe-smoking BBC presenter Peter West particularly vexed him and would inevitably be greeted with a contemptuous growl of, 'Here he bloody well is, wearing Victor Silvester's trousers,' a remark that was as scornful as it was incomprehensible.

What had drawn Hirst into his conscience is hard to fathom. My grandfather was born in 1900. He was old enough to have seen Hirst in action, but that seemed unlikely. Yorkshire hadn't begun playing matches at Middlesbrough until the '50s and I couldn't imagine him making the long trek to Scarborough or Leeds as a youngster, not when there were dance halls to scrap in. His small collection of books offered no clues. Alongside well-thumbed favourites such as *The Ring Pictorial History of Boxing* and a book about the Wild West featuring the paintings of Frederic Remington, there was just one volume on the game, Monty Noble's *The Fight for the Ashes 1928-29*. I have no idea how it got there.

I wonder if he might have seen the great man in the '20s when he ran coaching courses all around Yorkshire and pitched up on Teesside for a couple of days each summer. More likely, though, was that he'd come across him on a cigarette card – Hirst featured in several sets issued before the Great War – and simply taken a shine to the man. Looking at the photographic image on the 1912 set issued by Smith's Tobacco it's easy to see why that might have been. When he was older, Hirst expanded to the roly-poly proportions of a panda, but at his peak he had bullish shoulders, a powerful chest and forearms like a couple of York Hams. He looked like a steam-tug. It was a physique my grandfather – even in his sixties – shared.

There was something in his character that would have appealed, too. Hirst was tough, doughty, warm and friendly all at the same time. He was kind about others and shrugged off compliments like a spaniel shaking off river water. His talent was a gift and he believed himself lucky to have it. To see him smile made everybody happy. He did not swagger and he did not preach. He wasn't one of those men whose heads were so swollen by success and vanity they were – to hear my grandad tell it – forever getting them wedged in doorways. 'They've just give Geoffrey Boycott his county cap,' my grandad once announced. 'They couldn't find one big enough, so they stuck a peak on a blue umbrella.'

Hirst was born in Kirkheaton, just outside Huddersfield. It's a kindlier corner of the White Rose county than the smoky towns to the west that bred the likes of Fred Trueman, Ray Illingworth, Johnny Wardle and Brian Sellers, the cricketers whose uncompromising, unsmiling image would come – sadly to some of us – to be seen as the acme of Yorkiedom.

Kirkheaton is a lovely spot where, in summer, the hedgerows are filled with dog roses and the air with the trill of ascending skylarks. To watch cricket here is to be transported back into a J. L. Carr world musky with blossom and warmed by the sun and quiet decency. Wilfred Rhodes was born in Kirkheaton too (on occasion the duo played together for the village side, skittling out opponents for a handful of runs). These days the area round about is most famous as the setting of *Last of the Summer Wine*. If you squint a little you might picture Hirst and Rhodes, joined by their cheery pal from a few miles down the road in Berry Brow, Schofield Haigh, wandering around the moorlands like Roy Clarke's Clegg, Compo and Foggy, getting into mild scrapes and chuckling in wry bemusement at the vicissitudes of existence. It's not so far from possibility.

In the summer of 1970, Haigh's name was unfamiliar to me. He never cropped up when the great deeds of Yorkshire cricket were brought out and burnished. Yet he was the third highest wicket-taker in the county's history, one of only 33 players ever to have taken more than 2,000 wickets.

Haigh's friendship with Hirst and Rhodes was so close the local press called the trio the Three Musketeers or, more classically, the Triumvirate. The Kirkheaton pair were the only bowlers in Yorkshire whose deeds had eclipsed his and their shadows had almost blotted him from the oral history.

Haigh, like Hirst, was amiable and easy-going, filled with self-mockery and mirth. Everybody liked him, whether friend or foe. Yet on a helpful pitch – and there were a lot of them in the days when tracks were left open to the elements throughout a match – he was considered by many observers – including Sir Pelham Warner – to be the most devastating medium-pacer England has ever produced. On a damp wicket he broke his off-cutter almost at right-angles and hit the stumps more often than anyone before or since (74 per cent of his wickets were unassisted, either clean bowled or LBW). In the 16 seasons the Triumvirate played together, from 1898 to 1913, Yorkshire won the County Championship seven times and it was Schofield Haigh who topped the bowling averages most often during that glorious spell. Only one man who took more than 500 first-class wickets has a lower bowling average than Haigh: Wilfred Rhodes's heir, Hedley Verity.

The trio practised together long before the season had begun, appearing at Kirkheaton as early as Pancake Day with their bats and pads. When it was too wet for cricket they'd head up on to the moor tops and play knur and spell, a kind of rough-hewn working-class golf, in which a clay ball was flicked into the air and belted with a club that looked like a cross between a mallet and a polo stick. The winner was the one who hit it the furthest.

After a game they might have leaned on a gate between drystone walls, puffed on their pipes and gazed across the sheep-speckled heather to the smoke curling up from the chimneys of the mill villages where they'd first played cricket. It was somewhere up here, between the brown land and the green, that as a child I'd imagine Wilfred Rhodes's barn stood. The barn was part of the legend. 'One winter,' my father told me as the lawnmower whirred in the garden, 'Wilfred Rhodes borrowed a barn. He spent all winter in it bowling, looping the ball over a rope and dropping it on the handkerchief he'd placed on a good length. Accuracy. Accuracy, you see?'

I saw, but I ignored the implied lesson. My father was always banging on about line and length to me. But I wanted to bowl as fast as Keith Boyce or spin the ball like B. S. Chandrasekhar. I wasn't interested in all the boring, laborious stuff they'd had to do before they got there. I didn't want to be a cricketer. I wanted to be a genius.

'In the barn all that winter,' my dad said. 'Dedicated to his craft.'

In my mind, I smelled the barn. The musty odour of damp hay and mice, the sweet chemical tang of the mysterious thick brown liquid farmers always seemed to have stuffed in some dark corner ('Don't ever touch that, lads. It'll burn your skin right off your bones'). I saw Rhodes's breath white and silver in the icy dales air, heard the dull *thunk* of the ball hitting concrete, watched the white square of linen, bright in the gloom, fluttering as it was struck. Perhaps, like Kwai Chang Caine in *Kung Fu*, there would have come a time when Rhodes could do this exercise blindfolded, muscle memory so finely honed it appeared he was guided by a spirit: the Zen master of slow left-arm.

George Herbert Hirst had his own legend. In what might have been a Huddersfield and District League answer to that eerie moment in the history of popular music when Robert Johnson sat at the Mississippi crossroads waiting for darkness to fall and the devil to offer him a deal, it was said that in the winter of 1900–01 George Herbert went to Leeds for a few months and came back with a wide grin on his round face and a delivery the like of which the world had never before seen – the in-swinger.

Of course, the truth is not quite as magical or simple as that. Johnson learned blues guitar from listening to Charley Patton rather than trading his soul for it, and Hirst did not invent swing bowling. Swing was something a number of cricketers were tinkering with as Queen Victoria's reign entered its final years. But though Hirst may not have been alone in developing swing, he quickly became the new art's public face. His success and his personality popularised it. For that he has reasonable grounds to claim to be, as *Wisden* once suggested, 'the father of all modern seam and swing bowling'.

Whatever happened in the winter of 1900–01, it transformed Hirst's fortunes. Until that point he was little more than a standard-issue county bowler. He'd been quite nippy at first but slowed as his batting improved. Even his friend Rhodes called him 'a straight up-and-downer'. He took wickets for sure, but on good batting strips – such as those he encountered on a confidence-mangling tour of Australia in 1897–98 – the simple approach of his early years was not enough.

Quite what happened in Leeds that fateful winter is not recorded. However he went about perfecting this new skill, when he unleashed the booming in-swinger that would become his trademark in the spring of 1901 it created the same sort of sensation that Bosanquet's googly had the year before. Sammy Woods, the great Australia and Somerset all-rounder, summed up the feelings of batsmen across England that summer when he exclaimed, 'How the devil can you play a ball that comes at you like a hard throw-in from cover point?'

In his first season after mastering the strange new art, Hirst took 183 wickets at 16.38, with deliveries so extraordinary they left batsmen so befuddled they might have been struck over the head with a gong. In the next 12 seasons he only once took fewer than 100 wickets (and that only because injury caused him to miss several matches), topping 200 on one occasion and 150 three times.

There were any number of theories about how he did

it – some scientific, some as cranky as other Edwardian crazes such as phrenology. When the great man himself was asked about the arcane mysteries of his skill set, he shrugged self-deprecatingly and replied, 'Sometimes it works and sometimes it doesn't.'

Despite the famous last-stand heroics against Australia at The Oval in 1902 and the Edgbaston Test of the same year in which, alongside Rhodes, he helped dismiss Australia for 36, Hirst was never as effective playing for England as he was for Yorkshire. Lord Hawke said that Hirst didn't like Test cricket and didn't like playing Test cricket. It wasn't that George Herbert wasn't good enough for the international game, it was more that the international game wasn't good enough for him.

Hirst turned out for the Tykes from 1889 until 1922 and in those 33 years scored 36,203 runs and took 2,727 wickets. It was hardly surprising that Lord Hawke described him as 'the greatest county cricketer of all time'.

My father had just finished the 'We'll get 'em in singles' story when the lawnmower chuntered to a halt with a sound like Don Mosey beginning his post-day summary. A few minutes later, my grandfather came into the kitchen looking for lemon barley water. He could sense what we'd been talking about in his absence. He pushed up his sleeves and washed his hands. 'George Herbert Hirst,' he said. 'Only player in history to do the double double.' And we knew it was best to leave it at that.

The Men in the Postcard

Blake Lee House, October 1905

The postcards were on sale in stationers all round Huddersfield priced at one old penny apiece. I bought mine on eBay from a seller in South Wales for £14.99. The black-and-white photograph shows three smartly suited Edwardian men outside a large brick house shadowed by trees. One of them, broad-beamed and powerful as an industrial barge, seems to be on the verge of smiling. He stands with his hands in his pockets, paternal above the men to his front. The one to his right is short and slight and sits casually athwart his chair. His sparkling eyes, snub nose and bristling moustache call to mind a playful otter. The other man, to his left, is taller and slimmer. He has the gaunt, pale-eyed, serious face of an Anglo-Saxon saint. Perhaps that is just an imaginative projection, however, for this is Wilfred Rhodes, as close to sporting canonisation in Yorkshire as anyone is ever likely to get. The other two men are his great friends and team-mates, George Herbert

Hirst and Schofield Haigh. They are skilful, professional working-class men of great respectability. That is why they have been brought here today, to Blake Lee House, on the edge of the moors between Marsden and Buckstones, on a hillside leading up from Hey Green.

The tenant of the house, Mr Firth, is a leading campaigner for the Huddersfield Temperance Society. He has carried out extensive works to turn the imposing mansion into a guest house for those wishing to escape the sooty turmoil of the towns (and who wouldn't?). Blake Lee's large kitchens can cater for a multitude, regularly turning out knife-and-fork teas for 400 visitors. No alcohol is served, naturally.

Today's gathering is smaller, more select. There are two dozen guests, including aldermen and councillors (the Mayor of Huddersfield has sent his regrets. He is away, attending a conference on infant health in Paris – I imagine some grumbling about councillors and their expenses). The scene is a lovely one with views across the tree-lined valley, the gold and copper colours of autumn glimmering in dazzling sunlight. Little wonder one writer had said that for sylvan beauty Blake Lee surpasses even the Fairy Glen.

After a reception of home-made lemonade and confectionery, the sturdier guests are taken for a walk up on to the moors where they visit the sight of the Marsden Moor Tragedy (two gamekeepers brutally slain by a poacher a couple of years before – the demon drink an awful factor). Those of a less robust constitution wandered the lawns while the younger children play cricket. Mrs Hirst and Mrs Rhodes stay behind and chat. Mrs Haigh is not there; she is expecting and has taken bad. They are often together, these three women: Emma, Sarah and Lillian. Their husbands are away for weeks on end, sometimes whole winters. Like the wives of sailors, they come together for comfort and for company.

When the party reassembles, a photographer, Mr Shaw from Huddersfield, records the event for posterity. It is he, with the help of temperance campaigner Dick Firth, who arranges the three Yorkshire cricketers – the Triumvirate – for the photo. Perhaps he is a fan. Or is just hoping the postcard will make him a decent profit. It should sell well. They are giant local celebrities after all, and will continue to be so.

In the end, the Triumvirate will play close to 2,500 first-class matches between them, more than 500 of them together and, when cricket is suspended during the First World War, they'll work side-by-side in the same Huddersfield munitions factory. They are the three highest ever wicket-takers for Yorkshire, and are first, 12th and 33rd on the all-time first-class list. They have formed the most potent attack in county cricket, pitting their skills against the greatest batsmen of cricket's Golden Age: C. B. Fry, Prince Ranjitsinhji, Jack Hobbs, Frank Woolley, Gilbert Jessop, Victor Trumper, Clem Hill and, of course, W. G. Grace.

Between them, the Triumvirate will take nearly 9,000 first-class scalps, score more than 77,000 runs and pouch 1,669 catches. Left-arm medium-pacer George Herbert and slow left-armer Wilfred will take more wickets, but Schof's average will be lower, his strike rate higher. Bowling off-cutters, the diminutive medium-pacer is the more lethal when conditions are right. He took 14 Hampshire wickets in a day at Headingley the season before the photograph was taken. And it was Schof and Wilfred who bowled out Nottinghamshire for 13 at Trent Bridge.

Wilfred – a methodical, cautious batsman – will do the

double of 1,000 runs and 100 wickets in a season a record 16 times. The more merrily belligerent George Herbert will finish second on the list with 14. Schof will hit four first-class hundreds but, batting lower down the order, and perhaps lacking belief in his own ability with the willow, he does the double just once. It is Schofield's personality that counts most; the gutsy way he has overcome the fragilities of his own physique and fought on through long, hot afternoons in the field, always with a grin and some chaff. 'He always has a joke, even when in the tightest corner,' Lord Hawke comments affectionately. He is the heartbeat of the side.

The Triumvirate have been instrumental in transforming Yorkshire County Cricket Club from a motley collection of talented but dissolute vagabonds into the most formidable force in the County Championship during the Golden Age. They have set an example to their team-mates, practising and perfecting their craft as few have done before. To them being professional meant more than simply turning up and getting paid to play. They have made cricket, once a fast sport of gambling and drunkenness, into something respectable ('Hear, hear,' says Mr Firth).

Their impact on cricket outside Yorkshire is huge, too. George Herbert has changed the way the game in England is played by introducing swing bowling, while Wilfred's accuracy and mastery of flight has influenced a new generation of spin bowlers.

The characters of the three great all-rounders reflect the environment and the age they've grown up in. They are men to be taken seriously, but they were not entirely serious men. Schof's face is perpetually creased in a cheery smirk; George Herbert's smile is said to be so wide it stretches right round his head and meets at the back. In those days, Wilfred was taciturn in public, impish in private. Hirst and Haigh, born in the same year, are older than 'Young Wilfred'. They act like his big brothers, teasing him and jollying him along. Without them, Wilfred becomes introspective, gruff and, as time passes, increasingly irascible.

After Schof's death and George Herbert's retirement, Wilfred will become Yorkshire's senior professional, presiding over an era in which the White Rose county started to earn a reputation as a team characterised by abrasive dourness, given to grim, cautious cricket and sometimes aggressive gamesmanship. The Yorkshire of the grinning George Herbert, who famously said, 'Cricket is a game, not a competition,' will gradually give way to the Yorkshire most of us grew up with. The surly-looking men, the glowerers who didn't 'play cricket for fun' and, indeed, in the case of the worst of them gave the impression they didn't do much else for fun either. Many of these sour chin-jutters were outstanding players, but few inspired nationwide affection. 'It did your heart good to hear him laugh,' Pelham Warner said of Hirst. You couldn't imagine anyone saying the same of Fred Trueman or Brian Sellers.

Gentle and generous, wise and kindly, George Herbert, Schof and Wilfred would play cricket to a standard few could match and, when their strength failed, teach others (including four England captains and one prime minister) to attempt the same. When Wilfred spoke of cricket, Neville Cardus observed, 'History comes from his mouth in rivers.' He was, said J. M. Kilburn, 'a one-man university of the game'.

Their influence would stretch beyond the British Isles. They toured Australia, South Africa and the West Indies.

Wilfred Rhodes would spend four winters in India, as coach and professional to Bhupinder Singh, the Maharajah of Patiala, who in 1911 would captain the first Indian team to tour England. First George Herbert then other well-known Yorkshire cricketers joined him, living in an apartment above the pavilion at Moti Bagh cricket ground in Baroda, teaching locals to play the game, laying the foundations of cricket on the subcontinent.

But all that is to come. Now, it is a sunny autumn day in Yorkshire and, the photographs having been taken, it is time for a meat tea and entertainment from a tenor accompanied by the music of the piano, violin and banjo. Mr Dranefield, the vocalist, has a mellifluous voice and when he sings 'The Old Folks at Home', many in the assembly join in the chorus, swaying as their voices rise. Schof nudges George Herbert and winks, George Herbert fiddles with his silver watch chain and beams contentedly and Wilfred ... Wilfred watches the musicians keenly and studiously through his pale blue eyes, as if he's trying to fathom the mysteries of sound.

CHAPTER ONE

The Baby from the Brown Cow

Many legends swirl around George Hirst and Wilfred Rhodes. The first of them attests to the fact that George Herbert was born in 1871 on the opening day of the first ever Scarborough Cricket Festival, an event he'd adorn for four decades, where he'd take wicket 200 in the season of the 'double double', play his final game for Yorkshire and make his last appearance in first-class cricket, aged 58.

That 1871 match was played, not at North Marine Road, but in the old ground on Castle Hill between Lord Londesborough's XI and a team of Scarborough Visitors led by Charles 'Bun' Thornton. Thornton, who refused to wear gloves or pads, was one of the biggest hitters of a cricket ball in the Victorian age. At the Scarborough Festival in 1886, playing for the Gentlemen of England, 'Bun' would score a century with just 26 shots, one of which was a straight drive that was said to have travelled 162 yards before bouncing. Thornton had been born and raised in Herefordshire and had no familial or other connections with Scarborough, but he loved the seaside resort and would soon take over running the cricket festival, make a huge success of it, and along the way become a great friend and admirer of George Herbert.

So, if George Herbert had been born on 11 September 1871, the day Bun Thornton took the field in Scarborough for the very first time, it would have been a happy coincidence for cricket. Unfortunately, he made his entry into the world a few days earlier, on 7 September.

The other circumstances of George Herbert's birth are altogether more opaque. We can say with some certainty that he was born in the Old Brown Cow Inn, off St Mary's Lane in Kirkheaton. The Old Brown Cow was an alehouse that belonged to the Whitley Beaumont estate. In 1871 James Hirst ran the inn and farmed the six acres of land attached to it. This was part of a long-standing arrangement. When local magistrates threatened to remove the pub's licence in 1927, those opposing the closure claimed the Hirst family had been running the pub for over a century and that 50 members of the clan had been born in its rooms. The magistrates, unswayed by sentiment and tradition, shut the Old Brown Cow down. After the Second World War the local council made sure the pub would never return – whether run by Hirsts or not – demolishing it so they could widen the road to Leeds.

George Herbert was, by most accounts, the 10th child of the pub's landlord, James, and his wife, Sarah. He had four brothers (Thomas, James, Job and Henry) and five sisters (Mary, Hannah, Sarah, Amelia and Louisa). Hannah had died in infancy and Mary, the eldest, had been born before James and Sarah married and had her mother's maiden name, Woolhouse. After his father, James Hirst, died in 1880, George Herbert went to live with his sister Mary and her husband, John Berry, in New Street, Kirkheaton. In the 1881 census, George Herbert Hirst is listed as living at that address. He's also described as being the son of Mary and John Berry. This could be a simple error, or, in a plot twist straight out of Barbara Taylor Bradford, it may be that George's sister was actually his mother and those everyone thinks of as his mother and father were, in fact, his grandparents.

If there was gossip it does not seem to have bothered young George Herbert. And in Kirkheaton and its environs it was always George Herbert, never simply George. Some took this as a sign of deference, or Victorian formality. It may have been a bit of both. More likely, though, it was to make conversations shorter and simpler. There were thousands of Hirsts around Huddersfield, hundreds of them playing league cricket. In the days when men's forenames were drawn from a very shallow pool, with Georges, Josephs and Williams predominating, calling someone by both their given names was a short cut to understanding. It was far speedier than explaining who you meant through family reference.

In my grandfather's clan, where every other male seemed to be called Alfred, whole afternoons and evenings could pass after somebody said, 'No, not Old Alfie's Young Alfie, Young Alfie's Alfie, the one that married Our Alfie's lass. You know her, she was Fat Alfie's niece' and wind onwards from there until everyone was dizzy or had gone to the pub. Calling him George Herbert likely saved hours of spiralling confusion.

George Herbert's childhood among the sprawling mass of the Hirst family was a happy one. He recalled helping his father, James, drive the cattle to milking, but otherwise played cricket from noon till night. 'At the Old Brown Cow we played our cricket in the yard and on the intake field below.'

Kirkheaton squats on the slopes of the Pennines. The houses are made of grey Crosland Hill stone that glows on sunny days and grimaces on damp ones. There are a lot of damp ones. Nowadays, the valleys around Kirkheaton are the haunt of day-trippers, hikers and weekenders. On sunny afternoons, retirees park up on verges, fold out a picnic table and eat vanilla slices while looking out across the wild-flower meadows and sucking in the moor-top air.

It was a very different place when George Herbert was young. Smoke from the mills and factories and the hundreds of thousands of domestic chimneys curled up into the Yorkshire sky and fell back as soot. Tons of the fine black powder pattered down each day, darkening buildings, giving hedges and trees a funereal topcoat, dyeing sheep grey and playing havoc with the laundry. The people worked and played in it. They breathed it in. Coughs and sneezes left sombre blotches on cotton handkerchiefs. Asthma, bronchitis and other lung complaints carried off dozens daily. The manufacturing of cloth did not seem as inherently risky as mining or smelting iron, but it was hazardous all the same. The shuttle looms, rattling like machine guns, were a constant threat to the limbs of the unwary. In 1818, the village cotton mill had caught light, the fibres that hung in the air creating a fireball that burned to death 17 female workers, some of them as young as nine. George Herbert was born into a world that would have made Monty Python's 'four Yorkshiremen' wince.

The village already had a tradition of cricket. It was the birthplace of Andrew Greenwood and Allen Hill, two of the five Yorkshiremen who played in the first-ever Test match, at Melbourne in 1877. The cricket field, established in 1883, sat then, as it does today, on a flat headland facing towards the chimneys of Huddersfield. It's flanked by drystone walls and scoured by the moorland breeze. Across the valley, you can see the field and pavilion of Lascelles Hall. One of England's oldest clubs, Lascelles had a side so strong that three years before George Herbert's birth they'd beaten an All England XI and three years after it they took on the full Yorkshire team in a two-innings match and stuffed them by 146 runs. Among their stars were Ephraim Lockwood, John Thewlis and Billy Bates, the first Englishman to take a Test hat-trick. If George Herbert needed role models, he didn't have to look far.

He joined Kirkheaton Cricket Club in 1884 and spent so much time on the ground at Bankfield Lane, the little wooden pavilion was like a second home. George Herbert would later recall how at Kirkheaton when the players had 'nets' they were nets in name only. There were no actual nets. Every ball that was hit had to be fielded.

By then he had already left school. Aged 10 he'd been taken on as a wirer for a Kirkheaton handloom weaver who lived in a cottage on the road to Lascelles. His employer did little to encourage the youngster's cricketing ambitions. George Herbert would later recall that the man had no interest in the game and 'spent all his brass backing horses'.

His first proper cricket match was in 1885, an away fixture for Kirkheaton Seconds against Rastrick Seconds. George Herbert was supposed to play as a bowler, but wasn't needed. He made up for the disappointment by hitting 20 with the bat. He made more appearances for Kirkheaton Seconds that season, and the following year was promoted to the first team. By now he was working at Robson's Dye House across the valley from the Old Brown Cow.

Filling out as he hit his mid-teens, George Herbert had started playing rugby for Mirfield. The game had not yet split between amateur and professional codes. George Herbert played centre in a three-quarter line that included the future England star Dickie Lockwood. Lockwood was so impressed with Hirst he wanted him to move with him to a higher level at Heckmondwike, but by then George Herbert's focus had shifted back to cricket again.

The change had come in 1889 when George Herbert was 17 and Allen Hill arrived to coach Kirkheaton before the club's campaign in the Lumb Cup. Hill was the first man ever to take a wicket in a Test match. He'd played for Kirkheaton and Lascelles Hall before moving on to Yorkshire, where his fast round-arm bowling earned him 749 wickets. His career had been ended six years earlier by a badly broken collarbone. He was working as a wool weaver but when asked for his profession still proudly said 'cricketer'. Hill was genial and cheery. His coaching must have been good too because Kirkheaton ended the season with their first trophy, winning the Lumb Cup after defeating Cliffe End in the final. The match was watched by a number of Yorkshire players. George Herbert excelled with the ball, taking five wickets for 23. When Yorkshire played Cheshire at Fartown, Huddersfield, a week later, Hirst was invited to join them.

He travelled the short distance to the game in some trepidation, less because he feared the opponents, but because he was worried about his clothing. George Herbert had a pair of brown boots, white trousers held up with a snake belt and a thick cream jumper he'd have to keep on no matter what the temperature because the shirt underneath it was blue. He needn't have worried. He was better off than several of the other trialists – they didn't have shirts at all. George Herbert bowled decently in Cheshire's first innings, picking up three wickets, but when the game ended Yorkshire gave no indication they'd want a second look.

By now, however, his exploits at Kirkheaton – where on August Bank Holiday he'd taken nine Mirfield wickets for a handful of runs – had drawn attention and Elland took him as a 'Saturday man' for the 1890 season. This was not a full-time professional post, which would also have involved net bowling and tending the ground, but a pay-by-the-game arrangement. George Herbert used the first £4 he earned to buy himself a white shirt. He already had a canvas bag for his kit, which put him ahead of the great Tom Emmett, who in his first few appearances for Yorkshire had carried his equipment to matches rolled up in a newspaper. Emmett, it should be said, was also noted for the colour of his nose, which was said to be so red that any fly that landed on it burned its feet.

George Herbert was selected to play in two games for Yorkshire during the 1890 season. Against Staffordshire at Stoke in June he was given limited chances to shine. In his next outing, against Essex at Leyton, he performed poorly, failing to get a wicket or score a run.

In 1891 George Herbert moved to Mirfield as Saturday man. Yorkshire picked him for the match with Somerset at Taunton in late July. Again, his performance was mediocre, 15 runs and two wickets. Other cricketers in Hirst's time would make a great impact at Yorkshire only to be dropped as soon as they failed and never be seen again. His chances were running out.

The turning point came when he was picked in early May 1892 to play at Lord's against MCC and Ground. He batted well, scoring 20 and 43 not out, and took six wickets in the match. The performance at Lord's earned him a place in the Yorkshire team to play Essex at Dewsbury. He did well enough to retain his place when Sussex came to Sheffield. Things began badly. After Sussex had scored 177 in their first innings, Yorkshire were bowled out for 81 and forced to follow on. Ted Wainwright rescued the second innings by scoring a century and the visitors were set 137 to win. They were three down for 51, when Lord Hawke threw the ball to George Herbert. He had not had much of a game so far. He'd bowled 11 tidy but unproductive overs in the visitors' first knock, come in at number 10 to score a duck and one not out. Now, perhaps sensing it was his last chance, he charged in, bowled fast and straight, and ran through the Sussex batting like a ram through a wheat field, taking six wickets for 16 as they collapsed to 96 all out.

After he'd skittled out Sussex, George Herbert was so chuffed he abandoned his normal modesty and told Yorkshire's secretary, Joseph Wostinholm, 'I've got into the team now, and I am going to keep my place. If I can't do it with my bowling, I'll do it with my batting.' He was 20 years old and brimming with confidence. No matter what happened, he'd never lose it.

When George Herbert made his debut for Yorkshire in the 1889 season it was not a happy time for his native county. That great early chronicler of the White Rose game, the Reverend Holmes, called it, 'the low-water mark of Yorkshire cricket'. Yorkshire spent the first two months languishing at the bottom of the County Championship. They lost 10 matches and won just two, defeating Sussex in the penultimate match of the season to avoid finishing last.

The batting was feeble – a situation highlighted in the game against Kent at Halifax, in which Yorkshire were shot out in the first innings without a single batsman making double figures. The decency of the bowling, meanwhile, was undermined by fielding so hopeless it could have been as well done wearing blindfolds and oven gloves. Dozens of catches were spilled and hundreds of runs conceded by fielders whose co-ordination often seemed adversely affected by meal breaks. It was plainly time for drastic action, and luckily Yorkshire had just the man for the job.

Lord Hawke was tall and strapping, with a walrus moustache and keen, steady eye of a Wild West marshal. He had taken over the captaincy of Yorkshire in 1883, while still a student at Cambridge. An Old Etonian whose family lived at Wighill Park near Tadcaster, Lord Hawke would rise to a position of great prominence and power within the game and, along with Lord Harris of Kent, form a duo that was referred to – not with great affection – as the Dukes of Cricket. A Conservative politician, Lord Harris would serve as undersecretary of state for India and governor of Bombay. Lord Hawke would become president of Yorkshire County Cricket Club. To Hawke's mind, and to those of all right-thinking people, it was clear who had achieved the greater position.

That was for the future. For now, Lord Hawke found himself confronting a scene that might have daunted other young men. The Yorkshire team he had inherited was both supremely talented and a byword for roughness and dissolution. J. M. Kilburn commented in his usual mild way that the side had 'fallen prey to the temptations on offer to cricketers of the time'. Others put it more bluntly. Yorkshire's starting XI consisted of 'ten drunks and a parson'. The 'parson' was opening batsman Louis Hall, a nonconformist preacher from Batley who batted like he was facing Judgement Day. Walking into the Yorkshire dressing room in 1883 was like entering a Dodge City saloon when the cattle drives had arrived.

Lord Hawke took his time reaching for his six-guns, but in 1887 he kicked open the doors and came in shooting. His target was the greatest spin bowler of his generation, Ted Peate. Peate was born in Holbeck, Leeds, then one of the grimmest slums in the industrial world. He bowled slow left-arm with an action of such lazy elegance it practically purred. Peate played nine times for England. Most famously, or perhaps infamously, he came in last man against Australia at The Oval in 1882, with 10 runs needed and the accomplished Middlesex batsman Charles Studd at the non-striker's end. Peate was expected to block out the deliveries remaining in Harry Boyle's over and then let the stylish Studd – an Old Etonian evangelical Christian – try to make the winning hits. Instead, he took a series of mighty heaves and was clean bowled.

When asked what he had been playing at, Peate replied simply, 'I could not trust Mr Studd to get them.' Today this remark seems either mildly idiotic, or an entertaining illustration of the North–South divide, but in Victorian England it was viewed as pernicious truculence. Peate's file was marked. The following day the *Sporting Times* ran its death notice to English cricket. Ted Peate, from the smoggy, cholera-ravaged purlieus of Leeds, had inadvertently created the Ashes.

Undaunted by the furore about his behaviour, Peate returned to Yorkshire and the following season took 214 wickets – a first-class record. W. G. Grace cooed over the spinner's style and poise, while Yorkshire's wicketkeeper,

David Hunter, reckoned him 'the finest left-arm bowler I ever saw'.

Peate had once taken eight wickets for five runs against Surrey on a wet wicket, but he was equally effective on dry, hard pitches. Pace and flight as much as spin were his weapons and he was as accurate as the time signal. On the field he was a wonder of the age, off it a shambolic mess, disappearing into pubs as soon as play finished for the day and joining his gang of well-wishers, who bought him drink after drink. Soon the same mob started accompanying him to matches too, and their idol would join them in the beer tent during the lunch and tea intervals. In 1887, Peate was still bowling brilliantly, but his behaviour was so erratic and his entourage so brutish and foul-mouthed, Hawke banished him just three matches into the season. For Yorkshire there was no need to worry. His replacement was earmarked. He was a pitman's son from Morley, who not only bowled like an angel, but was a thumping left-hand bat and caught the ball as if he had suckers on his fingers. His name was Bobby Peel.

Nor was Hawke finished with his clear-out. After the 1889 debacle he took aim again. Out went four experienced players whose talents on the field had been compromised by their behaviour off it: Fred Lee (who'd hit 165 in a Roses match), all-rounder Saul Wade, Irwin Grimshaw (who'd scored a century in each innings in a match with Cambridge University) and off-spinner Joe Preston (best figures: nine wickets for 28 against MCC). It was perhaps a measure of the life of a professional cricketer at that time that only one of the men Lord Hawke fired during this spell would survive beyond the age of 50.

Hawke set about replacing the banished reprobates with

younger, more solid and decent professionals. George Herbert would be one of them. He was joined by opening batsman John Tunnicliffe, a devout Methodist, the loyal wicketkeeper David Hunter (whose chief vice was playing the concertina) and Tunnicliffe's opening partner, Jack Brown, from Driffield in the East Riding. Doubtless there were those at the time who bemoaned the fact that Hawke's policy meant there were 'no longer the characters in the game that there used to be', but for a young man such as George Herbert, making his first steps as a professional, the clear-out of these hard-living, rough-edged rogues must have made life a lot cosier.

Tunnicliffe had been such a prodigy as a boy, his local club Pudsey Britannia had changed their rules to allow him to play for them when he was 16. He was enormously tall for the time – around 6ft 4 – and as a youngster a massive hitter. In 1891, playing for Yorkshire Colts against Nottinghamshire Colts, he smashed a ball from Baguley over the old Bramall Lane pavilion and into the backyard of a brewery on the other side of the road. When he reached the Yorkshire first team that same year he modified his game, became more cautious and orthodox, getting his long leg well down the pitch. If Long John's batting was not always thrilling, his slip fielding made up for it. He caught equally well with right and left hand and, unusually among fieldsmen of the time, he was prepared to dive full-length to grab the ball. The sight of his large body, pale clothing and bristling moustache arcing above the earth called to mind less a salmon or a dolphin than a walrus.

His batting partner Jack Brown was his exact opposite in many ways. Compact and quick on his feet, he was forcing rather than forceful, an attractive player to watch with a range of drives, pulls and cuts. He was a brilliant outfielder too, fast across the ground with a flat accurate throw. Brown was the epitome of geniality and a well-known joker. His sledging of Shrimp Leveson Gower after the batsman had been dismissed for 70 – 'You have not been playing well enough to get out before' – is a small classic of the Victorian era. Perhaps it was the influence of Tunnicliffe or fear of Lord Hawke, but one day after nets Brown suffered a revelation, renounced booze, rushed home and emptied all the alcohol in his house down the sink. He continued to smoke like a damp bonfire. It would contribute to his early death.

It had taken George Herbert a while to establish himself, but by 1892 he was a fixture in the starting XI. A young man from Berry Brow, close to Kirkheaton, also made his mark that season. Robert Moorhouse's batting was characterised by an almost Brian Close-like toughness that earned him the nickname the Man of Bruises. He was limpet-like in damp conditions and against Surrey at Sheffield in June, on a wicket so sticky the ball rose from it with a sound like a plaster being pulled from a knee, he scored 39 from a Yorkshire first innings total of 98, and 38 when they made 91 in the second. So bad was the wicket and so effective the bowling of Yorkshire's off-spinner Tom Wardall – who took nine wickets in the match for 21 runs – that Yorkshire won by 58 runs. Moorhouse, meanwhile, had been so battered about the thighs by fearsome Surrey paceman Tom Richardson that he struggled to take his trousers off. In a later encounter with the equally ferocious Charles Kortright of Essex, Moorhouse would score a half-century despite having been hit so often on his left arm it had swelled to double its normal size.

A further and more dramatic reminder that cricket in the

era of uncovered wickets and limited protective clothing was a hazardous business came against the South of England at Scarborough. On a track that was as hard and uneven as corrugated iron, a ball from Tom Richardson kicked from just short of a length and smashed into off-spinner Ted Wainwright's temple. The all-rounder collapsed unconscious and had to be carried from the field. For several days afterwards he lay in bed and had to be fed with a spoon.

George Herbert created some mayhem himself with his fast, straight, left-arm deliveries and finished the season with 59 wickets for the county. Peel took 65, the off-spinner Wainwright 90. Tunnicliffe and Brown scored close to 1,400 runs between them. With their new-look, well-behaved side, Yorkshire won the County Championship for the first time since it had begun 20 years earlier.

In his early seasons with Yorkshire, George Herbert had batted at 10. He was uncultured, but he had a good eye and powerful shoulders. Early on he'd clubbed 35 against Gloucestershire and beamed with happiness when he heard W. G. Grace say, 'I didn't know this little beggar could bat as well.'

His technique improved as he watched others at the wicket and his batting grew in confidence. In late July 1894, county cricket saw the side of George Herbert that would come to characterise him in the public mind – the calm battler who was at his best when backed into a corner. The opponents were again Gloucestershire. On a Leeds wicket that was on the malevolent side of spiteful, Yorkshire had been reduced to 19 for nine in the second innings by the fast bowling of Captain A. H. Newnham when David Hunter joined George Herbert at the wicket. Hunter was perhaps the first of the breed of zany wicketkeepers who, like madcap goalkeepers, would become a common thread in English sporting life.

Born in Scarborough, he was the son of a builder and learned his cricket in the stone yard and later on the beach where, according to Lord Hawke, he and his siblings would play until the tide washed away the stumps. His elder brother Joe kept wicket for Yorkshire for about 10 years in the 1870s and 1880s, retiring at the end of 1888. He died tragically young in 1891. David Hunter followed him into the Yorkshire gloves and kept the job for 21 years. He was held in high esteem and great affection across the county. He was neat in his appearance and in his work behind the wicket. His hands were extremely soft and after he took a ball that beat the bat he would encourage the bowler in terms of warm endearment, 'Well bowled, honey!' Away from cricket, Hunter was a noted breeder of canaries and pigeons, a champion clog dancer and toured France as a member of a hand-bell ringing troupe. He was reputedly a decent bare-knuckle prize fighter too.

Walking out to join George Herbert, the eccentric Hunter surveyed the field, prodded at the ugly pitch, studied the snorting Captain Newnham and commented cheerily, 'We shall liven things up a bit!' He and George Herbert then proceeded to heave and slash their way to a partnership of 42. Set 94 to win, the visitors were dismissed for 67 thanks to Wainwright, who took seven wickets. Hirst took the other three. The stand between Hirst and Hunter had won Yorkshire the match. Nor had the West Countrymen seen the last of him that season. In the return fixture at Bristol, W. G. saw once again that the little beggar could bat when George Herbert thumped 17 fours to reach his first first-class hundred. He learned his craft in the middle. Harnessing his natural attributes – a keen eye, bullish shoulders and chunky forearms – he pulled and hooked with genial violence.

George Herbert's season had begun wonderfully with the ball. In the May Roses match at Old Trafford he'd taken 10 for 56 with bowling that bristled with aggression. In July he was instrumental in helping Yorkshire defeat Somerset in a single day at his 'home ground' of Fartown, Huddersfield. He took five for nine in 6.1 overs in the visitors' first innings and five for 44 in the second. When Yorkshire travelled down to Taunton later in the summer, George again tormented them. On a damp wicket he made the ball fly from a length and finished with seven for 32.

Even in these early days George Herbert commanded attention. No one could quite say why. It was true he had fair, wavy hair and a silky moustache, but he was no George Lohmann, the Surrey medium-pacer whose broad shoulders, slim hips and high cheekbones made even the resolutely heterosexual Pelham Warner gush like a schoolgirl. George Herbert was moon-faced and, as Alfred Gibson noted in *London Opinion*, 'Short, square, stout, almost squat, and as unlike an ideal athlete as one can well imagine. He looks beefy, stiff and immobile.'

It was not his looks that attracted attention, rather it was something indefinable that seemed to shine around him. Jack Hobbs would comment that Hirst was 'the most domineering personality' he had ever encountered. The great batsman did not mean that George Herbert was a blusterer or a bully, more that he possessed that quality George Plimpton attributed to movie stars – he seemed to fill any room he entered. He did not do this on purpose. He was not garrulous or flamboyant.

It was natural and beyond his control. He had a yeoman charisma. As James Boswell wrote of another sturdy and humble Yorkshireman, Captain Cook, 'He did nothing to catch the eye, yet drew it wherever he went.'

In 1895 George Herbert took 150 wickets and scored over 700 runs. He displaced the off-spinner Ted Wainwright as the chosen opening bowling partner for the subtle slow left-arm of Bobby Peel. George Herbert's bowling was characterised then by bustling energy. His approach to the wicket began with a vigorous hop, a pounding step and dynamic leap, and built up velocity from there. Against Middlesex at Leeds he took 12 wickets through sheer force. His five for 63 against Lancashire at Bramall Lane was a masterpiece of muscular endeavour. Bobby Peel was the rapier, George Herbert the battering ram.

Peel's benefit match against Lancashire at Bradford took place in August and featured a typical late summer appearance from schoolmaster Ernest Smith, a Morley-born amateur with a double Blue from Oxford. Smith had a florid range of drives and whirling cut shots combined with the fancy footwork of a sand-dancer. He was said to have hit more sixes over the Bramall Lane pavilion than any man in history. In their first innings, Yorkshire had lost three quick wickets when Smith strode out to the middle and thrashed Johnny Briggs and Arthur Mold all around the ground to reach his fifty in 45 minutes, putting on 99 with John Tunnicliffe. The match raised £2,000 for Bobby Peel.

At the start of the 1895 season Yorkshire sent a telegram to a young batsmen named David Denton, ordering him to come to Fenner's immediately for the county's match with Cambridge University. Denton had first appeared for

Yorkshire the previous season against Warwickshire, when he'd come in at number 10 and hit 22 in such impressive fashion the watching veteran George Ulyett said that young-sters like this one were the reason he'd retired. The merry, self-deprecating Ulyett had hit 18 centuries in his career yet still claimed Yorkshire only picked him for his whistling, he was not a bad judge of talent.

Denton had begun his career as a cricketer while working for the soap manufacturer Hodgson & Simpson. Like George Herbert he was unschooled and uncoached but he prac-tised like a demon, going straight from work to the cricket ground, batting and fielding until it got dark and then head-ing home for food and bed. Sometimes he didn't eat his tea till 10 o'clock at night, scandalously continental for the West Riding. Denton was a notoriously edgy starter, often pushing half forward to pacemen and edging the ball into the slips. The frequency of times he was dropped when playing this non-shot had led to his nickname of 'Lucky'. It was said that when he walked to the wicket the opposition captain would call out, 'Here comes David Denton. Who's going to be the first to miss him?'

Whether Denton offered any chances at Fenner's is not recorded, but he hit 77 not out against the university and fol-lowed that with an unbeaten 44 against Lancashire at Sheffield. Except when ill or injured, he never lost his place in the side again, riding his famous luck to score more than 36,000 runs, including 61 centuries. With the Honourable F. S. Jackson establishing himself as one of the best amateur all-rounders of the Golden Age and Tunnicliffe and Brown regularly posting century opening stands, the greatest Yorkshire team in the history of the county was slowly coming together.

Yorkshire were a strong and well-organised side now. The batting was powerful and the fielding both close to the wicket and in the outfield, where Denton was swift and alert, was excellent. It was just the attack that was holding them back. It was good, no doubt, but it needed something a bit special to make it truly formidable.

CHAPTER TWO

The Sunday School Pro

When Schofield Haigh, the new professional of Aberdeenshire Cricket Club, stepped off the train in the Granite City in the spring of 1891, the club officials who greeted him glanced anxiously at one another. The Yorkshireman appeared so slight, young and baby-faced that one onlooker joked the club must have plucked him from 'a Sunday School Nursery XI'. Schof grinned as he shook hands with the welcome party. He seemed a pleasant sort of chap, for sure, but as to being a professional cricketer, well, they couldn't help wondering if there hadn't been some sort of mix-up.

When Aberdeenshire had decided to hire a Yorkshire professional they had gone to the great Yorkshire opening batsman, Louis 'the Parson' Hall for a recommendation. Born in Batley in 1852, Hall was a long, skinny fellow with a lugubrious face that called to mind a cartoon hound with an empty stomach. Caricatures of him looked more realistic than their subject. He was said to be so made up of skin and bone that if you'd pushed a pin into him it would have fallen out for want of cushioning.

Hall had left school aged nine and worked alongside his father in the mill. He began playing for Batley when he was 20 and earned the nickname the Batley Giant, less for his height (he was barely above average) but for his upright stance at the wicket. He stood like a totem pole, and looked like one too.

Hall had made his Yorkshire debut in 1873 but performed poorly and dropped out of view for several years, apparently downcast by his failure. His fortunes were revived when he took up the post of professional with Perthshire in 1876. Two years later he'd made 78 out of a total of 169 for a Hunslet XVIII against the touring Australians, whose formidable attack included Frederick Spofforth, Frank Allan and Harry Boyle. Hall's batting lacked style and he was so pathologically defensive spectators of rival counties groaned at the sight of him. Yet amazingly, in an era when wickets often resembled ploughed fields, he carried his bat on 15 occasions in first-class matches. Austere and forbidding, he was, according to Lord Hawke, the first teetotaller ever to play for Yorkshire. Given all this, it would be easy to categorise Hall as the Geoffrey Boycott of the Victorian age, except that the Batley Giant was universally popular with both team-mates and opponents.

Brought back into the Yorkshire side after his heroics for Hunslet, Hall was characteristically immovable for the next 14 seasons, forming a brilliant chalk-and-cheese opening partnership with the flamboyant George Ulyett.

After retirement from first-class cricket, Hall opened a sports shop in Batley and served as a Liberal councillor. He continued playing club cricket and took his own side on an annual tour of Scotland. Hall had many contacts at the Scottish clubs. His opinion was respected. It was on his say-so

that Perthshire had hired Jack Brown, the hard-hitting opening batsman from Driffield, who was now making a name for
himself in the County Championship.

Hall had encountered Schof when he'd taken a team from
Batley to play Armitage Bridge, of the Huddersfield and District
League. He told the Aberdeenshire committee that the lad was
a quick bowler, a tidy bat and a willing and energetic fielder.
Now, as they led the cheery little fellow away, they wondered
if perhaps Hall had been speaking of an older brother.

They had no need to worry. Louis Hall was a singular chap
who'd named his two children Londesborough and Edith in
honour of Lord and Lady Londesborough, the founders of the
Scarborough Cricket Festival, but he had an eye for talent.
By the time Schofield Haigh left Scotland nobody would be
making jokes about him, except perhaps Schofield Haigh
himself. By then he had terrorised batsmen from Edinburgh
to Peterhead and the locals had found a new nickname for
him, the Forty-pounder Gun.

Schof Haigh was born at Church Terrace, Berry Brow, on
19 March 1871. He was the youngest of six children. Berry
Brow was a jumble of stone houses sprawled over the hills on
the eastern bank of the River Holme. On sunny days more
romantically inclined visitors said it put them in mind of the
hilltop villages of Italy (sadly, much of the picturesque part
of Berry Brow was demolished by the council in the 1960s).
There was a station, on the Huddersfield to Sheffield line, a
post office and a cricket field, where Schof's elder brother
John captained the local Tradesmen's XI.

Berry Brow was a hotbed of Methodism and temperance
(so much so that one of the town's alehouses had been iron-
ically named Exchange Evil for Good by the landlord) and

the Haigh family worshipped at the Salem New Connexion Chapel, presided over for much of the Victorian era by a charismatic preacher called Little Abe Lockwood, who attracted so many devoted followers he was nicknamed the Bishop of Berry Brow. A millworker and coal miner, Lockwood preached of damnation while waving a red handkerchief, a symbol of the fiery pit into which sinners were headed. Schof was headed somewhere else first, though it would take him some time and many false starts to get there.

Schof began playing cricket in Berry Brow's main street, where games would last until a policeman drove them away. Later he moved to a makeshift pitch in a local quarry where the other participants included Bobby Moorhouse and his brother Fred, who'd play for Warwickshire.

Schof left school as soon as he could and got a job as an apprentice millwright and patternmaker. Cricket obsessed him. He practised in the morning before going to work, during his lunch hour and as soon as he knocked off for the night. When the foreman was busy elsewhere he'd even practise in the mill, bowling a bobbin at a wicket he'd marked on the wall. He began playing for the Tradesmen's XI, then for Berry Brow, a club which Schof later claimed was so cash-strapped they had only a single pair of pads for the entire team, one leg guard per batsman. When one batsman came out with his pad on his right leg, the opponents assumed he was left-handed and moved around accordingly. The batsman then took his guard as a right-hander. 'You've got your pad on the wrong leg,' an opponent shouted. The batsman shook his head. 'Bugger, I thought I'd be batting at the other end.'

When he was 18, Schof moved to the higher-class cricket offered at Armitage Bridge. The club had recently seen its star fast bowler, John Beaumont, move south to play for Surrey (he'd take more than 400 wickets for them) and had a number of other talented youngsters including the Moorhouse brothers and the splendidly named Crowther Charlesworth, who'd go on to become a legendary figure at Warwickshire where his dashing hitting helped the county win their first title in 1911. It's said Warwickshire took Charlesworth on Schof's recommendation. He repaid the favour by waiting until Haigh had retired to blast his first double hundred, against Yorkshire in 1914.

The standard of cricket in the Armitage Bridge first team was extremely high, the competition for places intense. Schof, by now a nippy medium-pacer and forceful middle-order bat, made his debut against a formidable Lascelles Hall side that included Ephraim Lockwood. He took four wickets for four runs and retained his place until Louis Hall came to see him with an offer from Aberdeen that he couldn't refuse.

The fresh-faced 20-year-old who turned up for the first day of practice at Aberdeenshire's Mannofield Park was just 5ft 7 in height and had the chubby cheeks and whispy facial hair of an adolescent. Schof's initial performances seemed to confirm the committee's early misgivings. On damp wickets and in the unfamiliar surroundings he struggled with both bat and ball. His breakthrough came against Huntly towards the end of May. In a two-innings match he picked up five wickets in the first innings and three in the second. There were ups and downs after that, but his talent became ever more apparent while his affability and warmth made him popular everywhere he went. In August he finally hit his stride. Against the aristocratic Grange Cricket Club of Edinburgh he struck a half-century and a few weeks later was instrumental in a hearty stuffing of Stoneywood. Coming to the crease after a couple of early wickets had fallen, Schof smashed 75 not out from a total of 128 and then helped skittle the opposition out for 46.

High scoring was not a feature of cricket in north-east Scotland, where a batting average in the high teens might well see a player top the season's averages, and Schof's innings was hailed as a marvel. 'His display was an out and out splendid one,' recorded the *Aberdeen Evening Press*, 'and he very well deserved the applause that greeted his return to the pavilion.'

Over the course of the 1891 season Aberdeenshire played 37 matches, winning 20, drawing 10 and losing seven. Schof had taken 57 wickets at 6.8 apiece and scored 368 runs for an average of 16. His performances had been fitful, but his cheeriness and the improvement he'd shown as the summer progressed were enough to win him a contract for the following season.

Schof returned to Mannofield in the spring of 1892 broader, stronger and with more self-confidence. At this stage of his career, like his contemporary and friend George Hirst, he was concerned only with bowling fast and straight. On better pitches and against better batsmen, it might not have been effective, but in northern Scotland the extra speed he had gained as his body filled out was enough to shatter the spirits of the opposition. Schof took 69 wickets at 6.45 each and was said to have bowled only three wides all season. In 32 matches opposing teams managed to score more than 100 on just four occasions. Peterhead were blasted out for just 15.

Schof's batting, too, was impressively consistent and often spectacular. He scored more runs than any other batsman, averaging 21.6. His benefit match against Caledonian at Mannofield on 14 August was a grand affair with a sumptuous marquee luncheon hosted by the Marquis of Huntly. Schof struck 47 not out and took three wickets. His popularity ensured a huge crowd and he was handed gate receipts of £50 (worth around £6,500 today). The highlight of his season came a few weeks later when he was selected to play for North Eastern Counties against Louis Hall's North of England in a two-day match at Mannofield.

Hall's side was a powerful one that included Lancashire's strapping right-hander Frank Sugg (who two years earlier had been one of *Wisden*'s 'nine great professional batsmen'), his county team-mate, slow left-armer Johnny Briggs (the first bowler to take 100 wickets in Tests), Yorkshire opener 'Long John' Tunnicliffe and Wilf Flowers, who'd score over 50,000 runs for Nottinghamshire.

Against opposition of such high quality, the home side struggled. The one bright spark was Schof, who top-scored when the North Eastern Counties were skittled out for 92 and then took six wickets for 36 runs. Louis Hall – one of his victims – had been monitoring the young man's progress. He had heard good reports. Now he knew they were true.

Schof was back at Mannofield for the 1893 season. Cricket in the northern half of Scotland had traditionally struggled to attract the public and the local press frequently lamented both the inclement weather and the lack of a Caledonian W. G. Grace, who might ignite a passion for the game in locals. Aberdeenshire went the whole rain-affected season undefeated. Schof might not have been as crowd-pleasing as the bearded doctor but he was impressive enough. He took 103 wickets at 4.68 and hit 393 runs at 19.65.

In 1892 Schof had struck 66 not out against Perthshire. The committeemen at North Inch had made a note of him. Founded in 1824, Perthshire were Scotland's grandest club. Nicknamed the Big County, they'd win the Scottish County Championship twice as many times as any of their rivals and their match with Forfarshire, optimistically billed as 'the Scottish Roses Match' by the press in Scotland, attracted crowds of 5,000 and more. Perthshire offered Schof a lucrative contract for 1894. He'd enjoyed his years at Mannofield and made many friends. They were sad to see him go, but nobody in Aberdeenshire could begrudge the cheery Yorkshireman the chance to advance his career.

Bowling faster than ever and batting with greater confidence, Schof had a fine season at North Inch, finishing the season with 128 wickets at 4.103 and making 583 runs at 34.3. Against Uddingston in August, Haigh hit the headlines by taking seven wickets for seven runs including a hat-trick. The performance won him a two-guinea prize from the *Sunday Chronicle*. In the match against Stirlingshire he took eight for 13, against Drumpellier eight for 25, before thrashing the bowling around 'as if it were rot'. Against a Crieff Nondescripts team that included well-respected pro Peter Higgins, he blasted a century in under two hours.

By now his performances had begun to attract attention in his native county. In September the *Huddersfield Chronicle*, admittedly not an unbiased observer, was calling for Schof to be given a trial by Yorkshire.

In the tradition of pros in club cricket, Schof was allowed to pick a fixture for his benefit. Unsurprisingly he plumped for the derby with Forfarshire at North Inch. A crowd of over 6,000 watched the match in which he took three for

44. At a dinner after the match, Schof was presented with gate receipts of £67 by the Lord Provost of Perth, John Dewar. In his speech at the presentation, Dewar – from the whisky family – told the audience that Schof was the finest professional Perthshire had ever had and that the money was thoroughly deserved. A Perthshire councillor quoted in the *Huddersfield Chronicle* said that Haigh was hugely popular and that it was hoped by everybody that he returned the next season because we 'like the laddie'. The view was widely shared. The *People's Journal* described Haigh as 'the best all-round professional in Scotland', while John Bull in the *Scottish Referee* magazine lamented, 'We are afraid [Haigh's] performances are far too good for him to remain in Scotland even with Perthshire next season.'

Schof had undoubtedly benefited from his first season with Perthshire. He was playing against better players and on better wickets than he'd done with Aberdeenshire. According to the Scottish correspondent of *Cricket – A Weekly Record of the Game*, Haigh had been content at Aberdeenshire to 'bowl at a great pace without bothering about anything else'. Now, against batsmen who were not unnerved by speed alone, he was compelled to add guile. He developed an accurate yorker, learned to vary his pace subtly and added to his arsenal a well-disguised and flighted slow ball that would become a devastating weapon.

The best description of Schof in action during that time comes from a game late in the season in which he turned out for a Rossie Priory team that also included the famous footballer Lord Alfred Kinnaird, a tall, red-haired Old Etonian who had famously replied to his wife's remark that she feared that when he played football he might break a leg with the quip, 'Rest assured, my dear, that if I do it shall not be my own.'

Rossie were playing a Strathmore side that included a journalist from the *Scottish Referee*. In his report of the encounter, he records that the appearance of the great Haigh did not at first impress. Rather he was 'a small, dapper man' apparently struggling to carry 'a kit bag that was twice his size'. They all had a good giggle at his expense. Strathmore batted first, however, and the sniggering soon stopped as Schof steamed in and let fly. Suddenly, 'The little man was a 100 tonner broken loose from one of Her Majesty's Ironclads.' The cherry hurtled down the pitch as if it had been fired from a cannon. The writer himself was dismissed by a straight ball of lightning speed that struck the stumps with such force 'the groundsman was left to clean up the splinters'. Schof finished with eight wickets for 19 runs. Against all expectations Perthshire announced that Haigh had agreed to return to North Inch the following season. It would prove to be a grand hurrah.

In May 1895, Haigh helped Perthshire skittle out a strong West of Scotland side for 86. The *Dundee Advertiser* noted that 'Haigh, Scotland's champion bowler of last year, again carried the palm, securing no fewer than eight wickets for 18 runs. His first six overs resulted in five wickets for only five runs scored.'

In June against Stirlingshire Schof was again the star, striking 125 not out in a total of 202 for nine and following it by snapping up five wickets and taking two superb catches in the slips. In July he took seven wickets for 23 and hit 79 as Perthshire crushed Drumpellier.

By now Yorkshire had finally begun to taken notice. Schof was called down for a trial match against a Middlesbrough

XVI. Another Huddersfield player, Willie Lancaster – who also played as a pro in Scotland – grabbed the headlines by hammering 136 (including two sixes and 17 fours) and taking four wickets for 40, but Haigh did well enough, scoring 41 and taking eight wickets, including a hat-trick in the Middlesbrough side's first innings.

A game for Yorkshire Colts against Derbyshire followed and then in early July, with the Hon. F. S. Jackson and Bobby Peel called up for the annual Gentlemen v Players match at Lord's, Schof found himself playing for the full Yorkshire side against Derbyshire at Derby. Conditions were perfect for batting. The *Sheffield Evening Telegraph* went so far as to call the sky 'Italian' and the pitch was as flat as a billiard table. An expectant crowd watched the much-trumpeted young pro with some suspicion. He was a star in Scotland, but so what? Schof shut them up. He took five wickets for 73 in Derbyshire's first innings and two for 30 in the second as well as scoring 25 and 36 batting at number 10.

Back in Perth, Schof continued to excel and was called up to play for Scotland against Lancashire. The visitors batted first. Things began slowly for Haigh. He'd conceded 63 runs without troubling the batsmen. Then suddenly he found his form and took eight wickets for 15 runs with five of them clean bowled. Yet Scotland still lost by an innings, the batsmen flummoxed by Johnny Briggs, who finished with match figures of 14 for 65. The *Scottish Referee* lamented that the fixture had ever taken place and wondered if in future visiting English sides might bat with broom handles as a handicap. Schof alone escaped the ridicule. 'His reputation is certain to be given a lift by this magnificent performance.'

Sure enough, on 9 August the *Athletic News* reported that

Mr Connell, secretary of Leeds Cricket Club, had signed Schof as the club professional for the 1896 season. The correspondent wrote, 'Two or three other Yorkshire clubs of note have shown their willingness to give Haigh a place on their staff while . . . he had one or two liberal offers for clubs in Lancashire.'

On 31 August, Schof made his final appearance for Perthshire in his benefit match. He received a pay-out of £51 and 5 shillings. Presenting the award, Perth's county clerk, William McCleish, told the assembled throng, 'It is safe to say that Perthshire Cricket Club never had a better cricketer, one who was such a jolly good fellow, or one who was more esteemed in the city.' He lamented that Haigh was leaving, 'But merit must go where it is most in demand, and where it is best paid'.

In thanking the club and its supporters, Schof commented sweetly, 'In leaving this fair city I am sure I do not leave behind a single enemy.' In his final season, despite disruptions caused by his county call-ups, he had scored 487 runs at an average of 29.3 and taken 94 wickets at under five runs apiece. He was top of the bowling averages and second in the batting and had scored twice as many runs as any of his team-mates. In an unspoken tribute to his abilities, Perthshire replaced him for the following season with not one professional, but two.

After saying his farewells to his Scottish supporters, Schof travelled to Scarborough to play for Yorkshire's Players against the Gentlemen. The festival that year was attended by what the *Hull Daily Mail* described as 'a galaxy of fashionables'. Haigh bowled well, taking five wickets for 73 in the first innings and two for 21 in the second.

Schof continued to turn out for Armitage Bridge whenever he got the chance. The club had been busy raising funds and laying a bowling green in a bid to make the club popular 'with those who do not play cricket or are past their prime'. At a gala day in November, the club chairman spoke warmly of Schof, who he believed would become 'one of the best cricketers as England has produced'. The chairman had spent a good deal of time north of the border and 'from what I was told and read in the newspapers I found that Schofield Haigh was the best bowler who had ever gone to Scotland as a professional'.

In April 1896, Schofield Haigh was called up to play for Yorkshire Colts against Nottinghamshire Colts in a two-day game at Worksop. He hit a half-century in the first innings and picked up four wickets when the home side batted for the second time. His performance was noted by the Yorkshire committee.

On 9 May, Yorkshire concluded their game with Warwickshire at Edgbaston and travelled down to Taunton for their next match with Somerset. Somehow during the midday meal David Denton gave a lie to his nickname of 'Lucky' by contriving to cut his finger so badly he was ruled unfit to pay. With F. S. Jackson away playing for Lord Sheffield's XI against the touring Australians, Yorkshire were a man short. A telegram was sent to Leeds requesting Schof's presence in Somerset. He travelled down by the early train and arrived in Taunton just in time for the start of play.

He must have wished the train had broken down in Birmingham. In front of a handful of spectators, on a day of beating sunshine, Somerset's great Australian all-rounder Sammy Woods thrashed the Yorkshire attack to all points of the ground and sometimes out of it – one huge swipe depositing a delivery from George Herbert into the River Tone. Schof bowled 10 overs and came off relatively unscathed with one for 36 as Somerset blasted 323 in just over six hours. His old Armitage Bridge team-mate Moorhouse scored a century and he didn't bowl in Somerset's second innings as Yorkshire survived their early struggles to win by five wickets.

Yorkshire's next match was against Gloucestershire. The game was moved to Bristol because there was a smallpox epidemic in Gloucester. Jackson returned and Schof was dropped to 12th man. Yorkshire won the match easily without him. He was called up for the county again in early June for the match with Cambridge University for which a number of key players were rested, but he was once again anonymous.

Schof's performances for Leeds at least kept his name in the newspapers. By mid-July he had taken 73 wickets for 5.21 apiece and his batting average after 13 innings was an impressive – for the time – 32.10. Stand-out performances came against Pudsey Britannia when he took nine wickets for six runs and against Ossett when he claimed seven for 16.

Yorkshire gave him another chance and, against County Durham at Barnsley, he finally made an impact – quite a crater-sized one. Facing opponents who were admittedly not of the highest calibre, he sent down 40 overs in the match conceding just 50 runs and taking 14 wickets. Off the back of this performance, he was picked for Yorkshire's next match against the Australians at Bradford. Schof took two wickets for 55 in the first innings and was out for a duck when Yorkshire batted. It looked like the match might prove to be another false start, but when the Australians batted a second time on a pitch that was beginning to disintegrate Haigh bounced in and took eight wickets for 78. Yorkshire still lost by close to 150 runs, but Schof had done enough to keep his place.

In the game against Derbyshire at Bramall Lane Yorkshire batted first and scored 298. Schof took the new ball with George Herbert, clean bowled the first three Derbyshire batsmen and then returned for a second spell to clean bowl two more and have a sixth caught by Denton. He took six more scalps when Derbyshire followed on and Yorkshire won convincingly.

Schof, observers noted, took a run of around a dozen paces commencing with an awkward-looking jump and increased the length of his stride as he approached the crease. In delivery his arm was rather low, but the ball came through fast and with a considerable degree of spin on it. Among these standard deliveries Haigh occasionally inserted the cleverly disguised slower, flighted ball that would become one of his signatures.

As well as destroying Derbyshire's batting Schof had also impressed enough with the bat for a reporter from Sheffield to declare, 'In batting he possesses much of George Herbert's vigour without that batsman's measure of ability, though he can hit well all around the wicket.'

In the next match against Warwickshire at Headingley, Schof had 11 more victims, nine of them clean bowled. After that, the baby-faced lad from Berry Brow became a regular, helping to make an attack that with George Herbert, Peel and Wainwright, backed up by F. S. Jackson and Frank Milligan – a gifted amateur all-rounder who'd be killed in the Second Boer War – was one of the most formidable in England. They were helped by the presence of Hunter behind the wicket (in those days still insisting on standing up at the stumps no matter how fast the bowler – he'd later take a more conventional approach and stand back to the quicks) and alongside him Tunnicliffe at first slip. Most observers regarded 'Long John' as the greatest slip fielder cricket had ever seen. He took 678 catches during his career and, when forced to keep wicket in six matches when Hunter was injured, managed nine stumpings.

Schof came face-to-face with the formidable W. G. Grace for the first time when Gloucestershire arrived at Bramall Lane in late July. Haigh took the second over after Peel. He decided to surprise the Doctor with a fast yorker. He ran in and let fly. The shiny new ball slipped out of his hand and flew at Grace shoulder high. Fencing at it in self-defence the Doctor snicked straight to Hunter behind the stumps. George Herbert, whose failure ever to dismiss the great man was a source of irritation to him (after he'd retired, when asked why he'd never got W. G. out, Hirst replied with what might have been his only public display of testiness, 'Well, he never got me out, either') watched as Grace departed and shook his head at the injustice of life.

Aside from that small vexation, George Herbert was having a grand year. On New Year's Day, he'd married Emma Kilner in Kirkheaton Parish Church. The couple had moved to a modest house at Square Hill, Kirkheaton and by the start of the cricket season they were expecting their first child (a son, James, born on 6 October). George Herbert celebrated his new status by doing the double for the first time. He scored 1,122 runs and took 104 wickets. The latter tally was a drop from the season before. There were mumblings about that. Many in Yorkshire felt bowling was the real meat of cricket. Taking wickets won matches. Some onlookers felt young George needed to grit his teeth and not get drawn in by the easy gratification of stroke-play. He could leave that to the gentlemen for whom cricket was leisure not graft.

With Bobby Peel matching George Herbert by doing the double in a season in which he hit three centuries and took 10 wickets in a match three times, and F. S. Jackson and Jack Brown in formidable form with the bat, Yorkshire cruised to their second County Championship, winning 16 of their 26 matches and leaving Lancashire in a distant second place.

Despite the great work of George Herbert, Peel, Jackson and Brown, Lord Hawke was in little doubt over the turning point of the season. 'We won the Championship ... more by batting than bowling. It was only the advent of Schofield Haigh that made our attack effective, speaking generally, though all my boys had their day with the ball – I mean those who were called on to bowl.'

Over what was for Schof a short season – he played in just 13 county matches – he'd picked up 71 wickets at 15.28, good enough to top the Yorkshire averages. He'd taken five wickets in an innings seven times and 10 in a match twice.

Towards the close of the season, Schof played in a charity match for Leeds District against Castleford District and took seven wickets, six of them clean bowled. The match was played to raise money for the Micklefield Disaster Fund, in aid of the families of the 63 miners who'd died that April in an explosion at Peckfield Colliery. It was a grim reminder, if any were needed, of the sort of life that cricket had helped Haigh, Hirst, Tunnicliffe, Brown and the rest to escape.

Despite his devastating performances for Yorkshire the previous season, observers were still in two minds about Schof. There were many who doubted he'd survive the rigours of the county circuit. George Atkinson, a Ripon-born Yorkshire fast bowler from the early days of first-class cricket, had watched Haigh in his opening season for Yorkshire and said, 'I don't speak derogatory, but he takes a tremendous long run, and he is much too strained in bringing his arm round; he is wrenching every muscle in his body. He cannot last many years.'

There was a chance to gather fresh evidence in the second week of May when a trial match between Yorkshire and a local District XVIII was arranged at Thirsk. Schof played in the Yorkshire side. The District XVIII included George Herbert and James Shaw, a Yorkshire slow bowler who came from Linthwaite, near Huddersfield.

Yorkshire batted first and were bowled out for 144, mainly thanks to George Herbert who picked up six wickets. Schof came out in the late afternoon and opened the bowling with Peel. His first over was a sensation. He took a hat-trick, each victim clean bowled. He'd finish with thirteen wickets for 40 runs. Yorkshire were then bowled out for 123, George Herbert taking his match tally to ten. When the District XVIII batted for the second time, Schof took four wickets in an over (including his second hat-trick of the match) and finished with the extraordinary match figures of 20 wickets for 66.

Schof was not only quicker than he'd been the year before, but the variations of pace, the sly slower ball and the lethal yorker all seemed to have been sharpened. More than his ability, it was his temperament that drew attention. One Yorkshire cricket writer noted that circumspection and modesty were the keys to progress for the young cricketer and that, of these two virtues, Haigh had both. 'Steady and straightforward are adjectives that describe the man, and his happy and unassuming disposition make him many friends.' As it had been in Scotland, so it was in Yorkshire.

Nevertheless, it remained true that Schof's dramatic action took a lot out of him. His run-up was seven or eight paces and ended with an enormous step that gave some the impression of a gymnast about to do the splits. In his delivery stride he held his right arm behind his right leg while his left hand pointed directly skywards. He dragged his right foot along the ground so hard he had to put a brass plate on his boot to protect it. Schof was short and sturdy. But he was not as robust as he looked and lacked the massive reserves of stamina that characterised George Herbert and later Wilfred Rhodes. As a consequence, 1897 would be a season of peaks and troughs for him. He didn't reach the heights of 1896 until 21 July – the day of Queen Victoria's Jubilee – when Yorkshire played Surrey. That day, with a holiday crowd of 30,000 crammed into Headingley, Haigh took seven wickets for 17 runs, clean bowling Hayward, Baldwin, Leveson Gower, Chinnery, Keys, Lees and Wood in a dozen devastating overs, five of which were maidens.

Schof was still learning the characters and vagaries of the county circuit and his friend George Herbert was happy to help in his education. When Haigh encountered Jack Board, Gloucestershire's great wicketkeeper-batsman, for the first time, George Herbert was on hand with wise advice. Board was a genius behind the stumps, but had a reputation as one of the jitteriest runners in county cricket. When he was at the non-striker's end he backed up three or four yards before the bowler had released the ball. Seeing this as he ran in, Schof went over to consult with George Herbert, who was in his usual position at mid-off. 'Hey, George, I can run this fellow out, you know'.

George Herbert smiled. 'Aye,' he replied. 'But you mustn't. Just leave him be and he'll run all the rest out for us.'

George Herbert was having a great and at times comical season. In the game against Derbyshire at Derby in June, Yorkshire were set 154 to win and found themselves with nine wickets down and 16 runs still needed. Hunter sauntered out to the wicket to join George Herbert having seen the Derbyshire committee lining up champagne bottles on a table in the pavilion ready for a victory celebration. George Herbert was on 49. He told Hunter to block and he would get the runs. Hunter responded by hitting three consecutive fours. He then took a three at the end of the over to retain the strike and hit the first ball of the next over for the winning run. George Herbert finished 49 not out. The champagne went back in the cellar.

The game against Somerset at Taunton served to illustrate the attitude of even the best amateur players. With Hawke absent suffering from lumbago, the more flamboyant Jackson captained the side. Yorkshire were set just 115 to win. When Brown and Tunnicliffe put on 49 for the first wicket, Jackson decided there was no point in him hanging around and went off to the station with his fellow gentleman Frank Milligan to catch the train to London and get some extra rest before the next game against Essex at Leyton. As the train passed the County Ground, they saw to their horror that Yorkshire had lost five quick wickets. George Herbert and Schof were at the crease. Luckily for the amateur pair, the pros saw Yorkshire home and embarrassment was spared. Despite Jackson and Milligan's early arrival in London, the team lost to Essex by three wickets.

In late August, against Derbyshire at Bradford, Schof again hit the heights with match figures of 11 wickets for 80, a performance that included his first first-class hat-trick. The visitors had reached 120 for four in their first innings when Haigh changed ends. He took five wickets without a run being scored from him.

By then he was opening the bowling with George Herbert because Bobby Peel was no longer a member of the side. The incident that would shape Yorkshire cricket for the next 30 years occurred in the game against Middlesex at Sheffield on 16 August.

Ted Peate's replacement had proved more than a match for him not only on the field but off it, too. He drank heavily, though unlike his predecessor who'd often disappear into the beer tent during matches for a liquid lunch, Peel confined his boozing to the evenings and mornings. His habit of having a few tots before the start of play was perhaps a means of warding off a hangover. During late July and early August of 1897 Peel had missed nearly a month of cricket after apparently sustaining an injury in the Roses match of 19-21 July. He'd later claim that he was so badly hurt, he'd been forced to spend three weeks in bed. The nature of his sickness is unrecorded. Some people around the county – including, possibly, Lord Hawke – suspected a sustained bender. Peel finally returned against Middlesex at Sheffield. He scored 40 in Yorkshire's first innings, then took five for 71 in Middlesex's reply of 247.

Yorkshire began the final day having scored 29 for one in their second innings. They declared at lunch, leaving Middlesex needing 302. In the afternoon, Peel bowled just seven overs as Middlesex batted out time. The following day it was announced that Yorkshire had suspended him for the remainder of the season.

Over time, accounts of the incidents that had provoked these measures would grow ever more florid and comical until they saw a wobbly-legged and glassy-eyed Peel escorted away by Lord Hawke after urinating on the square. At the time, however, no details were given and the public were left baffled by the decision.

One man who perhaps had a better insight than most into what had gone on was George Herbert. Yorkshire's pros had been staying together during the match at a hotel. George Herbert was eating breakfast on the morning before the start of the final day when Peel reeled into the dining room smelling of gin and struggling to stay upright. George Herbert knew from experience that Peel often took a 'sharpener' early in the morning, but on this occasion he had clearly gone over his tipping point. Worried that his team-mate would land in hot water, George Herbert bundled Peel back upstairs and tucked him up in bed.

He then went to Bramall Lane where he told Lord Hawke that Peel had been taken ill. Hawke was sympathetic and George Herbert let out a sigh of relief. The feeling did not last long. When the team walked out into the middle, George Herbert saw to his consternation the figure of Bobby Peel, ruddy-faced, grinning blearily and with his cap askew, standing by the wicket. Swiftly diagnosing the nature of Peel's illness, Hawke ordered him from the field. The all-rounder refused to go. Instead, he solemnly marked out his run and bowled one of the beautifully flighted deliveries for which he was celebrated. Unfortunately, he had aimed at the sightscreen rather than the wicket. His Lordship had seen enough. Peel was led away.

When he got back to the hotel after the close of play, George Herbert found his team-mate fast asleep in bed. The next morning he told him to write a letter of apology to

Lord Hawke. Peel refused point-blank. 'Then you're finished, Bobby,' George Herbert said. His friend laughed at the idea. He was, after all, Bobby Peel. Yorkshire could not do without him. Besides, as he told the newspapers, reports of his drunkenness were exaggerated. He had drunk only a couple of gins before the start of play and nothing at all with lunch.

Despite Peel's talents and protests, George Herbert's verdict proved the correct one. The suspension quickly became a sacking. The great all-rounder left Yorkshire and was banished into the darkness. Or Lancashire, as it is known to the rest of the world. He would play as a professional for Accrington in the Lancashire League for a season (part of his fee was withheld for unspecified misdemeanours) before coming back to Yorkshire to play for a variety of clubs around Leeds.

Lord Hawke bore Peel no malice. 'It had to be done for the sake of discipline and for the good of cricket,' he'd write later. 'Nothing gave me so much pain . . . What hurt me was publicly censuring a valuable comrade and a real good fellow.' He'd prove that he meant it several decades later when, as president of Yorkshire, he approved the appointment of Bobby Peel as a talent scout and youth coach for the county.

Lord Hawke had now fired the two slow left-arm bowlers David Hunter rated as the greatest he'd ever seen. If he'd wanted to show the world that no individual was bigger than Yorkshire County Cricket Club he had done so in the most emphatic fashion. He had found Peel to replace Peate. Now he just needed to work a similar trick and find a replacement for Peel. Preferably a man who was quiet, dedicated and didn't pour whisky on his cornflakes.

CHAPTER THREE

The Boy in the Barn

In later years, when Wilfred Rhodes was asked to name the person he most admired, he would surprise the questioner, who probably expected to hear a name like Hobbs or Barnes, by replying, 'Thomas Edison'. The American inventor was intelligent and dogged – when faced with a problem he came up with a solution through observation, calculation and experimentation. This was Wilfred's method too. He watched, learned and tested, never giving in to fatigue or despair, always pushing on until he had reached his goal. Bowling would be his phonograph, batting his motion picture camera. The only coach he ever needed was himself. He was cricket's ultimate autodidact.

The child with eyes as pale blue as a husky's was born in Kirkheaton in 1877. His father was a coal miner, a bearded and serious Victorian patriarch. Rhodes senior had a passion for cricket and captained Kirkheaton's second team. When Wilfred was an infant he moved the family – wife Elizabeth and Wilfred's elder brother Hollin – out of the village to a farm cottage on the road to Hopton and made a wicket in the field behind the house. He took his son to watch his first cricket across the valley at Lascelles Hall and for Christmas gave him a bat, ball and stumps so that he could practise.

Wilfred went to school in Hopton and then to Spring Grove in Huddersfield. He watched Yorkshire play at Huddersfield and Dewsbury and, when he was just turned 10, walked the dozen miles from Kirkheaton to Bradford to see W. G. Grace play for Gloucestershire. On a tricky Park Avenue wicket the great man was disappointingly out for a duck.

A bright and studious child, Wilfred stayed on in education long past the point when George Herbert and Schof had begun working life. He was marked out as a future school-master and when he turned 16 a berth was found for him as a pupil-teacher at a school near Batley Carr. Sensing his teaching duties would interfere with his cricket, Wilfred turned down the opportunity and instead took a job in the Mirfield railway yards. Here he'd clean the engines and occasionally serve as a fireman. Inspired by local lad George Hirst's success, Wilfred dreamed of playing for Yorkshire.

Like George Herbert, Wilfred bowled left-arm 'as fast as I could' and batted right-handed. If Hirst ever wondered about this anomaly his thoughts have gone unrecorded. Wilfred addressed the topic in his usual fastidious manner, watching others and puzzling. When playing knur and spell, he noted, both he and George Herbert swung right-handed. However, when they played lawn bowls, George Herbert used his left hand to deliver a wood, while Wilfred used his right. Yet catching was a different matter. Wilfred found it easier to move to his left and only felt confident taking the ball one-handed on that side. Others, he'd observe, did things in reverse. Clem Hill, for one. The great Australian batted left-handed but his flat fast throws from the boundary were delivered with his right arm. Wilfred puzzled over the matter for years, but for once did not reach a conclusion that satisfied him. Had he seen Jimmy Anderson bowling right and batting left, he'd have even more to chew over.

By 1894, Wilfred was playing for Kirkheaton Seconds under his father. On Saturdays he worked till 2 p.m. Matches started an hour later. When the time bell rang he'd pick up his kit and jog to wherever his team were playing. One day the manager left early and put Wilfred in charge of the bell. That day Kirkheaton were playing away from home at Golcar. Eager not to miss the start, Wilfred rang time half an hour early and trotted off to play. That afternoon he hit his first ever half-century and picked up 5 shillings in 'talent money'. His happiness was short-lived. On the Monday the locomotive attendant called him into his office, reprimanded him for his misconduct and fired him.

Wilfred took a job helping a local farmer with his livestock. On trips to the market on a horse and cart he'd always stop when he saw men practising cricket and join in for half an hour or so. Once at Mirfield it was said he bowled the club captain three times in a row and was peremptorily told to bugger off when the skipper discovered he wasn't a club member.

In 1895 Wilfred was promoted to Kirkheaton's first team. He created a stir in his first season, picking up 87 wickets at around 10 apiece. He had set his heart on making a living from cricket and told anyone who'd listen of his ambition. He was called for a trial by Barnsley, playing in a benefit match for the club's retiring pro Jim Ackroyd. Wilfred took five wickets in the match but was out for a duck. While acknowledging he was a player of potential, the Barnsley committee told him he was too callow for the task.

Fortunately there were other clubs in other parts of Britain who were not so picky. Galashiels Cricket Club had been set up by local millworkers in June 1853. The club had moved to their Mossilee ground in 1882. The Border League was formed in 1895 and initially consisted of Gala, Kelso, Hawick, Melrose and Selkirk. Langholm and St Boswells would join soon afterwards.

There were strong ties between the West Riding of Yorkshire and the Scottish Borders, grounded in a shared industrial heritage – wool and textiles. Selkirk Cricket Club had been founded in 1851 by a pair of Yorkshiremen who were installing new looms in the local tweed mills. The first player to score a century for the club at its new ground in Philiphaugh was a Yorkshire professional named Parratt, who'd come up to work on those looms.

The formation of the new league and the growing intensity of local rivalries (fought out most notably on the local rugby pitches) led Galashiels to task John Tetlow, a card manufacturer from Cleckheaton who had business dealings in the town, with finding them a new Yorkshire pro to replace George Goulder, who was leaving at the end of the season to play as professional for Meltham, near Holmfirth.

Back in Yorkshire, Tetlow made enquiries with Arthur Shaw and J. L. Byrom, two well-known administrators in the Huddersfield and District League. They pointed him in the direction of Wilfred Rhodes. Galashiels posted off the contracts. Wilfred was just 17 when he signed them, 18 when he boarded the northbound train the following spring. He was the youngest professional ever to play in Scotland and he had never been out of Yorkshire in his life. Neither fact daunted him. Even as a gangly teenager, Wilfred had an impenetrable insularity that protected him from the outside world. Though he had an elder brother, Wilfred's character was that of an only child. He was reticent and watchful, self-contained, alone even in a crowd. He had set himself to making a living from cricket. He had practised through the winter whenever he got the chance and travelled to his new job 'with what you might call hopeful confidence'.

Wilfred was still a smooth-cheeked boy, and the Gala committee must have reacted to his appearance in much the same way the Aberdeen men had when they first clapped eyes on Schofield Haigh. But Wilfred's talents were more quickly obvious. When Arbroath United made the long journey south in June they found the young pro in formidable form. He batted fluently to score 57 and then took four wickets for 46 runs as the visitors held out for a draw. Later that month he took five wickets against a strong Watsonians side and in Gala's two meetings with arch-rivals Selkirk he picked up 12 wickets, five in the first match and seven in the second. His benefit game was against Grange from Edinburgh. A large crowd watched the match at Mossilee. Wilfred was unsuccessful with the bat but took three wickets as Grange got the better of a tight-fought match by eight runs. The season had been a great success. Wilfred had taken 92 wickets at seven runs apiece with his left-arm medium-pacers and helped Gala win the league title for the first time. The club invited him back the following year on improved financial terms.

Wilfred returned to Yorkshire in good fettle, but with a thought in his mind. On the soft, slow Scottish wickets, he'd discovered that a slow delivery, tossed up, would often get him a wicket. It planted the idea in his mind of changing the way he bowled. In the nets at Galashiels he practised spinning the ball more often. Typically cautious, he refused to try anything so experimental in an actual match.

The Scottish season ended earlier than the season in Yorkshire and when Wilfred returned home he went back to playing for Kirkheaton in the Huddersfield and District League. Here, for the first time – the county season having closed – he bowled in tandem with George Hirst. The combination proved far too potent for the opposition. Friarmere were dismissed for 49, Golcar for 23, Primrose Hill for 19 and Honley for 46. These four late-season wins were enough to secure the league title for Kirkheaton. George Herbert was evidently impressed with Wilfred and told the teenager he should apply for a place in a Yorkshire trial when he had finished his time in Scotland.

The winter before he'd gone to play for Gala, Wilfred had got a job working on a plate-laying gang on the line between Mirfield and Cooper Bridge. When he worked night shifts he took advantage and used the daylight to practise his cricket. Returning to Yorkshire after his first season in Scotland he again went to work with the plate-layers on a new line that was being cut between Huddersfield and Leeds.

When the season with Kirkheaton finished, Wilfred made the decision that would alter the course of his life – he decided to become a spin bowler. 'I had a natural length from being a schoolboy – my length got me my wickets in my early seasons in club cricket.' He knew now that at a higher level such a simple approach would not be enough. And so he set out to teach himself to bowl slow left-arm.

Having sought advice on how to grip and spin the ball

from a number of older cricketers – he'd acknowledge in particular the help of veteran Huddersfield pro Jim Stubbins – Wilfred set himself to the Edison-like study of turn. Later he'd say of bowling, 'There is only one road to success, and that is practice.' He was the living proof of that.

Next door to the Rhodes family home was a door-less old barn that had been used as a cart shed. The barn was six or seven yards long with a bumpy earth floor and sloped slightly upwards towards the rear. This dark, rough place would become Wilfred's personal indoor net. After a night shift, he'd come and bowl in it for hours on end, pacing out 22 yards from the blackness at the back of the wall into the pale winter daylight and banging in a stump.

Cricket balls were expensive and Wilfred had just one, an old chocolate brown thing that suited his purpose perfectly. He chalked white stripes across its surface so that as it flew from his hand and into the gloom of the shed he could observe how much spin his fingers had imparted on it and the angle of the revolutions. By this process, he learned how to bowl an orthodox left-arm delivery that took the ball away from the right-hander, a top-spinner that hurried on, and a back-spinner that slowed and rose from the ground. It was dull, monotonous work, but as the winter wore on and the ball thudded into the stone again and again and again, Wilfred slowly and surely learned how to regulate the spin exactly as he wanted.

Since he was bowling slightly uphill, Wilfred did not work on flight or length, and because the floor was uneven he couldn't tell how the ball might come off a genuine wicket, so line was of little consideration either. For the first step it was purely the spin, judged by the white lines revolving on the old brown ball, that Wilfred studied. He bowled. He watched. Sometimes a delivery rebounded back to him. Sometimes it didn't and he trotted into the darkness of the barn to fetch it. He bowled until there was a callus on his spinning finger that was hard as a horse's hoof. He'd have it for the next 40 years. On he went through the winter. The ball left his hand. The ball pitched. The ball struck the wall. Hour upon solitary hour, day upon drab day, he carried on, buried in his singular, repetitious task. *Bump, thump, bump, thump, bump, thump* ... Like Captain Virgil Hilts in Stalag Luft III, Wilfred was the Cooler King of Kirkheaton.

In early spring, when the weather turned milder, Wilfred moved out of the barn. He dug up a strip of decent turf from the meadow behind his parents' house and laid it in front of a haystack, bedded it into place with a heavy roller borrowed from a farmer and trimmed the surface with a scythe. It would not have passed an umpires' inspection, but it was flatter than the floor of the barn. With the haystack as his wicketkeeper, Wilfred took his striped ball outdoors and into the weak March sunlight, gradually adding length, line and flight to his lonely daily routine.

He'd come to believe during those months that a bowling action was essentially machine-like, with each movement linking to the next like the parts of a loom. If one link was damaged a bowler would lose his action completely. Wilfred had seen it happen – and like all professionals he lived with the nagging fear of it happening to him.

In Scotland during the 1897 season Wilfred bowled slow left-arm, learned to vary his pace subtly and further modified and refined his control. A bowler had to learn many things – a good length ball is one that gets a batsman in two minds, undecided whether to play forwards or back, but that length varies according to the pace of the pitch and the height of the batsman. He bowled and watched and stored the information away, his mind clicking like a calculating machine. He took fewer wickets – 77 compared to 92 the season before – but that was hardly the point. Wilfred wasn't seeking instant results, he was improving himself. His batting that season made up for the slight drop-off in penetration with the ball. He opened and shared in a record first-wicket stand of 178 against Royal High School. Wilfred's contribution was 65 not out, his highest during his time with Gala. When the team from Edinburgh batted, Wilfred was at his mesmeric best, taking seven wickets as the visitors slumped to 55 for eight at stumps. He'd end the season with close to 400 runs at an average of just over 25.

Galashiels were contesting the title with bitter rivals Selkirk, but the Souters proved too good for them. In the first encounter that season, Selkirk batted first and Wilfred took nine wickets as they were scuttled for 71. Sadly Gala couldn't capitalise. They batted lamentably and were all out for 37.

In September 1923 a letter appeared in the *Yorkshire Evening Post*. The writer was a former commercial traveller from the West Riding. He recalled a visit to Galashiels some three decades earlier when he was taken by one of his customers to Mossilee. On the way to the ground the man asked if he lived in Yorkshire.

'I replied: "I live in Leeds."

'"Well," said he, "our cricket professional comes from Yorkshire. He is a very good player and a beautiful bowler."

'I said: "What is his name?" My customer replied: "Wilfred Rhodes." I told him I had never heard of Rhodes.'

The writer concluded: 'If Rhodes taught them cricket, he also learned valuable lessons from them. He was only a lad then, and he acquired from them all the virtues of a canny Scot. Those early lessons in Scotland have helped make Rhodes the greatest all-round cricketer in the world and the cleverest cricket captain in England today.'

As the 1897 season wore on, it became increasingly clear that Wilfred needed to move on. While many Yorkshire people downplayed success in Scotland, other wiser observers were watching. When Galashiels played Grange, Wilfred met Augustus Grant-Asher, an Oxford Blue who'd hit a double hundred when the club played MCC in 1892. After watching the young Yorkshireman bowl, Grant-Asher advised him to apply for a county place.

Wilfred needed little encouragement. In the August of 1897 he had seen a newspaper notice that Warwickshire were inviting applicants to join the ground staff. Wilfred wrote in enclosing details of his experience with Kirkheaton and Galashiels. Warwickshire sent out enquiries about him in Yorkshire and Scotland and, evidently impressed, wrote back and asked if he would be available to play the following season. Wilfred replied that he would. It seemed a future was opening up for him in Birmingham. Then in October a letter arrived from Warwickshire. Due to budgetary restrictions they would not be able to offer him a place after all. It was a piece of penny-pinching the club would come bitterly to regret.

Other attempts to further his career also hit the buffers. His trial match as prospective pro for Slaithwaite of the Huddersfield and District League was washed out without a ball being bowled.

George Herbert's encouragement to apply for a county

trial with Yorkshire ended with a game for Yorkshire Colts against the county at Bradford in late September. Wilfred took just a single wicket and was outshone by another young slow left-arm spinner, Albert Cordingley from Eccleshill, near Bradford. He caught the train back to Huddersfield with his chin on his chest. Yorkshire were looking for the new Bobby Peel. 'It seemed to me,' he'd later recall, 'that I had missed my chance.'

Wilfred spent a miserable winter on the plate-laying gang, wondering if cricket was his future after all. Then as the nights began to lighten came good news. Yorkshire wanted to see more of him. He had been allocated a place as a professional at Sheffield United Cricket Club in the Yorkshire Council (his rival Cordingley had been given a similar berth at Leeds) and was invited to attend pre-season nets at Headingley.

George Herbert may have had an influence. Travelling back from a miserable tour of Australia that April, the great all-rounder praised his Kirkheaton club-mate to a reporter from the *Sheffield Daily Telegraph*. 'Hirst spoke very highly of young Rhodes. It appears he lives next door to the Huddersfield professional and [says] we may look forward to some very good cricket from Rhodes. He bowls a fine ball at medium pace and makes it do a bit of work both ways.'

The latter suggests George Herbert was still thinking of the Rhodes he'd played with in the 1896 season, but, accurate or not, it was the sort of high-level support Wilfred needed as he began what was to be the most important few months of his life.

Later, Wilfred would recall the nets at Headingley that spring as a rough baptism against the best of the county batsmen; a valuable lesson about the difference between bowling to club cricketers and top professionals. He'd remember returning home chastened, having been forcefully made aware of how far away he was from realising his ambitions. He thought he'd learned a lot, but had discovered that, as Schof would observe, 'The more you get to know about cricket, the more you see how little you know.'

Others, however, record a different impression of the young Rhodes that day at Leeds. Alex Wormald, of Kirkstall Cricket Club, was also present for practice. He remembered that five nets were set up in a row on the part of the ground where the practice sheds would later be built. All the first-team regulars were there except for Hirst and Denton.

The heir apparent to Bobby Peel, Albert Cordingley, was bowling in number one net. Wilfred had been allocated to number five net, with Wormald, Schof, amateur bats-man Frank Milligan and a trialist named Collinson from Mytholmroyd. A crowd of members and reporters gathered at the back for the first net to run an eye over Cordingley. Lord Hawke arrived and announced his intention to bat in each net in sequence. As His Lordship moved down the nets, the watchers followed him. When finally he went to take guard in the number five net, Schofield Haigh told his charges in his usual jaunty manner, 'Now boys, let's knock His Lordship's bob down.'

Wilfred followed Schof's instructions to the letter, flight-ing a delivery that pitched on leg, span and clipped the top of Lord Hawke's off peg. Hawke looked at the bowler with a mix of admiration and indignation. 'Did you do that on purpose?' he asked gruffly. Wilfred replied that he had. 'Then you'd better do it again,' Hawke instructed. Wilfred obliged, bowling Hawke a second time with an identical delivery.

Wormald told this tale many years afterwards when Wilfred had retired. Perhaps he had embroidered things a little, but the truth is that, whatever Wilfred thought about the impression he'd created, Yorkshire kept inviting him back. If he hadn't bowled Lord Hawke out to order, he had plainly done something to impress the great man. Lord Hawke would later recall that Rhodes had 'done nothing in particular, but in April, at our practice, he had given unmistakable proof of his skill'.

Following the net session, Wilfred and Cordingley were selected to play on opposite sides in a trial match between a Yorkshire XI and Bedale and District XVIII. Wilfred played for the former, his rival for the latter. This gave the Bradford man the chance to impress Yorkshire's batsmen, while Wilfred was effectively skittling out club players. Rhodes returned match figures of six for 37. Cordingley took five for 75, but among his victims were Jack Brown and David Denton. A few days later, Wilfred and Cordingley played for Yorkshire Colts against Nottinghamshire Colts at Trent Bridge. On the first day, Wilfred took four wickets, Cordingley just one. Then rain came and washed out day two.

The two spinners were selected for Yorkshire's southern tour where – or so Wilfred believed – they would be played in alternate matches. The first of the games was against MCC at Lord's, commencing on 12 May. In the nets at the Nursery End on the morning before the first day, Hawke asked F. S. Jackson to run his eye over the two bowlers. It seems Hawke favoured Cordingley, reasoning that his greater experience would make him less likely to wilt under the pressure MCC's formidable stroke-makers – who included W. G. Grace – were sure to apply.

Jackson went into his net and faced the young players. He attacked them just as he would any bowler. To his eye Wilfred seemed the cooler. He reported his findings to Hawke. The Yorkshire captain still favoured Cordingley. The two men had an exchange of views. For once, His Lordship backed down. Wilfred was selected. That at least is how the tale goes. Hawke would later recount it in his autobiography as an example of the sort of myths that sprout in cricket. 'So far as I recollect, I never had any doubt as to which I was going to try, but there is the story for what it is worth.'

When he was told of his selection, Wilfred's reaction mixed happiness with cold terror. He was daunted by the task ahead, not least because it meant coming up against W. G. Grace, a man he'd last seen as a paying spectator at Park Avenue. He was 'so nervous I barely knew where I was'. Feeling as if he was in some kind of dream, Wilfred walked out on to a field that seemed to him to be bathed in a misty glow. Fortunately, his nerves soon began to calm and the ground came back into focus. When called on to bowl the youngster was tidy and quickly picked up the wicket of the great Albert Trott. Lord Hawke offered him plenty of encouragement and gave him sound advice on field placings. Hawke would comment later, 'Wilfred's analysis of four for 24 was excellent. It was not the wickets he took but his beautifully easy action and fine variety that at once impressed us all. Both W. G. Grace and W. L. Murdoch were opposing, and both great judges told me how highly they thought of him.'

Even after decades of top-class cricket, Wilfred would never be able to shake off the sort of butterflies that fluttered in his guts that day. Instead, he would learn to control them, playing every game in what he described as a 'state of steadied

nervousness'. It was why by the end of the season the greatest tiredness he felt was not of the body but of the mind. By
September, even though his legs and arms were still fresh,
he'd feel 'fed up' with the game.

The match against Somerset was played on a soft track at
Bath that might have been made to order for Wilfred. He
was brought into the attack after three wickets had fallen
and took the next seven. He followed that by taking six in
the second. After the game, umpire Bob Thoms presented
Wilfred with the ball he'd used in the first innings and told
him to get it inscribed and mounted. Wilfred was so excited
by his success he promptly lost it. Cordingley, the man who
had seemed destined to be 'the new Bobby Peel', barely
played for Yorkshire again.

On that southern tour Wilfred would say he learned more
about cricket than he had in the previous 19 years. The wickets gave him confidence and the advice of his team-mates
transformed him from the self-taught and rather mechanical
bowler who – like the lad in the barn – plodded methodically
onwards regardless, into a cunning predator who could alter
his style to suit the wicket and vary his line and length to
account for the different batsmen he faced.

Wilfred was always watching and making mental notes.
He eyed other bowlers for tips – might he practise a faster
delivery like that of Trott? Or work on shaping the ball away
with his arm like Old Jack Hearne? He observed batsmen
for quirks and weaknesses – which strokes they favoured and
the field placings that would block them. He studied cricketers like a naturalist studying wildlife. His mind became a
reference library, precise and detailed. When other cricketers spoke of Prince Ranjitsinhji they would say, 'He was a

majestic stroke-player.' Wilfred, while allowing that Ranji's eye was so keen he could see the stitches on the ball in flight, would say, 'He was a majestic stroke-player, but . . .' and then give a forensic analysis of the Jam Sahib's foibles (for example, his penchant for teasing the bowler by placing a ball in the exact spot from which a fieldsman had just been moved). He saw the skull when others saw only the skin.

In a game against Gloucestershire, Wilfred found himself bowling at W. G. Grace again. He sent down a good length delivery and gave it some top spin. The Doctor, anticipating a ball that turned away from him, played down the wrong line. The ball thumped his pad. Wilfred appealed. W. G. stroked his great beard and glared at the umpire. He was plumb in front and knew it, but that hardly mattered. The umpire glanced at Wilfred, he looked back at W. G. and yelped, 'You're out, you're out, you're out! You'll have to go!' like a housemaid shooing a grizzly bear out of the scullery.

W. G.'s approach to the game was not always gentlemanly but there was a certain twinkling humour to his gamesmanship. In a match at the Hastings Festival – which Grace rather regarded as his personal fiefdom – Schof had asked the Doctor's permission to leave slightly early so he could catch a train that would get him home to Huddersfield that day. The request was still under consideration when W. G. skied a mighty hit into the deep right to where the Yorkshireman was fielding. As Haigh circled underneath it Grace's famously high-pitched West Country voice could be heard above the crowd, 'If you catch that, Haigh, you shall miss your train.' Schof spilled it and was back in Yorkshire before midnight.

Alongside his display at Somerset, Wilfred also ran through a powerful Surrey side at Bradford in early June, finishing with match figures of 12 for 70, took nine wickets in the match against Leicestershire and 11 against Essex. In Yorkshire's final game of the season, against MCC at Scarborough, he took five for 59. He finished the season with an incredible 154 first-class wickets.

Hawke considered that no bowler had made such an impact since Lancastrian medium-pacer Allan Steel had topped the English bowling averages during his freshman year at Cambridge University. While, 'No one since in English cricket has created the same sensation in his first season.'

The press marvelled at his youthful mastery. In the *Strand Magazine* C. B. Fry summarised the feelings of facing the quiet young destroyer: 'Hostile meaning behind a boyish face – ruddy and frank; a few quick steps and a lovely swing of the left arm and the ball is doing odd things at the other end; it is pitched where you do not like it, you have played forward when you do not want to; the ball has whipped away from you so quickly; it has come straight when you expected break; there is discomfort.'

Wilfred had created this sensation by mastering old cricketing virtues – line, length, flight, spin – rather than by inventing some new method – as Bernard Bosanquet would with his googly. His was a craftsman's brilliance, based on the perfection of simple methods rather than the invention of novel ideas. And that, in a nutshell, was Wilfred Rhodes.

CHAPTER FOUR

The Triumvirate Triumphant

The success of one Kirkheaton man in 1898 made up for the lacklustre displays of another. While Wilfred had been enduring a miserable winter of doubt working on the plate-laying crew in the chill damp of the West Riding, George Herbert had suffered an equally unhappy time in the blazing heat of Australia.

Leaving his wife and newborn son behind, he'd departed for Australia on his first overseas tour as a member of an England party led by the dashing Middlesex batsman Andrew Stoddart and including notables such as Archie MacLaren, Prince Ranjitsinhji, Johnny Briggs, Old Jack Hearne and his Yorkshire team-mate, Ted Wainwright. Stoddart's previous tour of Australia in 1894-95 had seen England win a thrilling series 3-2. At Melbourne, Stoddart had struck the highest score ever made by an England skipper and, on a sticky wicket at Sydney, Bobby Peel had been revived from a drunken stupor with cold showers and coffee to bowl England to victory by 10 runs.

On paper, the two teams seemed as evenly matched as they'd been in that series. But after securing an easy win in the first Test thanks to an innings from Ranjitsinhji that sparkled like the Kohinoor diamond, England's form evaporated in the baking air. They lost the next four encounters with Australia as the tour turned into an unmitigated disaster filled with so many misfortunes it's a surprise to read that none of the players was injured by a runaway pig. The travel between venues was long and torturous (one train journey lasted 29 hours), the umpiring poor, the crowds noisy and hostile and the outfields in the up-country matches more suitable for speedway racing than cricket. The Australian summer was so hot that at the end of a day in the field Old Jack Hearne of Middlesex lay in a cold bath for 90 minutes to cool down. In the steamy nights, the players slept fitfully, itching with heat rashes and sometimes wrapping themselves in damp blankets. The local wildlife proved troublesome, too. Tom Richardson shot a six-foot-long black snake that the locals assured him was deadly poisonous.

Stoddart – considered by many the equal of W. G. Grace – barely scored a run following the death of his mother, while the lion-hearted Surrey paceman Richardson, who had terrorised the Australian batsmen on the previous visit, struggled to get the ball to bounce above waist high. Wainwright, who ripped the ball so hard his fingers bled, could not spin the ball on wickets that offered all the grip of an ice rink and Hirst could get neither lift nor movement from them. In first-class matches, the two Yorkshiremen took 10 wickets between them.

The one bright spot of the tour for George Herbert came when he was at his lowest ebb. During the afternoon of the second day of the third Test at Adelaide, as England's attack was flogged all over the park by the Australian batsmen, he pulled a thigh muscle while bowling and was in such pain he couldn't complete the over. Back in the pavilion Hirst was attended by a doctor who told him the only cure was complete rest.

Rest was not in George Herbert's nature. Against medical advice, he went out to bat the next day with Wainwright as his runner. In an innings that combined courage and bloody-mindedness, Hirst scored 85 not out, hitting 11 fours with earthy pulls and hooks. He walked back to the pavilion to a standing ovation. His innings had lasted over three hours in heat that made the sweat sizzle on his forehead. Hardly what the doctor had prescribed.

George Herbert's struggles on the field had been exacerbated off it by the Australian press, which portrayed the England squad as not only unsuccessful but also shambolic. One evening newspaper claimed that Hirst and Archie MacLaren had got into a fight that left the Lancashire batsman with two black eyes. Apparently unchastened by this experience, MacLaren had then set upon Prince Ranjitsinhji and the resulting fracas had ended with both men wrestling on the floor. George Herbert was upset by this malicious nonsense, but he was more deeply hurt by suggestions from reporters that he had exaggerated his injury at Adelaide and did not need a runner at all. Cheating was anathema to Hirst and being accused of it ruffled even his genial exterior.

The tour had been draining both physically and mentally. The consequence was a season for George Herbert that was as close to a disaster as he would ever come. From 9 June until the end of August, Hirst batted 23 times and scored just 207 runs. He took only 36 wickets in the season and they cost over 25 each. The cricket press in England were downcast to see the doughty all-rounder in such a state, less because of the effect it had on the national team or on Yorkshire, but because he was so universally popular. Seeing George Herbert struggle made everyone sad. Neutrals willed him to succeed. They wanted to see his broad smile again. In September there were at last signs that his old, robust form might be returning.

With George Herbert out of sorts, it had been left to Schof to offer support to Wilfred. In early May he showed his devastating ability on a rain-affected pitch at Southampton. The game was the benefit match for Hampshire's Harry Baldwin. He was the first player in the county's history to have been awarded one and by the finish must have wondered why he'd bothered. The first day was lost to rain and the entire match was concluded in six hours on the second. Yorkshire scored 157 and then bowled out the home side for 42 and 36. David Steele was the only member of the home side to get a double-figure score. Schof made the ball leap and twirl like a Cossack dancer, taking 14 wickets for 43 runs.

In another low-scoring match, against Surrey at Bradford in early June, Schof showed his prowess with the bat. The first day was a washout. On the second, Surrey were all out for 139 – Wilfred and the rejuvenated Wainwright taking all the wickets. By the close, Yorkshire were 142 for eight, with Schof and George Herbert the not out batsmen. The pair would add 192 for the ninth wicket – a Yorkshire record. George Herbert struck 130 not out in four hours and 20 minutes – it was the one highlight of his ghastly year. When Schof was caught by Abel off the bowling of Brockwell for 85, the innings was declared at 297. Wilfred and Wainwright then bowled Surrey out for 37 to secure an innings victory.

Schof was picked for the Players in the annual fixture with the Gentlemen at Lord's, which began on 18 July, the start altered to allow W. G. Grace to celebrate his 50th birthday. Haigh too had other things on his mind, a week after returning from London he married Lillian Beaumont.

Yorkshire won their third County Championship with some ease, despite defeats to key rivals Surrey and Middlesex. Throughout the season the starting XI barely changed. Despite his loss of form, George Herbert played in 23 matches, Schof and Wilfred 26 apiece.

In 1898, Tunnicliffe and Brown had put on 554 for the first wicket against Derbyshire at Chesterfield, a first-class record that would stand until toppled by Percy Holmes and Herbert Sutcliffe at Leyton in 1932. Yorkshire were so delighted they gave both men a silver cup. Bizarrely, Tunnicliffe appears to have batted all day on no more sustenance than a biscuit and a 'two-penny sandwich'. The caterers at Chesterfield had been overwhelmed by the demands of the crowd, who had eaten everything else. The episode had consequences. Lord Hawke responded by introducing proper lunches for his professionals, who had previously been expected to forage for themselves. It was a measure that not only ensured that 'his boys' were always well fed, but also kept them away from the temptations of the well-wishers in the beer tent who had done such damage to poor Ted Peate.

The lunches were part of a raft of measures His Lordship would introduce to improve the life of Yorkshire's professionals. He wanted them to become respectable tradesmen, pillars of the community, what we would today call role models for an aspiring working class. Part of that process was seeing that the pros were properly rewarded and looked after. Lord

Hawke was a paternalist after the style of Lord Leverhulme or the Cadbury family. Yorkshire County Cricket Club was his Port Sunlight, his Bournville village.

As well as ensuring that Yorkshire's players were paid around 50 per cent more than those at their rivals, Hawke also introduced a points system for the payment of bonuses. At most counties, professionals could expect to get an extra payment if they scored a fifty or took five wickets. In Hawke's opinion this was not an accurate reflection of the value of performances. He reasoned, logically, that a century scored on a billiard-table track in bright sunshine was of less value than 40 scored on a gluepot beneath gloomy skies. Under his system, the contribution to winning took precedence over the effect on the averages. The points were totted up at the season's close and a bonus of up to £60 was paid out. In an era when the average annual wage was less than £40, this was a handsome sum indeed.

Hawke's most significant step was to introduce regular winter pay for the Yorkshire pros in place of the previous, discretionary, 'hardship allowance'. This turned professional cricket from a precarious existence into a viable career. Hawke's players got £2 a week throughout the off season. Lancashire and Nottinghamshire soon followed his example, but other counties steadfastly refused to pay players who were, in their view, 'doing nothing'. Sir Spencer Ponsonby-Fane, an important figure at Somerset and treasurer of MCC, spoke for the dissenters, commenting that winter pay was utterly ridiculous since it was 'paying a man to idle away eight months out of twelve'. Pelham Warner took a slightly more moderate view. He believed that winter pay was fair, but that it should be kept to a bare minimum so as to encourage professional cricketers to search out winter employment away from the game. The devil, after all, made work for idle hands, though not those of amateur gentlemen obviously.

Hawke's activism on behalf of the professionals extended beyond Yorkshire. When the England professionals – including the heart-throb George Lohmann – threatened strike action over match payments before the 1896 Oval Test, Hawke commented, 'I am one of those who think players should be paid liberally.' While others grumbled about the players' demands, Hawke suggested they should get £20 per game rather than just the £10 plus £5 expenses they were seeking. His Lordship was an unlikely shop steward, and it was a measure of how strongly he felt on the matter.

Hawke enjoyed the company of the pros – Hunter, Tunnicliffe and George Herbert in particular – and treated them as a schoolmaster might a class of potentially unruly but essentially decent children. It was said that when a professional wanted to marry, Lord Hawke insisted on meeting the potential bride to see that she was suitable. She would be brought to Wighill Park to have the rule run over her. Lord Hawke wanted a life of solid decency for 'his boys'. It wouldn't do if they went head over heels for some damned floozie.

Hawke was an autocrat and there was sometimes a patronising edge to his tone when he spoke of his professional team-mates, yet his reforms at Yorkshire had done much to help the players, whose wages now placed them on a par with trained and educated white-collar workers. Thanks to Hawke, George Herbert, Schof, Wilfred and the rest truly had entered the ranks of the professionals.

Lord Hawke led a party to South Africa over the winter of 1898–99 and Schof was invited to join it. As well as Schof and the skipper, the team contained three other Yorkshire players: the Hampshire-born all-rounder Frank Milligan, the dashing amateur Frank Mitchell (who would emigrate to the Transvaal and captain South Africa in England in 1912) and Clem Wilson, a stroke-making clergyman one of whose middle names was Macro.

Also in the team was Albert Trott, a brilliant all-rounder who was beset by various Bobby Peel-like personal problems, most notably with booze and betting. Trott could smash a ball vast distances (he'd cleared the roof of the new pavilion at Lord's) and his medium-paced bowling moved so consistently in towards right-handed batsmen off the pitch it was said that 'even his cigarette smoke broke from leg'.

Jittery Jack Board was in the team as wicketkeeper. His back-up was A. G. Archer. A great pal of Lord Hawke, Archer had no county experience and had failed to make the Haileybury first XI but, His Lordship explained, he 'had worn the gloves with credit in many Free Forester matches and could get runs now and again'. Archer would have the rare distinction of making his first-class debut in a Test match. In a crowded field, he may well be the worst player ever to get an England cap. Other amateurs in the party were Pelham 'Plum' Warner and the man with the longest surname in Test cricket, Hugh Bromley-Davenport. Both had been on the previous South African tour with Hawke three years earlier.

South African cricket had improved greatly since then, but the selection process for the Test side was blighted by regional rivalries, while the strength of the provincial sides rested too heavily on imported English pros such as Jack Brown, Fred Tate, George Lohmann and Sydney Barnes. The success of these men – all excellent players – had bred a brooding resentment towards English cricket among the local populace. With simmering tensions between London and Paul Kruger, leader of the Transvaal and the Orange Free State, the country teetered close to insurrection both on the field and off it.

Lord Hawke was not by nature a diplomat and at times he seemed set on making things worse rather than better. He refused to meet Kruger (his previous tour had taken place during the fall-out from the Jameson Raid – unsurprisingly, Hawke was an admirer of Cecil Rhodes – and he took a dim view of the Afrikaner government in Pretoria) and Kruger publicly returned the snub by turning down the chance to watch England play. Meanwhile, a game against Western Province was scrapped because the English professionals selected by the province – including Yorkshire's Jack Brown – were wrangling over pay. A rumour circulated by the local press claimed Lord Hawke was advising his fellow countrymen on the negotiations, further inflaming passions against him.

More annoying for His Lordship was the gossip that England's amateurs were in fact being paid. This had been a source of vexation since the days of W. G. Grace, when the amateurs' 'expenses' often far exceeded the wages of the professionals. Lord Hawke, who had a substantial private income, opposed such shady practices, something that brought him into open conflict with other less well-off English amateurs. The suggestion he was a hypocrite made Hawke beetroot-faced with outrage. Looking back on the winter, His Lordship recorded with admirable understatement that 'there was a good deal of unpleasantness with the tour'.

On the field things were a lot easier. Hawke's men generally thrashed the provincial sides they came up against. Only Transvaal had the temerity to field a side of just 11 men against them and were duly hammered for their impertinence by an innings and 201 runs.

Schof made his Test debut at the Old Wanderers ground in Johannesburg on Valentine's Day 1899. The South Africans had a strong side that included the brilliant all-rounder Charlie Llewellyn. Hawke's men won a hard-fought match by 32 runs. Schof's performance, on the matting wicket, was adequate – five wickets for 121 runs.

The second and final Test was at Newlands in Cape Town. A record crowd came to watch. Jimmy Sinclair batted superbly for South Africa, scoring a century before falling to a brilliant Johnny Tyldesley catch. England were bowled out for 92 in the first innings but batted well enough in the second to set the home side 246 to win. It seemed gettable, until Schof and Trott combined and dismissed them for just 35. They were aided by some extraordinary fielding by Frank Milligan, who caught a Sinclair drive off Haigh with such balletic athleticism Hawke declared it 'one of the catches of a lifetime of cricket'. Schof finished the second innings with six wickets. South Africa's captain Murray Bisset praised the English pair, claiming that defeat would not have been so bad 'but your two bowlers have rubbed it in'.

In his two Tests, Schof had taken 14 wickets at 15.71, and in first-class matches 33 wickets at 12.69, including figures of eight for 34 against Cape Colony. The tour had gone well, but he had missed key events at home. In January his mother had died and less than a fortnight later Lillian gave birth to their first child, John. He hurried home armed with a sheaf of spears and assegais, which his children would later use in the back garden when playing cowboys and Indians.

It was the opinion of some wise men on the boundary that

Rhodes's brilliant entry into county cricket had simply been good fortune. The 1898 season had been wet and it was as plain as W. G.'s paunch to these deckchair experts that the young Yorkshireman was simply a damp track sorcerer who would be exposed as a charlatan when faced with a month of sunshine. By the end of what was, by British standards at least, a Saharan summer, the critics had fallen silent. Wilfred had finished with even more wickets than he had the year before, 179.

Things began well. In the second innings of the match against Somerset, Wilfred took five for 11 as the home side were bundled out for 73. In the next game against Gloucestershire at Bristol, the home side were bowled out for 44 and 74 with Wilfred taking nine for 31 in the match. It might have been more, but in the second innings Lord Hawke was so confident of victory he took Wilfred out of the attack, saying he wanted to rest him for the game against Essex that came up next. At Leyton, the refreshed Wilfred took the first nine Essex wickets to fall before Walter Mead – the only home batsman to make double figures – got out to Jackson, who later apologised for spoiling Wilfred's chances of a ten-wicket haul.

Things did not always go Yorkshire's way. After the Essex victory, they travelled up to Cambridge to play the university at Fenner's. Among the students' batsmen was a 24-year-old theologian from Gloucestershire named Gilbert Jessop. He had a dog-like face and wound himself around his bat as if imparting torque to some powerful machine. When the ball came he – in Wilfred's words – 'went off like a spring trap', jumping to the off stump and whirling the ball to leg like a modern T20 player.

Wilfred was bowling when Jessop came to the wicket.

With barely a glance at the field, he smashed Wilfred to the boundary three times in his first five deliveries. Later he collared Jackson with a series of mighty blows, including one off a well-disguised slower ball that sailed so far over the row of poplar trees that flanked Fenner's that Schof burst out laughing at the wonder of it. 'The Croucher' finished with 171, made in just 105 minutes with 27 boundaries. The next highest scorer for the students was future Yorkshire player Rockley Wilson. He made 24.

Speaking to a reporter from the *Aberdeen Press and Journal* a couple of years later, Schof commented cheerily, 'He's a caution and a terror, is Jessop. He plays sad havoc with our bowling averages ... He plays cricket like no one else I ever saw. The ball sometimes seems to be out of the ground or over the ropes before you even bowl it.'

The game against Middlesex at Lord's was another difficult few days. Middlesex batted first and piled up 488, with Warner stroking 150 and Trott clumping 164. Wilfred laboured like Hercules, sending down 65.1 overs to finish with seven for 147. Yorkshire lost by an innings. The game proved the undoing of Schof's old chum from Armitage Bridge, Bobby Moorhouse. 'He had never realised his early promise,' Hawke would comment later, 'though a serviceable cricketer he was not well balanced and apt to lose his temper.' The breaking point had come when Trott skied a massive hit towards Block D. Moorhouse, who was fielding in the deep, watched the ball soaring into the sky, yet made no attempt to get under it as it came down a few yards in front of him. When Hawke loudly asked him what he thought he was playing at, Moorhouse replied, 'I didn't think it was coming this far and when I saw it up there I just said, "Damn it!".' Hawke retorted angrily that if Moorhouse couldn't be bothered to take a catch, then he might as well fire him. And he did.

There were tribulations for the bowlers of both sides when Yorkshire met Surrey at The Oval – the only ground in the country where the pitch was dressed with artificial fertiliser. The two teams scored 1,255 runs between them for just 17 wickets. For the home side, Tom Hayward made 272 despite being clean bowled by Schofield Haigh when he was on 70 – the umpire judging wrongly that the ball had bounced back on to the stumps from Hunter's pads. Even this bruising injustice did not faze the affable Schof. Walking off at tea he turned to Lord Hawke and quipped, 'Well, I never thought I'd see that happen … me, clean bowling Hayward'

For Yorkshire, George Herbert and Ted Wainwright put on 340 for the fifth wicket as the visitors posted a total of 704. The stand took just three hours and 40 minutes. George Herbert's display was as chanceless as it was exuberant as he crunched 31 fours in reaching 186. For Hirst it began a run of three consecutive centuries, the others coming against Hampshire at Bradford and Nottinghamshire at Trent Bridge. In the first of these, George Herbert shared in a famous partnership with Ernest Smith. Yorkshire were five wickets down with fewer than 100 on the board when the two came together. They thrashed 183 in less than two hours, Smith making 129 and George Herbert 131.

That season Wilfred tasted defeat for the first time in a Roses match, Lancashire victorious at Sheffield thanks to a MacLaren century the slow left-armer characterised as 'delightful'. When he was selected for the Players against the Gentlemen at Lord's, C. B. Fry and W. G. Grace set about him with deliberate relish, yet he still finished the innings having bowled 55 overs for just 131 runs.

Wilfred made his Test debut against Australia at Nottingham on 1 June 1899. He had played barely a full season in county cricket and only club cricket before that. His rise had been so fast most cricket fans still didn't recognise him in the street. England's captain W. G. Grace considered it 'unique' in English cricket. There was talk that Wilfred, at 21, was too young, but the Doctor backed him to become a worthy successor to Johnny Briggs and Bobby Peel. It turned out to be W. G.'s last Test. He announced his retirement after memorably commenting, 'It's no use . . . my hands are too far from the ground.'

The match was a stern examination for Wilfred. The two sides were packed with giants of cricket's Golden Age. Alongside Grace was C. B. Fry, Ranjitsinhji and Billy Gunn. The Australian side was captained by Joe Darling and included Monty Noble, Clem Hill and Victor Trumper.

Wilfred took the new ball with Jack Hearne. He soon settled into his immaculate groove and got the wicket of Noble. Returning to the attack later, he claimed the last three wickets to fall to finish with figures of four for 58. He took three more Australian wickets in the second innings and then watched from the Trent Bridge pavilion as Ranji saved England from defeat with a 93 not out so suave it smelled of Jermyn Street cologne.

Wilfred retained his place for the second Test at Lord's. Things began well for him when he dismissed Aussie openers Darling and Jack Worrall, but Clem Hill and Victor Trumper then took command of the situation and Wilfred and the other England bowlers were driven, cut and pulled all over the ground as both men ran up hundreds. Wilfred finished with three wickets but conceded more than 100 runs in getting them. Australia strolled home by 10 wickets.

Rhodes was in the XII for the third Test at Headingley, but didn't make the team, watching from the pavilion as Jack Hearne took a hat-trick. When the Australians played Yorkshire at Park Avenue, George Herbert demonstrated his talents more fully than he'd done in the Tests, taking 13 for 149. Wilfred was in the party for the fourth Test at Old Trafford but again watched from the stands. This time he received his education from Bill Bradley, who bowled wonderfully on a track that was as docile as an old labrador.

Wilfred finished the season strongly taking 11 for 112 against Nottinghamshire at Trent Bridge. Playing for C. I. Thornton's XI against the Australians at the Scarborough Festival he mesmerised in the seaside sunshine taking nine for 24, his best figures in an innings.

Yorkshire finished third in the County Championship after falling away late in the season when they seemed certain to win it. The county's batting was as strong as ever, but aside from Wilfred, the bowlers performed fitfully. In the County Championship, George Herbert had a batting average of 44.06, but his bowling in the same competition was notably less penetrating and he took five wickets in an innings just once all season. Tired from his batting exploits and still niggled by the thigh injury sustained in Australia, he perhaps lacked the extra nip that had made him so successful early in his career. For the moment he looked less like an all-rounder than a batsman who could bowl a bit.

Schof too had struggled. The dramatic, bounding approach that many observers had thought would wreck him physically had begun to take its toll; his pace fell and the ball no longer scampered off the wicket as it once had. He was ever more gripped by anxiety about his future.

Schof looked so like George Herbert he might have been his brother. The difference was the dark hair and the fact that he was built smaller than George Herbert in every plane and angle, like a scale model. Lord Hawke would liken the two pals to Tweedledee and Tweedledum. In fact, they were more like Russian dolls – wide-hipped and bottom heavy – with Schofield the one who would pack away inside the other. His Lordship admired Schof's skill and good humour ('Haigh was one of the best-tempered, happy souls I ever came across, always smiling'), yet at times appeared to question his backbone.

In one of those moments when Hawke's paternalism showed its patronising edge, he wrote that Haigh seemed intimidated by George Herbert, apologising profusely when he made a misfield off his team-mate's bowling. 'He always followed Hirst both actually and mentally, having profound hero-worship for him and knowing [Hirst's] was the stronger character.' This seems a cruel assessment of a talented and loyal man. And Hawke was not always correct about the particulars of things. For instance, he believed that Haigh did not like to take the new ball because of the extra pressure it placed on him and because he lacked self-belief. The truth was more prosaic. Schof did not like to open the bowling because his hands were exceptionally small and he found it hard to grip the ball when it was shiny.

That Schof was assailed by painful doubt, however, is a matter of record. Some might think that the well-documented mental health issues suffered in recent times by

Test cricketers such as Jonathan Trott and Marcus Trescothick are a product of our times. 'They never got depression in my day,' some red-faced blusterer on the boundary will intone after a bibulous lunch. 'They just had a dozen pints and got a grip. Bloody modern snowflakes.' In truth, cricketers have always suffered crises in confidence that descended into darkness. Of the great Test players mentioned in these pages, a disproportionate number would die by suicide: Albert Trott, Arthur Shrewsbury, Andrew Stoddart, Aubrey Faulkner, Albert Relf and Billy Zulch among them.

When Ted Wainwright returned home from the disastrous Ashes tour of 1897-98, he went straight to Bramall Lane and, without even bothering to remove his overcoat, picked up a ball and bowled. When he saw it land on the soft English turf and spin a foot to the right he was so relieved he practically wept. He'd travelled home in terror that he'd lost his ability to turn the ball entirely.

Even Wilfred Rhodes was stalked by fear before each season began, a nightmare that he could no longer find his length and line. For Wilfred, as we know, bowling was a mechanical process in which every aspect linked to the other like the cogs and chains of an engine – if a single part of it malfunctioned the whole thing would break down. In Wilfred's careful and considered view a simple thing like the unnoticed shortening of his first stride by half a dozen inches could send a bowler toppling from celebrity to anonymity in the space of a season. And if the methodical Rhodes sometimes had moments of anguish in the middle, then who wouldn't?

Schof suffered more than most, or at least spoke more openly of it. Cornered by a journalist from the *Aberdeen Press and Journal* after he'd returned to Perth to play in a benefit match in 1900, he said, 'You've got to know a few tricks to keep your place in first-class cricket. It's not all plain sailing, I assure you. When you are doing well, why, of course, it's all right; but when you're getting neither wickets nor runs for a few matches, the professional's lot is not by any means a happy one, and he begins to have visions of being "shunted" from the team; and once you are "shunted" it's not an easy matter getting back ... Although we have our good times, we also have our bad ones.'

As he watched the batsmen play his bowling with increasing ease, Schof was stalked by the fear of being 'shunted', the loss of his livelihood and the camaraderie of men he liked and admired. He would be back in the mills, the silver plate and mounted cricket balls that sat on his shelves a painful reminder of what he had once been. He couldn't let that happen.

He decided to take measures. Towards the end of the season, he shortened his run-up and modified his action, removing the final dramatic plunge. He would no longer use speed as a weapon. From now on he'd outwit batsmen. Schof was a canny cricketer who understood the game, but it's possible he also had help from his friend George Herbert. Over the years, Hirst would shape the careers of a number of Yorkshire's most successful bowlers – George Macaulay, Hedley Verity and Bill Bowes among them – with advice on tiny changes to their method or approach. If there was a kernel of truth in Hawke's assessment of the relationship between the two men, then it seems infinitely possible that Schof was the first to benefit.

The close season brought a mixture of happiness and tragedy for Wilfred. In late September, his elder brother Hollin fell from the steam engine on which he was working as a stoker and died from his injuries. Wilfred identified the body at the subsequent inquest, which recorded a verdict of accidental death. The 24-year-old was buried in Kirkheaton Cemetery. Less than a month later, Wilfred and Sarah were married at Kirkheaton Church. He was 22, she was two years older. They set up home together in a shared farmhouse at the unromantically named Bog Hall.

In marrying Wilfred, Sarah joined Emma and Lillian in taking on the arduous role of the professional cricketer's wife. Her husband would be gone for weeks at a time, returning home with a bag of stinking kit and a body filled with aches and pains, and no sooner had he stuffed down his tea and slumped by the fire than he was off again. He missed birthdays, Christmases and anniversaries. He was unavailable to clean gutters, cut lawns, fetch coal, chop wood or repair broken machinery. His wife was his laundress, his caterer, his confidante and often his press secretary, too. Because when he was away on tour, reporters from the local papers would come knocking on the doors to ask if any letters had been received and, if so, what portion of them might be shared with curious readers. In those instances, mindful of public opinion, she'd put aside the mending, shoo the children into the kitchen and read a little from the latest missive from a far-away land. And in the following day's *Examiner* or *Intelligencer* there'd be a small item: 'Mrs Rhodes recently received a letter from husband Wilfred, who is "Down Under" with Mr Warner and the MCC. He reports that he is fit and well and has recently been on a possum hunt, though not a single one of the creatures was bagged for they concealed themselves craftily in the trees.'

The great innovation of the 1900 cricket season was the

replacement of five-ball overs with the modern six-ball version. Wilfred was pleased as the extra delivery gave him more time to work his schemes. He had plenty of them. For if opponents wondered whether the emotional upheaval of the previous autumn might have dulled Wilfred's appetite for bowling, they got a decisive answer the moment the season began.

On 7 May at Bradford, Wilfred ripped through the Worcestershire batting like scissors through silk, taking four wickets in the first innings and seven in the second. Two weeks later in Sheffield, he dismissed seven Derbyshire bats-men in the first innings of a rain-blighted match. In June he rattled through Lancashire taking eight for 43 in the first innings and followed that up by taking seven second-innings wickets against Essex at Leyton.

In the first three weeks of the 1900 season, Wilfred took 50 wickets. His century came up against Hampshire at Hull on 21 June. He finished the match with 14 for 66. And on he went, and on. Eleven for 77 against Derbyshire at Derby; seven wickets in Sussex's second knock at Sheffield; 14 for 192 against Gloucestershire at Bradford (the remarkable Jessop walloped a century in each innings); at Cheltenham he brought the number of wickets he'd collected against W. G. Grace's side up to 27 by taking six for 36 in the first knock and seven for 67 in the second. His appetite for victims had an almost diabolic edge. Lord Hawke would quote from a newspaper article of the time, 'That astonishing youngster (he is still only twenty-three) is scourging the world of batsmen with scorpions.'

One of his most remarkable performances came against Essex at Harrogate in August. Lord Hawke described the game as 'phenomenal' and that had a hint of understatement about it. Rain interfered with play so much that Yorkshire's first innings concluded at 171 all out at 1 p.m. on the final day. Wilfred, with help from Schof, then bowled Essex out for 65. Hirst, Smith and Denton clattered 42 runs in 22 minutes and Hawke declared, leaving the visitors needing 149 in two hours to win the match. When the visitors batted a second time, Wilfred surpassed himself, claiming eight wickets for only 28 runs as Essex were dismissed in 57 minutes. That Yorkshire's wicketkeeper, Arthur Bairstow, stumped both Essex openers for ducks is indicative of the desperate confusion Rhodes sowed in the minds of his opponents.

Even when Wilfred came up against a player who seemed to have got the better of him, as Ranjitsinhji did when making 72 and 87 for Sussex with a mix of elegance and impish glee, he stuck to his task, never wavering or losing self-belief. The Jam Sahib might have looked like he'd won the battle, but Wilfred still ended the match with nine wickets.

Psychology played its part. Wilfred was young but played like a veteran. No matter what the conditions, he always bowled as if the pitch was helping him. As he'd say, 'If the batsman thinks it's spinning, it's spinning.' His flight was bewildering, his length perfect. In Yorkshire, old men would tell you that Wilfred, 'unlike these Copes and Carricks and them', could 'pitch it on a sixpence'. When asked about that, Wilfred gruffly dismissed the notion as utter nonsense. Any bowler, he said, would be happy to be able to land the ball 'on the morning paper – folded out'. Yet to batsmen it must have seemed like he could land the ball wherever he wished, an unsettling notion that preyed on the mind. A lot of cricket was in a player's brain. As George Herbert was fond of remarking, 'There's more ways of taking wickets than is written in the rules'.

Wilfred was laconic and merciless. His pale eyes had wizardry in them. Passive and thoughtful, he seemed in his stillness to be endlessly plotting the batsman's downfall, so that even when an opponent danced down the wicket and smashed him over the sightscreen for six, it appeared not so much a triumph as another step towards the cunningly concealed trap that lay waiting. Wilfred commanded the fates. Like death and taxes, he could be evaded but ultimately never avoided. Even when the other bowlers took a pounding, Wilfred emerged as a hero. For the Players against the Gentlemen at Hastings he returned match figures of 12 for 159 in a game in which the amateurs scored 406 in their first innings.

He finished the season with 240 wickets for Yorkshire at 12.72. In all first-class matches he had 261. He was the first Yorkshire bowler ever to finish the season as leading wicket-taker in England, the first to take 200 wickets in a season for his county.

Wilfred's main support that season came from Schof. The little man had practised hard in the frost and dew of spring and came to the season in fine fettle – the drop in pace gave him greater mastery of the ball, more opportunity to exploit his trickery. The first match of the season against Worcestershire at Bradford was all over on the first day. In fact, it barely occupied two sessions. The visitors were bowled out for 43 – Schof taking four wickets (three clean bowled) and Wilfred four. Yorkshire then batted and were dismissed for 99, a total that owed much to a partnership between Ted Wainwright (34) and Hirst (24), with Haigh chipping in a handy 15. Worcestershire were then skittled out for 51 to lose by an innings. Schof added three scalps to his first-innings tally and Wilfred seven. Haigh and Rhodes were the only bowlers Yorkshire used.

Against Derbyshire at Derby, on a helpful pitch, Schof took three wickets in the first innings and six in the second. Against Middlesex at Leeds in August he finished with match figures of 13 for 94. At The Oval he was instrumental in scattering Surrey for 52, clean bowling six batsmen for 21 runs. By season's end he had taken 145 wickets in County Championship matches at an average of 14.16. With his new control he broke the ball prodigiously, a delivery that pitched six inches outside off stump often jagging back to hit leg. Wilfred pronounced him 'the best off-spinner I've ever seen'. And, since Wilfred didn't throw praise around like an actor who's just won an Oscar, that verdict has to be taken very seriously indeed.

Wilfred in fact probably knew more about Schof's bowling than the man himself. Watching from his position in the covers with his usual keen eye and analytical mind, Wilfred saw that Schof generally bowled with what was termed 'overspin' – the ball spun on an axis which on a clock face would have run from 4 to 10. The angle of the spin meant that the ball not only broke in towards the right-hander but also gathered pace off the pitch. On a helpful wicket, it might hop or scuttle; the batsmen, never certain which, were perpetually caught in two minds.

Mixed with his off-breaks Schof bowled a quicker ball, which he disguised as thoroughly as any jungle ambush. The watching Rhodes observed, 'This delivery looked, when in the air, as if it was going to drop on a good length, but the pace behind it was such that it usually finished as a yorker.'

Batsmen were often so taken aback they were barely halfway through the shot when the bails went flying. In the days when leg before wicket applied only to balls that pitched in line with the stumps, the straight quicker ball caught out any batsman who had got into the habit of lazily padding away his off-breaks.

Devastating though the fast yorker was, Wilfred rated Schof's best delivery to be a slightly slower one that looped in its flight and dropped in the block hole. Sammy Woods agreed, saying it was the hardest to play of any ball he ever faced. Wilfred would watch it admiringly from his position in the covers. It was nearly always a wicket-taker, but Rhodes was not sure if Schof could bowl it intentionally, noting that 'it seemed to come out naturally whenever he was bowling at his best'. Hawke was less sympathetic and offered the caustic view that Haigh bowled the ball so rarely simply because he was 'lazy'. His Lordship was not a bowler. Wilfred was.

Despite his digs at Schof's character, Lord Hawke was well aware of his value as a wicket-taker and his relish for a fight. After a long and fruitless afternoon in the field, he'd often throw the ball to Haigh with the words 'Come Schofield, you haven't got your name in the papers yet, you know?', certain in the knowledge that Schof would respond with a grin, a shout of 'We're going to show 'em!' and soon after the bails would fly.

While two members of the Triumvirate ripped through the opposition batting (only two teams made more than 300 against Yorkshire all season), George Herbert was mainly an observer. His bowling was even less penetrative than it had been the previous year. Indeed, the Reverend Holmes pro-nounced George Herbert 'a complete failure with the ball'.

He took just 49 wickets for Yorkshire in the Championship at over 25 apiece. Luckily, his batting was even more merrily destructive than ever. In the same competition he hit four centuries and 11 fifties, piling up over 1,500 runs at an average of 43.69.

Yorkshire had begun the season unsure of success. The amateur all-rounders Jackson and Milligan were absent, fighting in South Africa (Milligan would die there, Jackson would contract dysentery and be invalided home), weakening both the batting and bowling. As it was, they sailed through the season unbeaten to win their fourth County Championship. That Lancashire finished second was a delightful bonus.

CHAPTER FIVE

Swerve

Of the Three Musketeers, George Herbert was the most congenial and easy-going. He had neither Schof's gnawing anxiety, nor Wilfred's hard-edged logic. Yet paradoxically he was the one who spoke least to journalists. Even those who sidled up to him as he sat on the boundary watching matches late in life went away with a small dish of mild platitudes, which they offered to the world as if they had been delivered from Olympus. Reporters' attempts to transform George Herbert's polite banalities into aphorisms filled with earthy wisdom inevitably call to mind the reaction of the Washington political set to Chance the gardener in *Being There*. If George Herbert had ever said, 'As long as the roots are not severed, all will be well,' it would without doubt have been a front-page headline in sports sections across Yorkshire.

George Herbert would go on to be one of Yorkshire's greatest coaches. His advice and insight would transform the careers of Herbert Sutcliffe and Hedley Verity as well as dozens of less celebrated cricketers. George Herbert certainly had wisdom to impart, just not to the idly curious.

George Herbert held to the old values of the dressing room. If he could not say a good thing about an opponent or a team-mate he said nothing, and even when he did praise them he often said very little. If he had insight, it was hard won and there was little to be gained from broadcasting his knowledge. When it came to addressing questions about himself, George Herbert was even more reticent. He had been brought up in a society where talking about yourself was viewed as a sign of arrogance and pretension. In his world, showing-off was almost as much a sin as greed. Nobody liked a big-head.

As a consequence, the dramatic change in George Herbert's bowling that occurred over the winter of 1900–01 remains both mysterious and miraculous – Yorkshire cricket's answer to transubstantiation.

What we know for certain is that George Herbert ended the 1900 season as what David Hunter called, 'A little man who bowled fast and straight, nothing more' and whose best years seemed to be behind him. He returned in May 1901 bowling a delivery that nobody had ever seen before – a booming late in-swinger that Hunter estimated could move as much as 4ft between the wickets. Batsmen were baffled and alarmed by George Herbert's new-found swerve. Its impact was revolutionary, more profound even than Bernard Bosanquet's unveiling of the googly in 1900. Hirst's swerver was the doosra of its day. It would change George Herbert's career and alter the history of cricket more profoundly, and perhaps more negatively, than any bowling innovation in history. It was the seed from which leg theory sprang and, from that, Bodyline. If things had turned out slightly differently, historians might have traced the fatal fracturing of the British Empire to a winter in Kirkheaton.

So, what happened to George Herbert in those cold months? The man himself was predictably and politely unhelpful. In a left-arm bowler, he explained, though there was a natural tendency to swing the ball in with the arm, it had taken him some while to be able to actually swerve the ball. 'The ability to do this seemed to come to me gradually – almost unconsciously in fact.' As to what made the ball swing, well, he seemed as baffled as the batsmen who faced him. 'With a new ball the swerve is most in evidence; why this should be I cannot explain. Then some days the swerve is more pronounced than others. I cannot explain that either, except on the theory that on some days a man is in better form than others. Sometimes a cross wind will help the swerve considerably. It is very difficult to explain how the swerve is brought about, or why it is more evident on some days than on others.'

When asked about a game against Sussex at Bradford in 1901 when his swerve was so devastating in one morning session that he took five of the visitors' wickets for 11 runs and left the batting side bewildered and broken, George Herbert shrugged and replied, 'I can't tell you what happened. I suppose it was just one of my funny days.'

There are other, smaller, moments that suggest George Herbert knew a bit more than he was letting on. The history of swing bowling is tangled, but reliable contemporary observers such as Pelham Warner and W. G. Grace generally place four names as keys to the development of swing – all of them were familiar to George Herbert.

The first was Walter Wright from Nottinghamshire,

who began playing for the county of his birth in 1879. Like George Herbert, he bowled left-arm at a lively speed with appreciable in-swing to the right-hander. Wright was said to be at his most effective with the new ball and once skittled six Yorkshire batsmen at Trent Bridge for just 10 runs in his first half-dozen overs. In 1886, after a series of disputes over pay, Wright left Nottinghamshire for Kent. He stayed for 12 seasons, taking 725 wickets. He was particularly effective at the Mote ground, Maidstone, where the slope across the pitch helped Wright's swing run 'down the hill'. George Herbert played against Wright many times and was clean bowled by him at Maidstone in 1892.

The three other men involved in the development of swerve all seem to have learned something of the art while playing baseball: Bart King, Monty Noble and Albert Trott.

In baseball, the screwball, which swings (or 'fades') into the right-handed batter is held in much the same way a seam bowler grips the ball – with the index and second finger down the centre. It may have been invented by a pitcher named Mathewson who came from Pennsylvania, where Bart King played his cricket. King bowled fast-ish right-arm and moved the ball into the batsman through the air. He was so successful on the Gentlemen of Philadelphia tour of England in 1897, one county allegedly attempted to engage his services with the enticing offer of marriage to a local widow with an income of £7,000 a year. On that 1897 tour, the Philadelphians played Yorkshire at Bramall Lane. The match was ruined by rain, but King bowled 12 overs and took three wickets, clean bowling Jackson and trapping Wainwright leg before. Hirst didn't play, but he may have watched and he'd certainly have heard about it from his fellow pros.

The Willesden-born Trott was a mercurial all-rounder who at his peak was arguably the best cricketer on the planet. Trott bowled slow-medium pace with a slingy round-arm action. Like King, it is said he learned to swing the ball while playing baseball as a young man. Later he would practise moving the ball through the air by placing a box in front of the stumps and trying to swerve the ball around it. Trott was the star of the Australian Test team of 1894-95, but for some reason was not selected to tour England in 1896. Miffed by the slight, he came to Britain anyway, got a place on the MCC ground staff, qualified by residency for Middlesex and during the seasons of 1898, 1899 and 1900 was widely regarded as the best all-rounder in England.

The bowler Trott famously hit over the new pavilion at Lord's was Australian Monty Noble, a man who, like Trott, was credited with introducing swing to Australia. Noble was considered by many the best exponent of right-arm medium-pace bowling in the world and he was apparently happy to share his secrets with opponents, as he did when teaching the in-dipper to Sydney Barnes.

Noble and George Herbert crossed paths for the first time during the miserable 1897-98 tour. On the train journey home from London after that awful trip, George Herbert let his guard down momentarily and told a journalist that Noble had 'made the ball swim in the air when bowling into a breeze'.

The precedents and examples were clearly there. George Herbert was not inventing something new but honing skills that already existed. The others may have swung the ball, his secret was that he swung it late, drawing the batsman into a stroke before the ball moved. George Herbert came in on a long, rhythmic run-up and, in the right conditions, his deliveries, bowled over the wicket with a loose, easy action, would appear to the right-hander to be angling straight across him and heading towards gully, before suddenly swooping inexplicably in at them from the direction of cover. The late swerve forced batsmen into ungainly last-minute changes of shot and half a dozen every season were caught flicking the ball between their legs.

George Herbert was not tall and lightning fast like left-arm swing bowlers of the modern era. He was no Wasim Akram or Mitchell Starc. If we were to pick someone he might have most resembled it was probably Gus Gilmour, the broad-beamed '70s Australian, or, in terms of height and pace, England's Sam Curran.

George Herbert may have brushed off questions of how and why, but others could fill in the gaps. Hunter, who got the best view of proceedings from behind the stumps, noted that at first George Herbert had swung the ball only slightly until 'he learnt to use the breeze'.

Warner believed that George Herbert was at his most effective in humid conditions under the brooding soot-heavy clouds of Leeds, Bradford and Sheffield. There is plenty of science to back that up. George Herbert clearly knew that atmospheric conditions played a part. On the return from the altogether happier 1904-05 trip to Australia he let slip to an interviewer that he couldn't get his swerve to work Down Under because the atmosphere was not as 'lazy and thick' as it was in England.

On days when the air was heavy as cream, Warner recorded, 'Hirst's fast left-handers would curl so much that he could place five, and on occasion six fieldsmen on the on-side.' A typical Hirst field when conditions were in his favour would feature a leg slip, three short legs, mid-on and long leg. Surprisingly to modern eyes he seems to have dispensed with conventional slip fielders altogether. David Hunter, meanwhile, abandoned his opposition to standing back and took dozens of catches down the leg-side as a result. The wicketkeeper was altogether less happy with the number of byes he conceded as the ball sped between bat and pad, and the rest of the Yorkshire team would watch his battles with George Herbert over the positioning of fine leg with wry amusement.

Unsurprisingly, the person with the most closely observed opinion on how George Herbert swung the ball was Wilfred Rhodes. Wilfred noted that while earlier bowlers had swung the ball straight from the hand (the kind of arm-ball used by conventional spinners), 'George's swerve was a different ball entirely . . . It used to go straight at the start, and, sometimes, it looked like it was going wide. Then, when it was just past the highest point in its flight, it would dip and swerve inwards.' The movement Rhodes saw never started until the ball began to dip.

His keen eye had caught something else about the delivery too: the position of the seam. George Herbert bowled with the traditional paceman's grip, the seam upright. However, midway through the ball's flight, at the point when it began to dip, the seam gradually tilted until it was at an angle of 45 degrees to the ground. It was when this happened that the ball swerved inwards.

Despite George Herbert's claims of ignorance, it's plain he not only understood what created his swerve, but he knew how to control it too. If he hadn't, his bowling in helpful conditions would have been erratic. It was not. Quite the contrary. When the ball was swinging, Wilfred was one of those fielding at short leg and noted that his team-mate's bowling was so consistent in its length and line that the fielders could creep in 'as close as they liked' without fear of injury.

George Herbert clearly knew what he was about, but he kept it to himself. To have voiced his understanding and explained his mastery might have appeared boastful. George Herbert was a humble man. Better then to effect naivety and brush off questions with a self-deprecating remark. 'Sometimes it works and sometimes it doesn't.'

Whatever the science of swing, or how George Herbert had come by his improbable swerve there was no doubting its effectiveness in 1901. Hirst, the up-and-downer whose career as a frontline bowler had appeared to be over, took 183 wickets in all first-class matches at 16.38 each, with deliveries so extraordinary even the sober *Wisden* described them as 'terrific'. In the County Championship he grabbed 135. He bowled superbly against Lancashire at Old Trafford, taking seven for 23 in the second innings as the home side slumped to 44 all out, and his 12 wickets against Essex at Leyton helped Yorkshire secure an innings victory after being dismissed for 104. Recalling that match, Lord Hawke would note of Hirst's bowling that 'some experienced competent spectators and the powerful batting side against him declared they had never witnessed anything like it'.

Lord Hawke often commented on the fact that George Herbert and Schof never seemed to bowl at their best together – either one of them was on top form or the other. In 1901, it was Schof who suffered. At the start of the season, he was troubled by a toe injury. Then in August his knee swelled up during the match with Derbyshire at Glossop. He made 159, the highest score of his career, against Nottinghamshire in the next match, despite struggling to run between the wickets, but shortly afterwards was told that he would have to sit out the rest of Yorkshire's season.

Aside from the century, Schof's brightest moment came near the start of the campaign. At Trent Bridge in June, George Herbert and Wilfred opened Yorkshire's bowling in the first innings. Hirst, however, struggled to keep his footing on the soft wicket and asked to be taken off after a single over. Schof came on in his place and, according to Lord Hawke, he and Wilfred then 'furnished the sensation of the season' by bowling the home side out for just 13. Haigh's contribution was a seven-over spell that saw him take four for 8. He might have done even better had not His Lordship spilled a chance off Tom Wass.

If Schof was off form, Wilfred was as remorseless as ever. His stand-out performances came against his favourite opponents Gloucestershire at Bristol in the second week of May (14 for 141), versus Leicestershire at Leicester later that month (13 for 96) and against Middlesex at Lord's at the start of June (12 for 134). He took his 100th wicket on the same day as the previous season, 21 June. Nor was he finished. Gloucestershire arrived at Hull in late July doubtless with a sense of dread. Wilfred took seven wickets in their first innings and five in the second. He also hit his first hundred for Yorkshire against MCC at Scarborough on 26 August. Hawke thought it, 'an admirable performance that gave him more pleasure than all his bowling achievements'.

Wilfred took 251 first-class wickets in all, as Yorkshire stormed to the title, winning 20 matches and losing just one.

They had pretty much secured the championship by the end of July, despite the fact the county's most celebrated batsman, F. S. Jackson, was unavailable. The first-choice starting XI that did the bulk of the work was considered by many – including Wilfred – to be the best the county ever had. Seven of this team scored centuries during the season – George Herbert hit a double ton against Worcestershire – and only Hunter the wicketkeeper had a batting average below 20.

Yorkshire's only defeat came, surprisingly, to Somerset at Headingley. It was their first defeat in the County Championship since they'd lost to Kent at Tonbridge midway through the 1899 season. When the two sides had met at Taunton, Somerset had come close to a shock, Hunter and Wilfred coming together late in the day to guide their side home by a single wicket. Now with Lionel Palairet, a model of the dashing off-side amateur, batting superbly in partnership with all-rounder Len Braund, they triumphed magnificently by 279 runs. After the victory was secured, White Rose supporters swarmed around the pavilion cheering for the visiting captain Sammy Woods, who had to come out on to the pavilion balcony half a dozen times to receive the ovation. The crowds in Yorkshire had yet to become the abrasive, abusive bunch who would provoke letters of complaint to Lord's. Cricket was still a game, a thing to be celebrated.

The Yorkshire attack's other major failure of the season came when they got what Lord Hawke had taken to referring to as their 'regular dose of Jessop'. The previous season Yorkshire had suffered ignominy at the hands of a rampant Croucher at Bradford. Jessop had blasted 104 in 70 minutes in the first innings. In the second knock, he'd been even more devastating, roaring to 139 in an hour and a half. During that second splenetic innings, Schof and Wilfred decided the only way to bowl to the dynamically violent Gloucestershire man was to stop him slamming the ball over midwicket by aiming outside off stump and making him 'fetch it'. They put the plan into operation, bowling wider and wider. And the wider they bowled the further Jessop walloped it. He smashed Wilfred straight out of the ground seven times before he finally misjudged one and was caught in the deep by Tunnicliffe.

After that debacle, Schof and Wilfred had another chat and concluded that in future they would bowl to the Croucher straight, full length and at middle or off stump, compelling him to drive.

When Yorkshire, as Champion County, played the Rest at Lord's in the final game of the 1901 season, Jessop was more explosive than ever. Schof and Wilfred's cunning plan proved as useful against him as an egg whisk in combatting a pouncing tiger. The Croucher thrashed 233 so fast the double hundred barely occupied a session. Wilfred went for more than four an over, practically an act of blasphemy. Five decades later, he'd still wince at the memory of it, and swiftly change the subject if anyone brought it up.

Despite this late hammering and the resurgence of George Herbert, Wilfred still topped the first-class averages. In the County Championship the Kirkheaton duo had taken 331 wickets between them. Unsurprisingly they were invited to tour Australia with Archie MacLaren's team. The Yorkshire committee objected. Wilfred was too young and they were mindful of the damage the previous tour had done to George Herbert's form and fitness. Lord Hawke, aware of the financial rewards of touring for the pros, made sure neither player was 'allowed to suffer financially through being kept at home, and both were perfectly satisfied'.

MacLaren was altogether less happy. He and Lord Hawke had clashed before and would do so again. The intervention had robbed the England captain of two great players, depleting his attack. When MacLaren returned home without the Ashes, he'd tell Wilfred that with the two Yorkshiremen in the team, England would have won the second and fifth Tests and taken the series.

Yorkshire's stance on the selections had direct consequences on the organisation of English cricket. Tours that had once been arranged and financed by individuals would now fall under the control of the newly formed Board of Control for Test Matches and MCC. The days when two England teams might arrive in a colony at the same time – as they had in Australia in 1887–88 – were over.

Schof came back strongly in 1902, developing, according to Lord Hawke, 'an insidious slow ball with a very deceptive flight'. That it was a wet summer was undoubtedly a help. He topped the Yorkshire averages and took 158 first-class wickets at just 12.55 apiece. Schof got fine support from Wilfred, who had more than 200 victims for the third season on the bounce and knifed through sides so often it became less time-consuming to note the matches in which he didn't take five wickets in an innings than to list those in which he did. Stand-out performances came, predictably, against Gloucestershire at Leeds (12 for 58) and Kent at Catford (12 for 54). George Herbert batted wonderfully and, though he didn't have as many of his 'funny days' as he had in 1901, still took 83 wickets.

Yorkshire had lost Frank Mitchell, who had emigrated

to South Africa (he'd captain their Test side in 1912), but the county's top order was still so strong that having to bat twice in a match was a novelty. During the season, opener Tunnicliffe had just 37 innings in 25 matches. His partner Brown played in 24 games and went to the wicket 36 times. George Hirst, meanwhile, got to the wicket on only 21 occasions in 28 matches. If he'd been in a worse side, he'd certainly have scored a lot more runs.

Yorkshire took the title again, losing just once to their bogey team, Somerset. Several times they fielded a team entirely of professionals – David Hunter normally captained. Hawke and Jackson were both eager to find new amateurs, but the ones they tried all 'had a damaging propensity to nibble at off-balls', His Lordship noted sadly.

Wilfred thought this team the best he ever played in. Over three seasons, they'd play 80 matches in the County Championship, win 49 of them and lose just two. 'The strength of the side lay in the team, not in one or two brilliant men,' he commented. Yorkshire were a match for any county on a dry wicket and better than everybody on a damp one. Wilfred attributed the team's versatility to the number of grounds Yorkshire used for home matches. By the 1980s players were complaining about it, believing that Yorkshire surrendered home advantage too often by playing on grounds – Middlesbrough, Harrogate, Hull, Dewsbury – that were as unfamiliar to them as they were to the opposition. Wilfred took a contrary view, believing that the constant shifting from place to place – he estimated that throughout his county career he only played two matches consecutively at the same venue twice – made the Yorkshire players expert at assessing conditions and adapting to them.

CHAPTER SIX

Singles

Wilfred unsurprisingly rated 1902 'the most thrilling season I ever had in Test cricket'. It was to be one of the most exciting Ashes series ever played, filled with startling genius, more twists and turns than an Olympic skiing slalom, and the sort of tight finishes that threaten manicurists with bankruptcy.

In the first Test at Birmingham towards the end of May, George Herbert at last made his mark as an international cricketer. The team was considered by many to be the finest England side ever assembled. MacLaren won the toss and batted on a wicket so amiable it practically chortled. Against expectations, Fry, MacLaren and Ranjitsinhji were dismissed with just 35 on the board. Johnny Tyldesley and Jackson calmed things slightly, but then the Yorkshire amateur was dismissed with the score barely into three figures. Lilley swiftly followed him back to the pavilion. In came George Herbert to join Tyldesley. For anyone else it would have been a daunting situation; not for him. Jack Hobbs would later remark on Hirst's calmness, how before going out to bat even when things were sticky, he sat with a smile on his face like a man anticipating a big dinner. Pressure was Hirst's element. He basked in it now, knocking up a century partnership with the Lancastrian in the hour that was left of the day. It poured down overnight. The pitch was damp, its placidity replaced with the threat of mischief. Before the wicket had begun to dry, Hirst and Tyldesley added another 25 runs and last-man-in Wilfred knocked 38.

The Australian innings began in poor light. By the end of it, they may have wished for total darkness. George Herbert and Wilfred bowled 22 overs, took 10 wickets and conceded just 32 runs as the tourists fell to 36 all out in little over 60 minutes. Wilfred took seven for 17, but the pair had bowled so beautifully together it was unfair to pick one above the other. C. B. Fry felt the figures did not tell the true story. 'It was Hirst who was responsible for the debacle. This is the best instance I know of a bowler getting wickets for his colleague.' A bewildered Australia followed on, but luck was with them. Rain washed out 12 hours of play and, since Tests that summer lasted just three days, effectively ended the match.

The Australians' next game was against Yorkshire at Leeds. The pitch was an 18-certificate horror. Australia batted first. Trumper, a master in all conditions, produced one of the performances of his great career to reach 38. When he was out, caught by Denton in the deep, George Herbert, in partnership with Jackson, ran through the rest of the side like gastric flu. A few slogs and swings late on brought the final total to 131. When Yorkshire batted they fared marginally worse. George Herbert and Wilfred each scored 12, worth 50 at least in better conditions, and the Australians led by 24.

The tourists had reached 20 for three when George Herbert

produced what he considered the best delivery of his career to clean bowl Trumper. The rest of the side reacted with panic. Hirst narrowly missed out on a hat-trick, bowling Monty Noble with an in-swinger that pegged back his off stump and then bowling Warwick Armstrong through the gate with the next delivery, another booming in-swinger. Bert Hopkins, who combined cricket with bee farming, appeared at the wicket. George Herbert's first ball saw the batsman prodding at a space where he imagined the ball might be, but it swung too much and missed leg stump by a whisker. Jackson then took three wickets in five balls. The Australians had been dismissed for 23. George Herbert had taken five for 9. Yorkshire needed 48 to win. It was no simple task. Taylor scored 11, Hirst held off the bowling for a not out 0, while at the other end Irving Washington made a match-winning 9.

In the second Test at Lord's, MacLaren again won the toss and elected to bat. Fry and Ranji were both out for ducks and then the rain came and washed out the rest of the game. When Yorkshire played the Australians for a second time, this match at Bradford, Schof took five for 49 in Australia's second innings, yet he still wasn't selected for the third Test at Bramall Lane, the place he might have occupied taken by Sydney Barnes. George Herbert bowled ineffectively, England got the worse of the conditions and though Wilfred took five for 63 in the tourists' second knock they still ran out comfortable winners by 143 runs, thanks in the main to the batting of Clem Hill and the swerve bowling of Noble.

Schof was destined not to be selected to play for England in a single Test, while others came and went as if selected by throwing darts at the county list. The official chronicler of Yorkshire cricket, the Reverend Holmes, was quite indignant, 'The non-inclusion of Haigh, one of the three greatest bowlers in the world in 1902, was universally dubbed an irreparable mistake ... Someone had blundered in not picking a bowler who hit the stumps as often as Haigh did.'

But who was the blunderer? Certainly not Archie MacLaren, who argued for Schof's inclusion in the XII selected for the fourth Test at Old Trafford. Lord Hawke, however, objected to the selection in the belief that, if the wicket were dry, Haigh would be kept as 12th man. Jackson, George Herbert and Wilfred seemed bound to be picked and the thought of another of Yorkshire's stars carrying the drinks when he could have been bowling Yorkshire to victory quite put His Lordship off his devilled kidneys.

Continuing the spat with MacLaren that had begun with his refusal to give permission for George Herbert and Wilfred to tour Australia, he now refused him the services of Schof. The England skipper must by now have realised that arguing with Lord Hawke was as pointless as Morris dancing and gave up. By then he had another problem. The selection committee had dropped Gilbert Jessop. MacLaren's comment that the selectors must believe England were playing a school for the blind fell on deaf ears. Taking the only revenge that opportunity had afforded, MacLaren got his own back on Lord Hawke by making George Herbert 12th man and in his stead playing Fred Tate of Sussex. It is a measure of what followed that since that match it has been very hard for any cricket writer to type the name Fred Tate without using the adjective 'hapless'.

Tate was no duffer – he'd take 180 wickets that season – but he started the match in poor spirits. It was plain that public opinion was all for Schof and George Herbert and therefore – unfairly – against him. He failed to take a wicket in Australia's first innings and made five not out when England batted. Things got worse in Australia's second innings when he dropped Joe Darling at square leg off Len Braund. Darling went on to add crucial runs with Syd Gregory as the tourists struggled to 86 all out, setting England 124 to win.

Hugh Trumble and Jack Saunders – a left-armer with a sus-piciously wristy action – made quick inroads into the England batting before Bobby Abel came in and slapped a rapid 21. With three men out England needed just 32 to win. But when the eighth wicket fell they were still 15 short of victory and wobbling. Wilfred walked out as calmly as he could to join wicketkeeper Dick Lilley. Three shots added seven runs to England's total, then Lilley sent a drive hurtling towards the pavilion. It seemed a certain boundary until Clem Hill dashed out of nowhere and flung himself full length to take an improbable catch.

Fred Tate came out to the wicket looking whey-faced and terrified. Eight runs needed getting. Wilfred was at the non-striker's end with four to his name. Tate took his mark and glanced around the field. The sky was dark, the boundary fielders shadows in the gloom. Rain began to fall, heavily. The umpires led the players from the field. Wilfred and the agitated Tate sat in the dressing room for what the Yorkshireman would later recall as 'the longest forty-five minutes of my life'.

When the game restarted, Wilfred walked out feeling reasonably confident. The damp outfield would make the ball slippery and hard to grip. All they needed to win was a couple of loose deliveries. Sure enough, Saunders' first ball squirted from his hand and went shooting down the leg-side.

Tate flicked at it and the ball flew to the ropes. Four more needed. Saunders ran in to bowl. It was his quicker one. Tate was caught out by the pace. He flailed at it too late. Behind him the timbers rattled. He never played for England again.

The final Test at The Oval would, if anything, be even more exciting – well, for the Englishmen anyway. The Australians made 324 in their first innings, with George Herbert taking the first four wickets and later clean bowling Syd Gregory. When England batted, it rained. The sodden wicket took on the texture of Shredded Wheat. The ball jagged, bumped and slid. England barely scraped past the follow-on. Australia fared little better against Bill Lockwood, but with a big advantage on the first innings they set England 263 to win. At lunch, the home side were five wickets down with just 49 on the board. The England dressing room was a glum place, Wilfred would recall, 'with one or two players muttering about the weather being as good as an extra man for the tourists'.

After lunch the entire complexion of the match was changed by the extraordinary Gilbert Jessop. Oblivious to the jumpy pitch and light so dim the fielders might have carried Davy lamps, he slammed 104 in 77 minutes in a remarkable display of power and judgement. At the other end, Jackson watched and batted doggedly. George Herbert felt the importance of his Yorkshire team-mate's innings was unfairly overlooked. '[His contribution] was rather lost sight of at the time owing to the tremendous hitting of Jessop, but we would not have won the match without him.' Jessop's departure brought George Herbert to the wicket and by his own mild estimation, he 'held the fort, taking it steadily and getting runs when we could'. Lockwood stayed with Hirst while 27 were added. Lilley stuck around long enough for 34 to be squeezed from the Australian attack. 'They say I had a big grin on my face at the end of every over. Well, it was a smile of relief not of happiness,' George Herbert said.

In the pavilion, Wilfred watched with mounting relief. He started to feel that he might not have to bat at all. He went down into the lavatories to – by his own account – wash his face. By the time he returned to the dressing room, the match had taken another twist. The Yorkshireman barely had time to buckle on his pads before the ninth wicket fell. England were still 15 runs short of victory and Wilfred was clattering down the pavilion steps to the gate, where George Herbert was waiting to greet him.

Just what George Herbert said at that moment is arguably the most debated sentence in English sport. Legend, of course, has George Herbert telling Wilfred, 'We'll get 'em in singles.' Wilfred – who was perhaps nettled by the suggestion that Hirst had needed to mollycoddle him – would later say he couldn't recall whether anything was said or not. George Herbert, meanwhile, changed his tune as the years went on. In 1938 he said, 'I can't remember my exact words. I don't think I said that. There was no arrangement between us when he came in, but I wouldn't like to contradict the report. Probably we said we would go on as usual and not get flurried.' In 1952 he was more categorical, telling the *Yorkshire Post*, 'A forcing batsman would never have said those words. If he could have hit a boundary he would have done.' Yet he'd also tell A. A. Thomson around the same time, 'You never remember what you say at times like that.' After George Herbert died, a letter writer to the *Daily Telegraph*, who had been sitting by the pavilion steps when the famous meeting took place, recalled that Hirst told Rhodes, 'One at a time,

Wilfred, we'll get 'em,' which was good enough to satisfy E. W. Swanton.

One thing George Herbert did seem sure about was that Rhodes's first words to him were, 'I was having a wash when Dick [Lilley] got out, so I hadn't time to get nervous.' Whatever was said, the two men proceeded quickly to the middle where Wilfred found himself facing Hugh Trumble bowling round the wicket. Trumble was tall with a high action. His off-breaks rose sharply off the soggy wicket. Three short legs were clustered in. Wilfred had barely adjusted his eyes to the light when a ball from Trumble jumped practically vertically from a good length and struck his glove, bouncing down to safety as Victor Trumper dived forward from his post close to the wicket. In the following over, another Trumble snorter found the edge and flew perilously close to Warwick Armstrong in the slips.

The rain fell steadily throughout without ever being heavy enough to stop play. The dampness handicapped the bowlers, but Trumble and Noble were steady despite the slippery ball. Trumble was almost machine-like in his accuracy, while Noble, George Herbert recalled, 'kept trying to tempt Wilfred with half-volleys outside off stump to an off-side field with slips, point, cover point, mid-off and third man. But they couldn't scare Wilfred and they couldn't tempt him.'

In an atmosphere that felt to him like it was 'charged with electricity', George Herbert remained in a pocket of calm. 'When a man is concentrating on his game he is not as excited as the people looking on,' he recalled. And the crowd *were* excited, those that could bear it. One of the old gatemen later told George Herbert that 500 spectators had walked out before the finish, unable to stand the tension. Legend also speaks of an elderly member biting through the handle of his umbrella and a police constable on the boundary weeping from the unbearable strain of it all.

Wilfred nudged a Noble delivery narrowly wide of Armstrong with two still needed. George Herbert called the run. When Hirst gathered the next single, pandemonium briefly broke out. A Church of England clergyman – thinking it was the winning hit – invaded the pitch and had to be lifted back over the rope by a couple of Australian fielders.

Finally, it was Trumble bowling to Wilfred, batting at the Gasometer End. For once he over-pitched and Wilfred drove hard between the bowler and mid-on. He set off for the winning run and didn't stop till he reached the pavilion. George Herbert, running in the opposite direction, was engulfed by the crowd who'd rushed on to the field as soon as they saw the batsmen cross. It took the Yorkshireman 15 minutes to fight his way back to join his team-mates, his 'shoulders sore from all the back-slapping'. George Herbert was proud of the way 'young Wilfred kept his end up'. The two Kirkheaton lads had seen England through. 'The runs had to be got, so we got 'em,' he said afterwards with sort of matter-of-factness reporters loved.

Until the heroics of Ben Stokes and Jack Leach at Headingley in 2019, this was the greatest match-winning last-wicket stand in English Test history. George Herbert and Wilfred would be forever linked by it and to it, whether anyone said 'We'll get 'em in singles' or not. They were cheered resoundingly and repeatedly by the crowd at The Oval and back in Kirkheaton that September they were each presented with an upright piano bought via subscription by the proud cricket fans of Huddersfield. Whether the pianos were ever played or not goes unrecorded, but reporters visiting their homes noted that the tops of both instruments were covered in silver bowls, cups, teapots and other trophies and mementoes of their wonderful careers. Even if Wilfred had wanted to play the piano that autumn his wife might have forbidden him. The couple had a new baby, Muriel, who'd been born at the height of the season.

Early in 1903, Yorkshire played MCC at Lord's. The rain was dismal and to protect the main field the match was switched to the Nursery Ground. The visitors were short of an opening batsman and Wilfred was drafted in. Displaying characteristic watchful diligence, he carried his bat for 98, robbed of a century when Yorkshire's number 11, Fred Ward, was bowled by Len Braund for a duck. That it would turn out to be poor Ward's only first-class innings was no consolation.

Watching from the pavilion, Lord Hawke shook his head. He actively discouraged Wilfred from batting, sending him out into the middle with the words 'Now, Wilfred, no more than twenty'. He wanted Rhodes fresh for a long session of bowling, but knew that Wilfred had other ideas. Once, at Leyton, when Hawke had issued his usual command, Wilfred had replied wistfully, 'I hope that someday I shall play for England for my batting.' To which Hawke might have responded, 'Not if I have anything to do with it, you won't.'

Wilfred was the most prolific wicket-taker in England, yet remained oddly unmoved by his success. 'One of the curious things about Rhodes,' Hawke observed, 'is that he himself has never enjoyed bowling half so much as he does batting. I always feared that development of his batting powers, which, from the first, were quite evident, would check his skill with the ball.'

That Wilfred loved batting was true enough. From the

start, he'd got more pleasure from a fifty than a five-wicket haul. Bowling was hard graft, its nuances too subtle for the spectators in the stands to appreciate. Wilfred had noted the rising noise that greeted Jessop's hitting, the almost child-like glee of the crowd as another mighty drive sailed over their heads. A bowler could take six wickets in an over and never generate a roar like that.

It wasn't really about glory, though. For Wilfred it never was. It was about practicalities. Bowling was difficult, especially on the improving pitches of the era. An injury could finish a bowler with one snap. He'd see it happen that very season with John Brown of Darfield, a very fast Yorkshire bowler who dislocated his shoulder straining for extra pace and never played again. Even if injury didn't end a career as dramatically as that, it could force a bowler to alter his action, lose his way and fade slowly from the side. Batting was a safer bet. George Herbert was once again the example Wilfred followed. Whether the conditions favoured his swerve or not, George Herbert always made runs. Even if his niggling injuries kept him out of the attack, he'd still have had a place in the side. Others, such as Schof, were just one knackered knee away from a shunting.

And besides, Wilfred really did like batting. He might have made it his living from the off, but as he said, 'You can practise bowling on your own, you can't practise batting on your own.' Hawke said, 'I have never known anyone enjoy batting more than Wilfred.' All he wanted now was the chance. But His Lordship had other ideas and after the experiment at Lord's, Wilfred was dropped back to number six. He didn't mind too much. It was a position from which he could practise his shots.

In May against Worcestershire, Wilfred bowled over 90 overs to finish with 14 wickets, but the marathon spell seemed to knock the guts out of him. The next six weeks were the bleakest of his entire career. He plodded on like he was walking uphill into a stiff wind with a cooker on his back. He could not get a wicket against Middlesex at Lord's and conceded more than 100 runs. He did little better against Sussex, who knocked 135 off him in exchange for a brace, while piling up 558 for eight at Park Avenue. He batted four times and contributed just 14 runs. In the next three Championship matches, against Warwickshire, Derbyshire and Kent, he took only six wickets. This was the sort of dark spell all professional cricketers feared. In the background he could hear the mutter of the doom merchants and the rumble of the shunter.

Happily, Wilfred's form returned miraculously and inexplicably at Trent Bridge, where he took seven Nottinghamshire wickets in the first innings and struck a half-century. He then hit 79 against Leicestershire at Dewsbury. The climax of his resurgence came against Lancashire at Bradford, he and George Herbert seeing off the imperious Sydney Barnes to guide Yorkshire to victory after Wilfred had taken eight wickets in Lancashire's second innings to go with the five he'd bagged in the first.

To add to Yorkshire's early-season problems, George Herbert had suffered a bad calf strain that kept him out of several matches, while John Tunnicliffe damaged a hand batting and the middle-order stroke-maker Irving Washington — whose parents must surely have had literary aspirations – was missing with the ailments that plagued him and would prematurely end a promising career. There were problems with Schof, too. His body creaked and his faith deserted him. After the glory of 1902, his summer was to be one of drudgery. Though he topped 100 wickets for the season, he failed to turn in a genuine match-winning display, his best performance coming against Essex at Sheffield in mid-August when he took five for 13 in the first innings and followed it with three for 11 in the second.

Like Wilfred, Yorkshire recovered their form as the season wore on, but it was too late and they finished third. Despite his injury, George Herbert had a wonderful season. His swerve returned and, though he had lost a little pace, he made up for it with know-how. He batted with merry power, his lashing on-side shots delivered like punchlines. He scored just under 2,000 runs at an average of 47.28, below only Fry and Ranjitsinhji in the first-class averages. Unsurprisingly, *Wisden* described him as 'Beyond all doubt ... the best all-round man of the year.'

It was a season of remarkable performances. Before he injured himself at Old Trafford, George Herbert had struck a century against Worcester and taken six wickets in an innings against Essex and Gloucestershire. When he returned he walloped 120 and took nine wickets in a match with Kent at Leeds. At Dewsbury, he scored 153 against Leicestershire before running himself out, at Bradford 142 versus Somerset, and at Trent Bridge on 99 he danced down the wicket to Nottinghamshire slow left-armer John Gunn, missed the ball and was stumped. He took his revenge when the two teams met again at Headingley, hitting a half-century and taking 11 wickets.

With Schof below his best, it was left to George Herbert and Wilfred to terrorise the batters. The game with Surrey at The Oval saw Yorkshire make a moderate 254 and still end up winning by an innings and 97 runs. George Herbert and Wilfred bowled unchanged throughout, finishing in an almost perfect division of labour with 10 for 67 and 10 for 81.

One of the most remarkable matches of Wilfred's career was the encounter with Worcestershire at Huddersfield. There was only four hours' play on the Friday and Saturday. The visitors were dismissed for 24 in the first innings (Wilfred picking up five wickets for four runs) and reduced to 27 for six in the second innings, still 25 adrift of Yorkshire's first-innings score of 76 for one declared. Jug-eared all-rounder Ted Arnold then held the Yorkshire attack at bay for 45 minutes to save the match. By the end, his thighs and knees were so puffy and bruised from all the George Herbert in-swingers that had whacked into his legs he could barely walk back to the pavilion. He'd scored 13 not out.

Essex were reduced to 36 for eight on the sort of soft Sheffield wicket they seemed always fated to encounter. The story in Yorkshire was that as the train travelled northwards, the Essex players would scan the skies. As they drew closer to their destination the heavens would darken, rain would begin to fall and they would be heard muttering sadly, 'Here we go again – caught Tunnicliffe, bowled Rhodes.' (Though on this occasion Tunnicliffe for once remained catchless.)

Against Lancashire at Bradford, Yorkshire needed 164 to win. They had lost half their wickets with 111 on the board when Wilfred came out to join George Herbert. The Kirkheaton men saw them home. Hirst, lashing the great Barnes around like he was a net bowler, got his second half-century of the game. He'd consider it one of the best innings of his career – not a big score, but made in tough conditions against fine bowlers and bringing victory to the team he loved.

After that match, Willie Cuttell told Schof that Yorkshire were the most fortunate team in England. 'You only win when you're lucky,' he said. Schof smiled his twinkling smile. 'Aye, and we only lose when we're unlucky.' That was Schof. He was a great chirper. Sometimes his banter flowed so unstoppably George Herbert would get fed up and shout, 'Talk back at him! Talk back at him!' to whoever was copping it.

Wilfred liked Schof a lot. 'A cheery customer and fond of a joke,' was how he described him. Haigh teased Wilfred too, but without much effect. However hard Schof tried, he could never quite break through Wilfred's austere exterior to the, likely, austere man within.

Schof was a joker, but most of the laughter fell on himself. He liked to tell the tale of the time he was asked to present a trophy to some local league winners and practised his speech to his father over and over again until he knew it by heart. When he stood up in front of the audience at the awards dinner, however, his mind was blank as a chicken's. Staring out at the faces looking expectantly at him, Schof felt sweat breaking out on his forehead. He tugged at his shirt collar. He took a drink of water. 'Before I come here tonight,' he croaked, 'only two people knew what I was going to say: myself and my father. Now only father knows. Here's your cup, boys.' Assessing his discomfort later, he'd say it was worse than scoring four ducks in the same innings.

Schof and George Herbert were a funny pair, always playing mild practical jokes on one another, or sharing self-deprecatory moments they'd later weave into comic tales. On one occasion at Northallerton, Schof arrived shortly before

George Herbert and told the gateman he was being stalked by a short, stocky man with sinister intentions. 'Whatever you do, don't let him in.' When George Herbert arrived a few seconds later, the gateman refused him admission, until more of the Yorkshire team arrived and explained who he was. Another time, late in their careers when their hair was whitening as their waistlines broadened, the pals had travelled to an away fixture together. On the train they had done a good job of persuading each other they weren't so elderly looking as they feared. They approached the ground with a spring in their steps only to be greeted by the gateman with the words, 'The umpires' entrance is over there, gentlemen.'

The rejuvenated George Herbert had topped Yorkshire's batting and bowling averages and Wilfred had recorded the first of his 16 doubles, scoring 1,137 runs and taking 193 wickets in county matches. Both men were selected for the tour of Australia that winter. It was the first organised directly by Lord's. This time Lord Hawke raised no objection.

Australia had held the Ashes through four series and they were bellicose about their chances of keeping them. After all, Fry, Ranjitsinhji and Jessop were missing from the touring party. Even with these box-office names England had been unable to defeat the Australians, so what chance could they have without them?

In truth, England's team was a solid one. It was captained by Pelham 'Plum' Warner, who George Herbert and Wilfred rated highly. Warner was a batsman as warm and solidly elegant as an Adam fireplace. He was sharp-witted and enjoyed talking about cricket almost as much as they did. On the boat out to Australia, Plum even had Wilfred, George Herbert and the other England bowlers drawing up plans of attack and field placings on pieces of paper – a genuine novelty in the days when any kind of tactical analysis was viewed as tantamount to cheating.

Also in the side was Johnny Tyldesley, who Wilfred rated as one of the best attacking batsmen England ever had, the forceful Tom Hayward of Surrey and Tip Foster, a glossy striker of the ball with the traditional gentleman's repertoire of drives and cuts. The bowling was tidy, with Wilfred and George Herbert joined by Surrey leg-spinner Len Braund, Worcestershire's medium-paced off-spinner Ted Arnold (his bruises healed, he was walking normally again), Arthur Fielder of Kent, who bowled out-swingers at military medium, Albert Relf, another medium-pacer who broke the ball from leg, and the original mystery spinner, Bernard Bosanquet of Middlesex.

Always sensitive to criticism, Wilfred noted with irritation that he was being dismissed by many Australians as the sort of bowler who was only any good on damp English pitches. They'd seen his fellow Yorkshireman Ted Wainwright struggling to move the ball half an inch on the native billiard table surfaces and reckoned this Rhodes fellow would be just as ineffective.

It was the first time Wilfred had ever left the British Isles, but anyone who thought his inexperience would count against him had overlooked his intelligence and resourcefulness. In Australia he didn't simply bowl as he would on a sloppy track in Sheffield, he studied the conditions and tailored his style to fit.

It was true, the pitches, unless rain-affected, offered little encouragement in terms of spin, but that meant the bowler had to work out other stratagems. Like Edison, Wilfred never came across a problem to which his mind couldn't, over time, find a solution. If the ball wasn't so easy to flight – he thought it might be the lack of moisture in the dry air – then you bowled flatter and got some extra bounce by pushing the ball through quicker.

He would continue bowling in this style when he returned to English cricket in the 1904 season, dropping the slow, looping deliveries that had brought him such success in his first six seasons. The style was lower risk and as time went on it would become the default setting of the majority of English county spinners. Wilfred's adoption of this simpler approach to bowling was perhaps part of his resolve to shift his emphasis increasingly to batting. It required less practice and concentration. Though successful in his new style, he would never take the same volume of wickets again.

Wilfred deployed his new method on a plumb wicket against Victoria and took five for 26. He rated that a far better spell of bowling than when he helped dismiss the same side when they met again for 15 on a 'sticky dog'. That meagre total would have been even less if his old foe Albert Trott hadn't been dropped in the slips off Rhodes's first ball – he went on to make the top score of 9. The drop denied Wilfred what would have been his first ever first-class hat-trick. He'd have to wait 20 years to finally get one.

George Herbert too had been dismissed by the Australian press on the basis of his previous unhappy visit. He quickly went about correcting that misapprehension, plundering 92 off Victoria's bowlers. At the Sydney Cricket Ground, he pulled and hooked with his usual chortling belligerence to score 66.

By now, it was becoming plain that this was going to be a

very different tour from the 1894–95 fiasco. The Australian summer of 1903–04 was one of the mildest anyone could remember – like England in June – and made playing much easier for the visitors. The youthful Warner proved an effective and enthusiastic leader, always keen to consult with the professionals. There was none of the previous divisions between gentlemen and players, either. Amateurs and pros stayed in the same hotels. A great spirit of camaraderie developed between them. They played and acted like a team. It was like being on tour with Yorkshire.

The first Test lived up to the expectations that inevitably followed the excitement of the 1902 series. Warner lost the toss. The pitch was a featherbed. The bowlers looked at it and rolled their eyes. Australia made a mess of their start, however, losing three quick wickets and it took a century from Noble to get them to 285 all out.

England began much as the Australians had done. They were 73 for three when Tip Foster arrived at the wicket. It was his Test debut; he was nervous. Later he'd produce a thrilling array of booming drives and cut shots that flashed like lightning, but early on he struggled. Rhodes's analysis was typically clear-eyed: 'He never quite settled down till he'd made fifty or sixty ... he hardly timed the ball.' As the wicket eased and Foster's anxieties calmed, he 'played cricket as fine as I have seen, and his driving was splendid. Up till then he had been playing uphill.' Foster received good support from Len Braund and Albert Relf, and was batting beautifully when England's number 11, Wilfred, came out to join him. The Australians may have thought their bowling was just about done for the day, but the Yorkshireman had other ideas. He made a chanceless 40 not out as he and Foster built a record last-wicket partnership of 130. When Foster finally fell for a then Test record score of 287, England had a first-innings lead nudging towards 300.

When Australia batted again, the wicket was perfect and Trumper was at his most majestic, scoring 185 not out. George Herbert summarised the sight of the Australian in full flow with his usual succinctness, telling Warner, 'It's not much use setting a field when that lad's going.'

The only bowler who managed to keep Trumper quiet was Wilfred. He bowled all afternoon; remorselessly tight, his line and length as immaculate as the Holy Conception. Even with Trumper in full flight his 40.2 overs cost just 94 runs and he took five wickets along the way. Even the magnificent Victor struggled to cope with the Yorkshireman's probing accuracy. At one point, when he had completed a run he said to Rhodes, 'Wilf, won't you give me a bit of peace?' To which Wilfred's response was characteristically terse: 'No.'

England scampered home by five wickets, though not without alarms. Tom Hayward made 91, George Herbert came in at 82 for four, on a pair, and flicked his first delivery, from gangling medium-pacer Frank Laver, narrowly wide of short leg. He steadied himself after that alarm and guided England to victory with an unbeaten half-century.

At Melbourne in the second Test, on a wicket he might have had imported specially from Sheffield for his own amusement, Wilfred was imperious, taking seven for 56 and eight for 68. Only Trumper offered any resistance, top scoring in both Australian innings, and England won easily. The Australian crowd, irritated by Rhodes's metronomic approach to bowling, began barracking him by counting down his steps 'One, two, three, *plunk* … one, two, three, *plunk.*' If they thought it would unsettle him, they had picked the wrong man. On he went unperturbed, ball after ball of perfect line and length, until finally they gave up and went to the bar. His match figures of 15 wickets for 124 runs are the best ever by a Yorkshire bowler in a Test (well, they are if you exclude Bradford-born Jim Laker). He might have got even more. So many catches were dropped off his bowling Wilfred lost count of them. He wondered if the trees that lined one side of the MCG and made sighting the ball difficult might have had something to do with it. Afterwards George Herbert joked that the only reason he hadn't dropped one himself was 'that none came to me'.

Though George Herbert fought a couple of typically valiant rearguard actions in the third Test at Adelaide, making 58 in the first innings and 44 in the second, England still went down by 216 runs. Australia's main weapon had been the generally under-used Bert Hopkins of New South Wales, who bowled in-curving medium-pacers. Deploying off-theory, in which he constantly pitched the ball a foot or more outside off stump, he sliced through England's second innings. Wilfred would later admit, 'We ought of have left him alone till he bowled nearer the sticks.'

The fourth Test – which began a remarkable six weeks after the start of the third – was dominated by Bernard Bosanquet, who hoodwinked the Australians with his googlies when they batted last, taking six wickets as they fell 157 runs short. Wilfred played a strong supporting role, taking four for 33 in Australia's first innings and helping Warner put on 55 for the last wicket in England's second knock. Wilfred was not entirely impressed with Bosanquet. He thought him erratic and incapable of keeping to a decent length, noting that he took some wickets with deliveries that bounced twice. Fielding at short leg, he watched with his usual diligence until he could pick the googly every time. It was a piece of knowledge that he could use when Yorkshire played Middlesex.

England lost the fifth Test at Melbourne. On a rain-ravaged wicket, Tibby Cotter, fast with a low, slinging action that made the ball skid off the turf, took six for 40 in England's first innings. Trumble – rated 'a brainy bowler' by Wilfred – did the damage in England's second innings, taking a hat-trick and four more wickets in what would be his final Test. One bright spot for England was the bowling of George Herbert, who took five for 48, his best figures for England. His favourite moment of the tour was his delivery that dismissed Victor Trumper first ball when the great man was 10 runs short of completing his 1,000 for the season. The ball pitched a couple of inches outside off stump, swerved in the air and hit the top of middle. Trumper played back to it but was beaten by pace and movement and perhaps by his attempt to force it away.

Wilfred had noted that the Australian batsmen pursued an attacking policy, constantly striving to dominate the bowling. The most aggressive of them all was Victor Trumper. The great right-hander told Wilfred he always aimed to hit his first ball for four to establish himself. It was a piece of information that had to be treated cautiously when it came direct from an opponent. Kidology was part of top-class cricket. As George Herbert constantly reminded Yorkshire's younger players, 'There's many a battle been won by a bluff.'

Wilfred and George Herbert both considered Trumper batting royalty. He was superb on any surface, picking from his vast range of shots like a master cabinetmaker choosing the correct chisel from his rack. One thing about Trumper that astounded Wilfred was the state of his bat. He often came to the wicket bearing something that looked unfit for a knockabout on the beach, the blade dirty, dented and knotted as if it had been found lying in a hedge. He also pulled the rubber grips off the handles of his bats, preferring to grip the rough binding. He prevented it from becoming slippery by rubbing it regularly during an innings with a lump of resin he kept in his pocket. It reminded Wilfred of his team-mate David Denton, who had once used a bat with a blade so hard the only way to get oil into the willow was by pricking the surface all over with a penknife. It was the level of his skill not the quality of his equipment that made a cricketer.

George Herbert was always a good character to have on tour – cheerful and kind with an easiness around people that defused arguments and prevented grievances from festering. This time he'd played well too, finishing with 569 first-class runs and 36 wickets.

Wilfred was the leading wicket-taker in Australia that summer with 65 at 16.23. He'd taken 10 in a match twice and five in an innings seven times. In the Tests, he'd taken 31 wickets at 15.74. Not bad for a spinner who was only any good when a stodgy wicket sucked the ball in and spat it out for him.

After a long journey home that saw them dock in Marseille and then take trains across France and England, George Herbert and Wilfred arrived back at Huddersfield station in the early hours of the morning. Waiting to welcome them home was a party of three: their wives Emma and Sarah, and Schof.

The 1904 season was one of personal glories for the Triumvirate. George Herbert, Wilfred and Schof would all do the double. These successes would follow an unsettling and upsetting event. On the third day of the match with Leicestershire at Bradford in May, the dashing and affable opening batsman Jack Brown collapsed as he walked to Park Avenue. He would never play again. That winter he'd die of heart failure aged just 35. Brown was a popular member of the side, a practical joker who'd once – on a tour of Australia with A. E. Stoddart's team – paid a member of the crowd to don whites and field in his place while he went and had a beer. The opener's cavalier approach to cricket and life masked a fragile constitution. Some traced this back to a bout of rheumatic fever he'd contracted as a young pro in Perth, though a combination of chronic asthma and heavy smoking cannot have helped.

Brown's dramatic exit affected the team. They drew their first four matches and were beaten by Middlesex at the start of June, a string of results that hamstrung their chances of regaining the title. Gallingly, Lancashire went the season undefeated to claim it instead. Yorkshire won just nine games and finished second.

Brown would not be the only absentee that season. Yorkshire had also lost the amateur batsman Tom Taylor (middle name Launcelot), who had abandoned county cricket to concentrate on his engineering business, and Irving Washington, who had gone to live in South Africa in the hope the warm weather would cure his various illnesses. With Jackson available for only a dozen matches, Yorkshire's batting was weaker than it had been for a decade. It was a situation that played into Rhodes's hands.

Wilfred was now bowling in the flatter style he'd developed that winter. He was accurate and consistent but lacked the sharp edge of earlier seasons. Still, he took 10 wickets in the matches against Essex, Hampshire and Warwickshire. His batting, meanwhile, had become more efficient. He had settled into his methods. These were self-taught, naturally, for Wilfred was a model of self-improvement. In the field and from the dressing-room balcony, he studied the batsmen he admired and made mental notes of their most effective strokes and how they played them. He'd then practise the ones he liked. Wilfred never spoke of how he did so, but it's hard to avoid the image of him standing in front of the bedroom mirror at Bog Hall, bat in hand, cap set squarely, executing a cover drive and checking how it looked, like a teenager throwing dance moves. Once he'd got the knack of them, Wilfred would try the shots in the nets, winnowing away those that didn't work for him and perfecting those that did.

At the start of the season, he hit a few half-centuries, then against Surrey at Park Avenue he struck a century with the sort of cavalier stroke-play that drew attention partly because it seemed so out of character. Against Worcestershire at Worcester he got the highest score of his career so far, 196. He was briefly promoted to open the batting but without much success and dropped back to number seven again. It was from this position that he scored a battling 76 against Middlesex. His study of Bosanquet's bowling in Australia was evident. The googly merchant took 10 Yorkshire wickets, Wilfred's was not among them.

Lord Hawke acknowledged that Rhodes 'was worthy of a place for his batting alone'. He still wasn't happy about it, though. 'What I had anticipated would happen when Rhodes was allowed to develop his batting happened, namely that his wickets cost five runs more apiece and he took 39 less.'

George Herbert was troubled all season by a strained leg but declined to sit down no matter what the medical men told him. His injury restricted his bounding run, his pace dropped to military medium, but he'd lost none of his ability to move the ball and he could still plug away with dogged accuracy when the air was thin and the breeze could not be harnessed. Though he often ran with a limp, George Herbert hit eight centuries for Yorkshire and another for the North against the South. Three of them were scored in trying circumstances. Against Kent, Yorkshire went in 178 behind on the first innings. They'd lost two wickets for 84 when George Herbert came to the middle. He made 157 and turned what had looked like certain defeat into a draw. His 103 against Middlesex helped his team effect another remarkable escape.

Schof showed his resilience and what football managers might call *bouncebackability* once again and recovered from the struggles of 1903 to strike form with both ball and bat. Towards the end of June, he and Wilfred bowled unchanged through both Hampshire innings at Headingley. Schof finished with 10 for 49 and Wilfred 10 for 39 as Yorkshire crushed the visitors by 370 runs. Three days later at Edgbaston, Schof smashed 138 and took three wickets in both innings. In the next match against Derbyshire, he scored another century and took five for 85 in Derbyshire's first innings.

The game against Kent at Harrogate in June was abandoned by the umpires on the second day after allegations that the pitch had been doctored overnight by the groundsman to help the home side. On the second day, shortly before the match was called off, Schof took a hat-trick bowling slow leg-breaks to avoid hurting anyone. Yorkshire vehemently denied any wrongdoing. Kent demanded an inquiry, but

MCC saw no purpose to one and whatever had, or hadn't, happened would remain a mystery, though mutterings about Lord Hawke's unholy influence at HQ could be heard down among the hop fields. Shortly afterwards, Schof completed his first and, as it would turn out, only first-class double.

Schof, George Herbert and Wilfred got good backing from Billy Ringrose, a medium-pacer from the Vale of Pickering, and swing bowler Hubert Myers from Yeadon, who Wilfred described bluntly as 'like Emmott Robinson but not as good'. Myers had been brought into the side as a batsman, only revealing his potential with the ball in the nets before a game with Oxford University. He'd end up opening the bowling with George Herbert. Against Gloucestershire at Dewsbury, he took eight for 81 in the first innings and 10 in the match. He'd eventually emigrate to Australia where he played a few seasons with Tasmania. Ringrose looked like a genuine prospect. Sadly, the physical demands of county cricket proved too much and he retired after three seasons, his ankles aching and his feet swollen despite the fact he had taken to wearing six pairs of socks when fielding.

For the Three Musketeers and for the rest of Yorkshire, the highlight of the season was George Herbert's benefit match against Lancashire at Headingley over the bank holiday weekend of August. On the first day, more than 30,000 packed into the ground, spilling out over the cycle track that then surrounded the field and on to the grass itself. To accommodate them all, the boundary rope had to be pulled in. Hawke thought the turn-out 'a worthy tribute to one of the best sportsmen who ever stepped on the field'.

Lancashire's captain, Archie MacLaren, won the toss and, completely misjudging the pitch, put Yorkshire in. They scored over 400. When George Herbert came in, he seemed momentarily shaken by the thunder of affectionate applause and cheering that had accompanied him to the wicket. He started unsteadily, but soon shook off the emotion to crash 65 with a series of mighty on-side blows. When Lancashire batted he rediscovered some of his old zest, getting the wickets of Spooner, Tyldesley and MacLaren in his opening three overs and finishing with six wickets for 42. In Lancashire's second knock, Tyldesley, aided by an Australian medical student, Les Poidevin, saved the game for the visitors, denying George Herbert the perfect end to his match. When the entry fees were tallied they came to a little over £3,703.

In a move that seemed designed to endear him still further to his legion of admirers, George Herbert announced his intention to invest a chunk of his money not in stocks and shares, or property, but in a Huddersfield toffee factory. A few years later, he was marketing his George Hirst 'health toffees', which promised to restore energy. In June 1906, Hirst's sales force handed out dozens of penny tins – complete with the all-rounder's portrait – to spectators at Lord's on the morning of Yorkshire's encounter with Middlesex. Over the next few days, a two-paragraph report claiming that 2,500 spectators were seen clutching the tins and predicting that the name Hirst would soon be as synonymous with sweets as it was with cricket appeared in hundreds of local and regional newspapers from Devon to Aberdeenshire.

The whole exercise suggested that if George Herbert had not been distracted by cricket he might have made a genius marketing man. The toffees seem to have disappeared into the fog of history. His deeds remain. That season he scored 2,501 runs at an average of 54.36 and took 132 wickets at

21.09. He was the first professional to score 2,000 runs and take 100 wickets in a season, a feat previously achieved only by the amateur Gloucestershire trio of W. G., Gilbert Jessop and Charlie Townsend. Hawke considered the achievement all the more remarkable 'considering how lame he often was'.

CHAPTER SEVEN

Doubles

With his bristling moustache, piercing stare and bald pate, the Hon. F. S. Jackson looked rather like the actor James Finlayson, whose belongings were so often destroyed by Laurel and Hardy. Not that Stan and Ollie would have got very far with Jackers. He'd have beaned them both with a couple of cover drives, or a brace of full bungers. Though he was born in Leeds and spent his entire career with his native county, Jackson paradoxically always seemed less of a Yorkshireman than Lord Hawke, who came from Lincolnshire. Blue-blooded and metropolitan in outlook, he belonged more to the nation as a whole than he did to any of its provinces. Despite that, he was well liked by the Yorkshire pros and enjoyed their jokes and teasing. When Jackson stood as a parliamentary candidate in Leeds and invited George Herbert to speak on his behalf, George Herbert agreed, stood up before a huge crowd and brought the house down by advising the assembly, 'Do not vote for Mr Jackson. Yorkshire need his batting.' Jackson chuckled about the incident whenever he thought of it, even though he failed to get elected.

Jackson's appointment to captain England against Australia in the summer of 1905, therefore, seemed so in the natural order of things it was a surprise nobody had thought of it before. As it turned out, Jackson was not the most tactically astute of England captains, but he was one of the luckiest, winning the toss five times.

Wilfred and George Herbert were selected for the first Test at Trent Bridge. George Herbert was feeling the effects of a strained thigh and his toe had been bruised badly by Tibby Cotter when Yorkshire had played the tourists at Bramall Lane a week earlier. A specialist doctor called in by MCC pronounced him unfit to play. England won comfortably thanks to Bosanquet who, despite Rhodes's scepticism, bowled brilliantly in Australia's second innings, taking eight wickets for 107. Wilfred's main contribution was with the bat. In company with Dick Lilley he helped raise England's first innings to a respectable 196 all out and in the second he shared in a century partnership with Jackson, making 39 not out.

At Leeds in late May, Schof destroyed Worcestershire in both innings to finish with match figures of 12 for 95. His heroics earned him a call-up for the second Test at Lord's. He came into the side in place of Jessop, who had been out for a duck playing a wild shot at Nottingham. The decision to dump the Croucher caused murmurings throughout cricket and can't have helped Schof's nerves on what was his Test debut at home.

England batted first and at the close of play on the first day were eight wickets down for 258. That night and early the next morning it rained heavily. By the start of play the sun was shining, the wicket drying. England quickly finished their innings so that Schof and Wilfred could take advantage of the sticky track. The expectation was that Australia would be bundled out in quick time. Jackson must have known from county cricket that Schof hated taking the new ball. Perhaps the England captain was impatient, or, like Hawke, thought Schof was just being silly. Whatever his reasons, instead of letting another of England's bowlers wear off some of the shine, he threw the glossy cherry straight to Schof, took up his place in the slips, licked his lips and waited for the carnage.

It never came. Or not from Schof and Wilfred anyway. The Australian openers opted for a policy of all-out attack. Wilfred went for four an over – headline stuff – while Haigh, struggling to grip the shiny, damp ball, took an even worse shellacking and the 50 came up in half an hour. Later, Wilfred would explain away the failure, saying that 'the critics' (you imagine his lip curling as he said those words) had failed to understand how cutely the Australian pair had manipulated the strike. Schof had wanted to bowl his off-breaks at the left-handed Clem Hill, while Wilfred fancied his chances against the right-handed Trumper. Realising this, the two experienced Australians had ensured it didn't happen, refusing singles and cannily remaining at what were for the Yorkshire pair the wrong ends. The press, ignorant of the subtleties of professional cricket, had not understood the problem, Wilfred concluded bitterly. This would have been a credible explanation for the situation, certainly. Except for one thing – Hill didn't open the batting, Reggie Duff did. Duff, like Trumper, was right-handed. For once Wilfred's analysis was wrong.

Jackson took Schof out of the attack after half a dozen fruitless overs and brought himself on. He got the wickets of Trumper, Hill and Noble in quick succession. There was minor belligerence from Armstrong and skipper Joe Darling, before Schof returned and clean bowled Bert Hopkins and Charlie McLeod and Wilfred finished off the innings by trapping James Kelly lbw. The visitors were all out for 181, a low total but hardly the rout that had been anticipated. More rain fell when England batted for a second time and the match was abandoned.

Fully fit again, George Herbert returned for the third Test at Leeds and Schof was retained despite his failure to exploit the wicket at Lord's. Wilfred, however, was omitted in favour of Colin Blythe. Many expert observers believed the Kent spinner was the better bowler, though it is doubtful if any of them were regulars on the Western Terrace. There was grim communal grumbling of typical southern bias.

England batted first. Jackson smacked a dazzling 144 not out and, with George Herbert who made 35, put on a valuable 69 for the fifth wicket as England failed to take advantage of the captain's innings and were all out for 301. Australia struggled to 195, Derbyshire paceman Arnold Warren the pick of the bowlers. Schof and George Herbert took a wicket apiece. When England batted a second time, Darling set defensive fields and had his bowlers aiming well outside off stump. Despite the fact that Tyldesley hit a century in under three hours, *Wisden* described the cricket as 'very flat and tedious' – a measure of what was expected of batsmen in those days. England declared at 295 for five, with George Herbert at the wicket undefeated on 40.

Jessop, among others, felt Jackson had declared too late. It proved the correct judgement. Australia made it through to the close of the match, finishing on 224 for seven from 91 overs, still a mighty 177 runs behind. Another hour of bowling might have won it for England. George Herbert took a wicket in each innings and a brilliant catch to dismiss Trumper, while Schof bowled economically without much threat. Arnold Warren had taken six wickets in the match and dismissed Trumper twice. He never played for England again, the first in a long line of Derbyshire fast bowlers with a right to feel aggrieved about the fancy caps at Lord's.

At Old Trafford, Wilfred returned, but Schof was dropped. His replacement was the bristling Walter Brearley, on his home strip. England batted first and ran up a total of 446. Jackson was again outstanding and George Herbert and Wilfred handy, contributing 25 and 27 not out. On the Tuesday morning, it rained heavily and then the sun came out. England completed their innings as fast they could, Wilfred and Lilley putting on 59 in 45 minutes. On a pitch that Brearley memorably described as 'bubbling nicely', George Herbert took the new ball in tandem with the mighty Lancastrian paceman. Big Walter soon had Trumper snicking to Wilfred in the slips. He then bowled Noble. George Herbert performed poorly and was removed after a couple of overs, never to return.

Australia were stumbling from the start and Wilfred must have been itching to have a bowl on a pitch that might have been commissioned for him. Jackson, however, delayed his arrival. When Wilfred finally handed his sweater to the umpire he struck almost immediately, dismissing Armstrong. He was then taken off again, the skipper's reasoning once again opaque. Joe Darling hit a brilliant counter-attacking 73, farming the strike to protect the tail-enders. With last man Kelly having reached 16, Jackson summoned Wilfred again. He dismissed Kelly with his fifth delivery. In total Wilfred had bowled just 5.5 overs. Still, Australia were all out for 197 and followed on 249 runs behind.

In the second innings, George Herbert was no more effective than in the first. This time Jackson used Wilfred a little more and was rewarded, the spinner trapping Trumper leg before when he was dangerously poised on 30 and then getting rid of Algy Gehrs and McLeod as Australia once again fell apart to lose by an innings and 80 runs.

At The Oval, Wilfred and George Herbert were retained. England batted. Cotter was at his most wild and hostile, smashing through the defences of MacLaren and Tyldesley. Fry flailed at him and got lucky. Hayward stood on his wicket. Jackson arrived. He and Fry put on 151 in quick time. Fry was out for 144, Jackson followed, then Reggie Spooner. George Herbert was done by Laver for five as England finished the day on 381 for seven. The next morning Wilfred batted serenely, coasting to 36 and putting on 72 for the eighth wicket with Ted Arnold of Worcestershire. The final wicket fell when the total had reached 430.

When Australia batted on the fast, even Oval track, George Herbert at last hit some decent form. Using all his skills, he had Armstrong caught in the slips for 18, clean bowled Darling for 57 and then took a smart catch off his own bowling to get rid of opener Reggie Duff for a defiant 146. Wilfred bowled 21 overs without reward, though he was as tight as ever on a tough day for the fielding side.

With a 67-run advantage on first innings England thrashed their way to 261 with six wickets down before Jackson declared. The task of bowling out Australia once again proved beyond England. George Herbert picked up the wicket of Noble as Australia closed out the match with four wickets down. Wilfred was victimless again.

England had retained the Ashes, though the contribution

of the Triumvirate to that success had been moderate. They had taken 20 wickets between them. Wilfred had averaged 48.66 with the bat, despite having a highest score of 39, and George Herbert 35. The trio would do much better in the County Championship, which Yorkshire won despite a rocky spell in June that saw them lose to Lancashire, Derbyshire and Kent.

As if to confound Lord Hawke, Wilfred had an extraordinary season with both bat and ball. In the first match of the County Championship against Somerset at Taunton he came in at number seven and struck the ball straight and hard, powering his way to a double century that included 32 boundaries. He also took seven for 101 in the match. He followed that feat with five wickets in an innings against Gloucestershire, Worcestershire and Cambridge University. Against Essex at Huddersfield, he took six wickets for nine runs in 50 deliveries. His good form continued for the Players against the Gentlemen at Lord's where he picked up eight wickets including his county team-mate and England captain Jackson twice. In the Champion County match at The Oval, that saw Yorkshire play the Rest of England, he bowled superbly taking 11 wickets. Yorkshire won by 65 runs – the first county ever to win the annual fixture.

Wilfred's feats were matched by George Herbert. His injury had still not properly healed, but he battled on with all his heart and strength. He took seven for 48 against Somerset and five for 43 against Surrey. He made five centuries, including a massive knock against Leicestershire at Leicester in May, when he came in with Yorkshire three wickets down and close to 400 runs short of the opposition's first-innings total. When he was finally out his team were nearly a hundred ahead. He batted for just seven hours, hit a six and 53 fours. His 341 was the highest score ever made by a Yorkshireman, the highest ever in a match featuring Yorkshire, topping the 318 W. G. had thumped way back in 1876. George Herbert also scored 232 not out against Surrey at The Oval. Only one other Yorkshireman made more than 40 in that match. If anyone thought the batting might have worn him out they were mistaken – he took five wickets for 43.

The return with Surrey saw a very different feat of batting heroics from George Herbert. Played on a rapidly deteriorating Headingley wicket, it was a game in which batsmen struggled. Yorkshire were set just 32 to win but found themselves up against the fearsome Neville Knox, the fastest bowler of his generation. The ball flew, batsmen swayed, ducked and yelped, but George Herbert stuck fast, scoring nine not out and leading Yorkshire to a five-wicket victory.

At Old Trafford, Johnny Tyldesley and Reggie Spooner both scored centuries as Lancashire piled up a handsome total in fine weather. A shower of rain made the hard surface of the wicket dangerous when Yorkshire batted and the situation was perfectly exploited by Lancashire's Australian bowler Alex Kermode, who bowled them out twice to give the home side a crushing victory by an innings and 52 runs.

The return match at Sheffield was a wonderful contest. With Walter Brearley bowling full tilt, Lancashire dismissed the home side for 76. The burly Brearley was one of Yorkshire's most feared opponents – a great Desperate Dan of a man who looked like he could fell a dray horse, or substitute for one. On damp wickets, he had local denture-makers rubbing their hands in anticipation, the ball snorting and rising like a startled pheasant from a good length. Yorkshire had no one to compare to him for earth-pawing, chest-beating hostility, and when Lancashire batted they scored 177.

The home side replied on the bumpy and dangerous track against Big Walter, who was straining so hard he split his shirt clean down the back. Jackson batted with flair and tenacity and Denton played what he considered the best innings of his career to score 96. Wilfred abandoned his normal caution and, with the ball screaming round his ears and thumping into his thighs, attacked from the second he arrived at the wicket. He even clobbered one delivery over the head of point and into the stands as he cantered to 74 in 75 minutes. The reply amounted to 285. Lancashire needed 185 to win. Against Wilfred and Schof they collapsed to 140 all out.

Predictably, Schof's fortunes took a slight dip after his fine season in 1904, but he still managed to turn in several devastating displays with the ball. The first brought him a dozen Worcestershire wickets. Three weeks later at Sheffield he repeated the feat against Nottinghamshire, this time conceding 40 fewer runs. In the next match against Warwickshire in Dewsbury, he and Wilfred bowled unchanged in the second innings both taking five for 26. Schof topped the first-class bowling averages at the end of the season. He had taken 118 wickets for Yorkshire in the Championship at 14.53. He'd also hit five first-class half-centuries. If he'd had George Herbert's happy confidence, or Wilfred's grave application, he might have become a top-class all-rounder. Wilfred certainly thought so. To his mind, it was only a lack of self-belief that held Schof's batting back.

Against Essex at Leyton, Yorkshire needed only a draw to win the Championship. The home side piled up 521 and then bowled Yorkshire out for 98. Johnny Douglas – a man

Wilfred greatly admired – pulled off a piece of bowling any of the Triumvirate might have welcomed as their own. He came on first change just before lunch. With the fifth ball of his second over he bowled Tunnicliffe. Lunch was taken. With his first ball after the break he trapped Hirst. In his next over the first three balls passed uneventfully then he took a hat-trick – Wilfred, Schof and Myers. He had taken five wickets in eight balls and conceded only three runs.

Forced to follow on, Yorkshire battled with skill and bloody-mindedness to save the match and win the title. George Herbert reined in his attacking instincts and batted for five hours for just 90. For the final hour, he was joined by the normally cavalier Ernest Smith, who obdurately made it through to the close without making a single scoring shot. 'His 0 not out is certainly the most historic and creditable "blob" in the whole history of cricket and he has subsequently called it his martyrdom,' Lord Hawke commented with a chuckle.

Schof's part in Yorkshire's impressive season and his excel-lent performances on his first tour there, earned him a place on Plum Warner's MCC tour of South Africa that winter. The party also included David Denton and other top-class cricketers in Albert Relf, Jack Board, Ernie Hayes, Colin Blythe and Walter Lees. There was also a pleasing smatter-ing of eccentric amateurs including Shrimp Leveson Gower and Teddy Wynyard of Hampshire, who bowled underarms, had won a DSO in Burma and was one of Britain's best figure-skaters.

Things began very well for Schof. In the first match against Western Province at Newlands he took five for 29 in the first innings, and when the two teams met again at the same ground he scored 61, adding 82 for the ninth wicket with Leonard Moon of Middlesex (another cricketer who'd take his own life). Shortly after that, however, he was struck down by dysentery. The travelling was arduous – the players covered 5,000 miles and spent 23 nights sleeping on trains – and gave Schof no time to settle, rest and recover. He battled gamely and played in all five Tests, taking four for 64 in the first innings of the second in Johannesburg, but he was never well enough to perform at his best.

Even if he'd been in peak condition, the tour would likely have been an unhappy one. On the matting wickets, England were totally outclassed by a South African side boasting some of the best leg-spinners of the age – Aubrey Faulkner, Reggie Schwarz, Gordon White and Bert Vogler – supported by the dogged batting of Dave Nourse and Percy Sherwell. England – whose only leg-spinner was the ineffectual Jock Hartley, an amateur who hadn't played county cricket since 1898 – lost the series 4-1.

Schof's contribution was meagre – six wickets at 43.83. He'd done even worse with the bat, claiming later that he went out into the middle 'and simply knocked a lot of fresh air about'. He was glad to get back to Huddersfield, where he presented Lillian with a large bag of ostrich feathers. The couple wouldn't get much time together. It was already the second week in April and preparations for the new season were about to begin. When his team-mates asked him about his winter, Schof responded, 'I enjoyed everything about it but the cricket.'

No doubt relieved to be back in familiar surroundings, Schof had a storming season, finishing with 174 wickets in all matches (138 in Championship games) with best match figures of 12 for 105 against Middlesex at Lord's. He topped the Yorkshire averages again, but nothing he could have done would have matched the heroics that summer of his friend George Herbert.

The Hirsts' third child, Molly, was born just as the season began. The new life in his Kirkheaton home seemed to inspire George Herbert. On 17 May, he hit a century and took 11 for 79 against Kent at Catford, following that by picking up 12 for 66 against Leicestershire at Leeds. The winter's rest had done him good and, although now in his mid-thirties, he was bowling as quick as he'd ever done. George Herbert was no Brearley or Cotter, but he couldn't be taken lightly either. C. B. Fry would regret his foolishness of writing in a newspaper early in the 1901 season that Yorkshire's only weakness was the lack of a truly fast bowler. A few weeks later, Sussex met Yorkshire at Bradford on a wicket that was like 'marble with an oiled top'. A nasty wind blew across the field. George Herbert had evidently read Fry's comments. 'George showed his paces,' Fry recalled. 'He hit all of us on the knee caps and skittled everyone except the Jam Sahib.' Ranjitsinhji made a creditable 35, Fry got 15; no other Sussex batsman got into double figures that day.

Though he rarely bowled anything like a bouncer, George Herbert had a reputation for hammering batsmen round the legs. Seeing the damage his friend inflicted – swollen knees, thighs that looked like an angry man had taken a meat tenderiser to them – Wilfred always bought the thickest pads he could find. Once, when George Herbert was batting against Lancashire at Old Trafford, he was struck a painful blow on the arm by Walter Brearley and heard a Lancastrian in the crowd bellow, 'That's right, give the bugger a bit of his own back.' 'I never in my life bowled a ball at a man,' George

Herbert protested afterwards. Of course he didn't. He bowled at the stumps, but if batsmen would wander in front of them, well that was their lookout.

George Herbert's 1,000th run of the season came against Kent in Sheffield on 27 June and his hundredth wicket the next day at Leyton in the match with Essex. Though he'd hit six centuries, it was his innings in adversity that he relished most. His 93 against Kent pulled the game round in Yorkshire's favour; his 89 not out against Derbyshire towed them to victory. Perhaps his best batting was the 58 against Brearley in the Roses match at Bradford; the top score of the match, it was instrumental in securing a six-wicket win. Sometimes even George Herbert's heroics were not enough; he took 14 wickets against Nottingham only to finish on the losing side by 25 runs.

Throughout the season his form never waned, his strength never weakened and his energy suggested perpetual motion was not a scientific impossibility. He rounded the season off with an amazing performance against Somerset at Bath, where he scored a century in each innings and took 11 wickets for 115 runs, six in the first innings and five in the second – an all-round performance that has never been matched.

George Herbert had achieved the double by the end of June, two weeks quicker than anybody had ever done before. As it became clear that the Kirkheaton lad might achieve a milestone that had eluded even W. G. when he was young and muscular and rampaging through the shires like some mythic beast ('They ought to make him play with a littler bat,' Tom Emmett had remarked mournfully), the public was increasingly gripped by his progress, keeping track of every wicket and run. There was no radio, and cinema was still a novelty, so George Herbert's deeds came to the people from the news stands each morning and evening.

Professional football was more popular than cricket, but it was not so well covered by the daily papers and periodicals. Indeed many of the smarter national broadsheets and magazines did not write about the professional game at all. By contrast, cricket was elegant and fashionable, diverting and fun, a fixture of the London season. Nobody went to a football match to show off the latest gown from Paris, or hat from Bond Street. Footballers such as Billy Meredith, Harry Hampton and Colin Veitch might be heroes in working-class neighbourhoods of the North and Midlands, but their names did not appear alongside glowing accounts of their successes in the *Pall Mall Gazette*, the *Strand Magazine* or *Tatler*. Yet in these publications in the summer of 1905, George Hirst – a former dye-worker who'd left school at 10 – was almost as ubiquitous as Lady Margot Asquith and Mrs Patrick Campbell.

It was clear too that people were not just following George Herbert, they were urging him on, willing him to succeed. He was extraordinarily popular, not just admired, but cherished. The thought of him brightened the day, it made people smile.

George Herbert had made his 2,000th run during his epic display against Somerset. His 200th wicket seemed a long time in coming. He had to wait till the end of the season. The Scarborough Festival pulled down the curtain on the summer. On 30 August, Yorkshire played MCC. George Herbert needed five wickets to achieve his great milestone. The visitors won the toss and elected to bat. With his second ball, George Herbert clean bowled MacLaren. Six deliveries later Henry Foster was caught by Ernest Smith. Then Spooner and Frederick Fane began batting sensibly. They'd put on 132 when Wilfred trapped Spooner. He got Meyrick Payne first ball, but Len Braund stuck around. The day wore on. The tension mounted. Wilfred got rid of Fane.

George Herbert returned to the attack and summoning all his reserves of energy clean bowled Teddy Wynyard. Two more wickets needed. The South African all-rounder Bert Vogler joined Braund. The duo batted stubbornly. They'd added nearly 50 when George Herbert produced an in-ducker that shattered Vogler's stumps. Shrimp Leveson Gower arrived. He adopted a cavalier approach, playing and missing, slashing the ball through the covers. The clock ticked on towards the close. Emma Hirst had sat through the entire day. Now she had to return to the hotel to put baby Molly to bed. As she walked away across Trafalgar Square, George Herbert ran in to bowl to Braund. The Somerset all-rounder was on 73. He clipped a George Herbert delivery into the air, straight towards the fielder. It was his MCC team-mate Foster on as a substitute. Foster did his duty. The roar of the crowd told Emma that her husband had made it.

When the season ended, George Herbert had scored 2,385 runs and taken 208 wickets. He had batted 58 times and sent down nearly 8,000 deliveries. Asked if he thought anyone would ever match his feat, George Herbert replied with a weary grin. 'I don't know, but they'll be very tired if they do.'

The strain had taken its toll. George Herbert had got through the last month of the season on grit and determination alone. One of his knees was so badly swollen he could barely bend down to tie his bootlaces. He told the *Huddersfield Examiner*, 'It gave me gip – after I'd got the runs and the wickets. The feat was a triumph of spirit over matter.'

Wilfred, like everyone else that season, was eclipsed by

Hirst, but his contributions were far from shabby. He scored 1,721 runs and took 128 wickets. Despite his achievements, he found himself facing heavy criticism. In *Wisden*, Sydney Pardon voiced the concerns of many. 'The fact remains that his continued advance as a batsman did not compensate for his marked decline as a bowler.' Wilfred, the almanack declared, had 'lost his quick spin off the pitch and, on hard wickets, batsmen did not fear him in the least'. Wilfred must now be acknowledged as an all-rounder, but 'it would have been better for Yorkshire if he had remained a specialist, made fewer runs, and still remained a great bowler'. The comments might have been dictated by Lord Hawke.

Despite the heroic efforts of George Herbert and the masterful contributions of Schof and Wilfred, Yorkshire narrowly missed out on another title, finishing runners-up to Kent. Kent won fewer matches than Yorkshire, but also lost fewer and eventually 'won the title by one run' after Yorkshire lost to Gloucestershire late in the season by that very margin. The defeat to Gloucestershire saw the unfortunate Billy Ringrose cast in the Fred Tate role. With a batting average in the lower single digits, he walked out at Bristol to face Gilbert Jessop bowling at his quickest with two runs needed to win. The first delivery was fast and wide down the leg-side. Jack Board dived full length and only just prevented it going for the byes that would have won the game. The next ball was straight and even faster. Ringrose prodded and missed. The ball thwacked his pads. He was plumb in front. Kent had their title. Ringrose dropped out of the Yorkshire first team at the end season.

In the end, George Herbert's matchless achievements were more than a compensation for the failure to land another title.

They would be remembered long after Kent's Championship would be forgotten. Lord Hawke marvelled at his work, 'Hirst was again paramount, indeed superlative ... it was not only what he did but how he did it, coming off when an effort seemed most necessary, and playing his best against the most formidable sides.' Across England cricket fans nodded in agreement. Not since 1876, when W. G. had been an unstoppable force, had the country followed the deeds of one man so closely or celebrated them so warmly. George Herbert's energy seemed to epitomise the Edwardian age. He had a locomotive power. His stamina was proverbial. David Hunter commented that he 'was full of spirit and mettle and I've seen him tug and drive till he could hardly trail'. Writing in *London Opinion* Alfred Gibson summarised: '[Hirst] weighs anything up to fourteen stone, but he can bowl at great pace for hours, and if he remains at the wicket half a day he is still as frisky as a kitten.'

George Herbert was the Duracell bunny of the time and one manufacturer recognised the potential. The idea that product endorsement is a new thing in the world of sport is untrue. When he completed his double double, George Herbert seized the opportunity to pick up some extra cash by advertising Phosferine Tonic Wine. According to Hirst, or at least in the words written for him by the company, Phosferine taken at the end of a hard day's cricket had helped him stave off exhaustion. It was 'wonderfully effective' and helped build up a 'marvellous reserve of staying power' as well as quelling any sense of nervous anxiety that might attack a sportsman during the dark hours of the night. In fact, according to the advertising, Phosferine Tonic Wine was capable of curing everything from depression to influenza. Sceptics in the medical profession decided to investigate. A study in the *British Medical Journal* in 1911 revealed that this miraculous remedy contained nothing more than diluted phospheric acid, quinine and a healthy shot of alcohol. Wherever George Herbert's amazing energy came from, it wasn't from the patented tonic.

CHAPTER EIGHT

Titles and Changes

Unsurprisingly 1907 started a little slowly for George Herbert. Nobody could begrudge him taking a more leisurely run-up and he didn't reach his best until high summer. At Glossop towards the end of July, he and Wilfred bowled Derbyshire out for 44 and 72, George Herbert taking 11 for 44. He followed that up by taking 15 for 63 against arguably his favourite opponents, Leicestershire, at Hull. The visitors were almost bowled out twice in a day and George Herbert took the second hat-trick of his career, all the victims clean bowled. His first hat-trick had come 12 years earlier against the same opponents.

In the second innings against Middlesex at Bramall Lane, while Wilfred bunged up one end with a display of immaculate line and length defensive bowling, George Herbert at the other bowled into a wind that might have been ordered specially for him. The ball ducked into the right-handers as if there was a guidance system in off stump and Hirst recorded the best bowling figures of his career, nine for 45.

The season was rainy and wet, which added to the sense of anti-climax following the gallop to the double double. Yorkshire lost more days to rain than they had in any other season in their history. Two home matches were abandoned without a ball being bowled and there was barely a game that didn't suffer disruption from the weather. In June, Yorkshire did not complete a single match as a damp, dark blanket of drizzle flopped across the country. It was not a season for forcing batsmen. George Herbert did not score a single century, though he played a number of fine innings under the gloomy skies. His 78 against Essex helped secure a victory that at one time had seemed unlikely. His 91 not out against Kent at Canterbury headed off what had looked an inevitable defeat.

Perhaps Wilfred was mindful of the criticism from the previous season, or maybe it was just the damp. Whatever the reason, his bowling improved as his batting tailed off again. He finished the season with 177 wickets at 15.57. He began as he would continue. On Yorkshire's traditional curtain-raising West Country tour he took 12 wickets against Somerset, nine against Worcestershire and picked up five for 72 in Gloucestershire's second innings in between. In the Whitsuntide Roses match, he bowled with concentrated brilliance in Lancashire's second knock to pick up six for 46. In the return at Headingley, he took 11 wickets and made 69, the highest score of the game.

Those who were relieved to see Wilfred going back to what he was 'best at' suffered a disappointment when he was promoted to opening batsman as Yorkshire struggled to find a replacement for the sadly departed Brown. The feeling was compounded when Wilfred responded to the challenge by compiling an immaculate 112 against Leicestershire. Happily for those who wished Wilfred to focus on bowling, his promotion proved temporary. Yorkshire felt they had found a new partner for Tunnicliffe in the shape of James Rothery from Batley.

Wilfred did not appear in the Test matches against South Africa that summer. The place of the left-arm spinner went to the exceptional Colin Blythe, rated by Ranjitsinhji as the most deceptive flighter of a ball in cricket. There was discontent in Yorkshire when the Kent man was chosen ahead of Wilfred for the Leeds Test, as he had been in 1905, but this time, on a damp wicket, Blythe proved the merit in the decision by picking up 15 wickets for 99 runs and beating Rhodes's Melbourne performance as the best-ever bowling by an Englishman in a Test match. No doubt there were those on the Western Terrace who muttered that 'Wilfred would have got all twenty', but most went away convinced.

George Herbert featured in three Test matches against South Africa that season, but only performed to his county standards in the final one at The Oval where he took three wickets in each innings.

Unsurprisingly, Schof enjoyed the damp summer. He took five for nine in the first innings against Essex at Leyton in July and later in the month finished the game against Warwickshire at Sheffield with 13 wickets for 40. He and George Herbert bowled unchanged in Warwickshire's second knock. At close of play, he hurried home. Lillian had just given birth to a third child, Reginald. At the season's close, he topped Yorkshire's bowling averages with 96 first-class wickets at 12.31.

Nottinghamshire won the title. Yorkshire were second again (tied with Worcestershire). The greatest team was breaking up. Brown had died, now Jackson, who'd only managed a single match that season, announced his retirement, while Long John Tunnicliffe left to take up a coaching position at Clifton School. On the upside, another talent had been unearthed in Kirkheaton, Ederick Bates. Ederick was the son of Billy Bates, a Kirkheaton man who'd played for Yorkshire and England in the 1880s before falling into depression and dying at the age of 44. A superb and stylish batsman, Billy Bates had been nicknamed the Duke and so Ederick's new team-mates dubbed him the Marquess as a jokey mark of respect. A forceful opening bat and a brilliant outfielder, Bates would make 114 appearances for Yorkshire, but save his best cricket for the years after the First World War when he'd moved to Glamorgan.

Wilfred's second trip to Australia that winter was no more successful than Schof's to South Africa. Arthur Jones was skipper of an MCC side that included Blythe, Barnes, Braund, Jack Hobbs and George Gunn. They played well in the early state matches, but could not match Australia in the Tests, losing four out of five. Jones went down with pneumonia early in the trip and struggled to recover. His vice-captain, Irishman Frederick Fane, seemed uncertain whether Wilfred was there as a bowler or as a batsman and ended up using him fully in neither capacity. Wilfred opened the batting in the second innings of the first Test and made a creditable 29, posting a half-century stand with Fane. But then Hobbs – on his first overseas tour – came in to replace him and he switched back to number seven in the order.

Rhodes liked and admired Hobbs but both men were introverts and, though they'd forge a fine partnership on the field, were never truly friends off it. Instead, he hung out with the whimsical George Gunn, who in character perhaps reminded him of Schof, and Sydney Barnes, a man he rated, not unreasonably, as the greatest bowler in history. Barnes shared Wilfred's gruff, no-nonsense manner. Like Wilfred, he took pride in himself and in his work. He was a craftsman and he knew his value.

Those who ran first-class cricket thought Barnes's temperament 'suspect', which only meant that he refused to do as he was told. He had little time for those who sat at Lord's and made the rules and he bridled at cricket's class system, noting how on hot afternoons the gentlemen fielded in the shade of the grandstand while the professionals laboured in the sun. He had quit the county game in 1903 and gone off to play for Church in the Lancashire League instead. When asked about his decision, he explained the economics simply and convincingly: 'We were paid £5 for a home match and £6 for an away match and you had to pay your own travelling expenses and lodgings out of that.' In winter, the players got nothing at all. Barnes preferred to play in the leagues and pursue his career as a draughtsman. It earned him more, gave his family security and left him answerable to nobody but himself.

Barnes was tough and uncompromising. In an age when the professionals were not expected to answer back, he spoke his mind. 'I don't understand you, Barnes,' Lord Hawke admonished him. 'You only play when you like.' Barnes looked His Lordship in the eye and snapped back: 'And I intend to go on doing so.' As time went on, Wilfred would come to share some of Barnes's sentiments about the way the game was run and the men who ran it. Though he might grouse privately, unlike the great medium-pacer he would never quite have the courage to break away, even when the opportunity came. Unlike Barnes, he had no occupation besides cricket. The leagues offered good money and better terms of employment, but playing for Yorkshire gave him nationwide status. He stuck with the devil he knew.

Regardless of the company, it was a miserable trip. Wilfred's bowling was under-used and, perhaps because he was not allowed to build up any rhythm, rarely rose above competent. He took just 31 first-class wickets on the tour, well below the numbers of Barnes, Arthur Fielder and even the amateur, Jack Crawford. In the five Tests, Wilfred took just seven wickets at a cost of 60 runs each. His batting did not make up for it, he barely averaged 20. Away from the Tests, he hit close to 1,000 first-class runs including two centuries and finished below only Gunn and Joe Hardstaff in the MCC averages, but it was hardly the stuff of headlines and Wilfred returned home troubled about his career and working over the changes he felt he needed to make in his approach to the game.

In 1908, Lord Hawke celebrated his 25th year as Yorkshire captain and 'his boys' rewarded him with an eighth County Championship. His Lordship enjoyed the season thoroughly and always viewed this particular team with the greatest affection. The side at the start of the new century had been the best he captained, but in His Lordship's mind it had per- haps been *too* good. Many opponents had been beaten before a match had even begun, others had surrendered meekly. Hawke was a country gentleman. He spent his winters hunt- ing and fishing. He wanted sport. With the great team of 1900–02 he had sometimes felt like he was fishing for salmon with dynamite, or gunning down rabbits with a Maxim gun. It was so easy there was no fun in it.

In 1908, it was different. The matches were competitive, hard fought. Lord Hawke spent many happy days in the field standing in the slips and chatting with the amiable David Hunter and whichever opposition batsmen they could draw in. His Lordship liked the veteran wicketkeeper immensely and when he was forced away on business would place Hunter in charge of the team – even if there were amateur gentlemen in it. Lord Hawke ensured that Yorkshire were a good deal less dogmatic about such things than other counties. Though his infamous comment about professionals captaining England would lead to him being marked down as an upholder of feudal values, Hawke was actually more liberal on the subject than most of the game's administrators of the time.

Hunter had a sharp wit and droll manner, and Lord Hawke enjoyed his polite mockery of opponents. Once, when Middlesex had come to Bradford, Plum Warner was batting to Wilfred. He played forward immaculately, his nose over the ball. 'Ah, Mr Warner, you play Wilfred better than any of the others,' Hunter told him. The next ball whirled down. Warner played forward again, but this time Wilfred had pitched the ball a foot shorter. Warner stretched an extra few inches to reach it but to no avail. The ball spun and beat the bat. Behind the stumps, Hunter gathered and whipped off the bails. The square leg umpire raised his finger. As Warner walked off, Hunter called after him, 'Good afternoon, Mr Warner. And such a pity when you were playing Wilfred so well.'

As well as allowing him to enjoy the comical chirruping of Hunter, Lord Hawke's position in the slips also afforded him a very good view of his favourite cricketer in action. George Herbert had a wonderful summer. Only Colin Blythe took more wickets and only Schof had a better average. He began the season by taking 12 for 19 against a Northamptonshire side which had just been admitted to the County Championship. Their batting proved as brittle as cinder toffee and Yorkshire bowled them out twice for an aggregate total of just 42 – the lowest in County Championship history.

Fewer wickets but better performances came against tougher opponents on the days when Yorkshire needed him most. Against Surrey at Headingley he took six wickets in the second innings, five clean bowled. At Bramall Lane in the Roses match, he bowled with genuine fury for 45 overs picking up 11 wickets for fewer than 100 runs, his hostility a response to a lifter from Brearley that had broken Schof's spinning finger. George Herbert had good times with the bat, too. He hit the ball with all his usual smiling violence against Derbyshire (58 and 128 not out), Leicestershire (89) and Middlesex (96).

It was Wilfred's 10th season in first-class cricket. With Brown and Tunnicliffe now gone, he responded eagerly to Lord Hawke's appeal for an opening bat – the winter in Australia had convinced him he needed to work harder on that aspect of his game. Bowling was a battle, especially on featherbed wickets. If you could bat, you could take advantage of such conditions. And batting, Wilfred was convinced, was a good deal easier than bowling. 'It is harder to be a moderate bowler than a moderate batsman,' he'd say.

Going in as opener, Wilfred hit three hundreds during the season. The problem was finding him a regular partner. The bright hope Rothery hit an impressive century in a rain-drenched encounter with Kent but was too often beset with sickness. Charles Hardisty from Horsforth made fifties but nothing bigger and would spend most of his career as a

The Brown Cow Inn, Kirkheaton *c.*1911. Run by the Hirst family for generations, it was the birthplace of George Herbert and, reputedly, forty-nine other Hirsts.

Bog Hall, Kirkheaton. The romantically named shared home of newlyweds Wilfred and Sarah Rhodes.

Young Wilfred, his innocent appearance belying his intention of scourging the batsman with scorpions.

The Triumvirate relaxing on the boundary. George Herbert appears typically paternal, a role that came naturally to him.

Wilfred enjoying a joke with Lord Hawke during Yorkshire's surprisingly successful 1908 season.

Wilfred in action in 1906 using the flatter, quicker style he'd adopted in Australia.

Schof's early dramatic catapulting action, as dangerous to the batsmen as it was his own body.

Schof placing his field – a packed leg-side if conditions suited him.

Yorkshire 1895. Lord Hawke (seated centre) is flanked by Bobby Peel and F. S. Jackson. John Tunnicliffe is on the far left of the row, Jack Brown and David Hunter are seated on the ground with George Herbert.

England versus Australia, Trent Bridge 1899. C. B. Fry, K. S. Ranjitsinhji, W. G. Grace and F. S. Jackson seated. George Herbert is in the back row, and a youthful Wilfred sits on the grass with Johnny Tyldesley.

George Herbert during his peak years of swerve.

Getting back and across, George Herbert demonstrates his favourite pull shot.

Plum Warner's unexpectedly triumphant Ashes team of 1903–04. George Herbert and Wilfred lurk at the back. Warner and Tip Foster on the far right. Bernard Bosanquet, imposingly tall, is in the centre.

Yorkshire on the eve of World War One. Major Booth (back row, fourth from left) was killed at the Somme, while Alonzo Drake (back row second from right) died of illness during the conflict.

George Herbert and Wilfred with the much-mocked
Yorkshire captain Major Arthur Lupton in 1925.

Wilfred with the brooding Abe Waddington,
a very different man from George Herbert or
Schof.

'Wilfred's finished'. Yorkshire's
smooth and scheming secretary,
Frederick Toone.

Wilfred walking out to bat with Abe Waddington at Toowoomba during the disastrous and acrimonious 1920–21 Ashes tour.

Wilfred's final home Test. England clinch the Ashes at The Oval in 1926. An England selector, he had been persuaded, against his better judgement, to pick himself.

George Herbert imparting wisdom at Yorkshire. Len Hutton called him
'the ideal coach'.

Two elderly greats. Wilfred with the proudly independent Sydney Barnes,
the man he considered the finest bowler of all time.

professional in the leagues of Northumberland and Durham. Benny Wilson had talent but retreated too easily into turgid defence. The matter would never be properly resolved. The only regular opening partner Wilfred would ever find would be Jack Hobbs with England.

Because he was opening the batting, Wilfred bowled less – 300 fewer overs than George Herbert – but he was still effective, picking up 100 wickets for Yorkshire in the Championship at 15.82. That Hawke was allowing Wilfred to concentrate on his batting without any sly asides owed much to the arrival on the scene of a new discovery from Teesside, Jack Newstead. He took 131 wickets with his fast-medium right-armers, including 10 against Leicestershire and Surrey, and also clobbered 733 runs, including a century against Nottinghamshire at Trent Bridge. It was enough to have him selected as one of *Wisden*'s Cricketers of the Year.

Newstead was 29 years old and had found his way into the Yorkshire side via a circuitous route that took in spells as a professional at Middlesbrough, several seasons with the Lord's ground staff and a summer in County Wicklow play-ing for the private XI of Stanley Cochrane, whose family fortune came from the invention of ginger ale. His time at Yorkshire was to be bright and brief. He'd take 80 wickets the following season and 32 the one after that. In 1912, he made just two appearances for the county and was dropped from the squad. The reasons for his sharp decline were a mystery. The more he tried to rectify the problems the worse things got. A career in the Lancashire League was ended by injury in the 1920s. Jack Newstead holds the singular and unpleasant distinction of being the only *Wisden* Cricketer of the Year not to receive an obituary in the almanack. As

Schof had told the reporter in Scotland, a professional's life was fraught with worry and careers like that of Newstead certainly added to the anxiety.

Not that Schof had much to concern him at the beginning of the 1908 season. For a couple of months something singular occurred: he and George Herbert bowled well together. At the start of the summer the two pals were in great form. In the first four matches of the Championship they took 60 wickets between them, 35 clean bowled. Sadly it came to an abrupt end when Schof encountered Walter Brearley at Sheffield. When he returned, he found he couldn't rip the ball as hard as he'd have liked. As a consequence of this, Haigh did not break 100 wickets for the second consecutive season, finishing with 93 first-class victims, 71 in the Championship. However, his average of 12.11 was good enough for him to place top of the first-class averages.

Yorkshire's batting was only moderate, but they bowled and fielded so brilliantly that only two men, James Douglas and Bernard Bosanquet, scored centuries against them. When the season had started, the Yorkshire players had thought so little of their chances of winning the title that George Herbert had advised Ernie Hayes of Surrey to choose the Lancashire match at The Oval for his benefit game as it was likely to decide the Championship. Yet the team had cantered merrily through the season, finishing unbeaten – an outcome Wilfred considered the biggest surprise of his career.

Lord Hawke was delighted with it all. At the close of the season, Yorkshire celebrated his quarter-century in charge by awarding him a benefit of £1,000, a figure topped up with a further £824 donated by readers of the *Yorkshire Evening Post*. As an amateur, His Lordship could not, of course, accept cash.

Instead, he selected six works of art, which were bought with the money on his behalf.

Wilfred had perhaps found the season less joyful than his captain. While Schof was terrorised by the thought of failure, his friend found that success too brought a monstrous pressure. By Wilfred's own estimation his average summer saw him playing around 115 days of cricket, batting more than 60 times and sending down more than 6,000 deliveries. Travel between games added to the workload. On one occasion Yorkshire finished a match with Somerset in Taunton at 6 p.m. and caught the train north. They arrived into Leeds at 2 a.m. and went straight to Dewsbury, where their game with Northamptonshire started nine hours later. When the festival matches came at the end of the season the Yorkshire pros might find themselves sandwiching a game at Hastings in between a couple of matches at Scarborough. They rarely slept in their own beds and often were forced to grab what rest they could on the journey or in the pavilion. This, Wilfred noted, did not leave them feeling physically tired, but placed a strain on them mentally. From his own point of view this was exacerbated during spells of collective or personal success. In 1908, he recalled, Yorkshire's unbeaten run preyed on the nerves. He and his team-mates became anxious about maintaining their undefeated record and 'at night sometimes I used to find myself picturing disasters and quite working myself up about it'.

The summer of 1909 was another one of downpours and unfinished matches. The pros hated the hours spent loitering in cold dressing rooms, where the scent of mildew hung in the air and the only heat came from a coal fire whose warmth barely penetrated the gloomy dampness. As Wilfred commented, 'Most men, I fancy, would rather be playing in a losing game than watching the rain come down.'

Despite the title of 1908, the Yorkshire team lacked the resilience of old. In the past they'd possessed a cast-iron self-belief that carried them through the rough spots. Now when they went down, they stayed down. The first sign that the pugnacity had drained from them came at Worcester in May. Left a target of 146 to win, Yorkshire slumped to 133 all out. More ignominious even than this debacle was the defeat to Surrey at The Oval. On a rain-dampened pitch, Yorkshire were set 113 to win. Batting against Razor Smith and Tom Rushby as if they'd been blindfolded and spun round in circles, Yorkshire staggered to 26 all out – the lowest score in their history. The last five wickets fell for no runs and the innings lasted fewer than 17 overs.

George Herbert had taken six wickets in the second innings of that match, but like his county he was below his best for much of the season. His leg was troubling him again and he seemed to be lacking some of his old effervescence. It was noticeable in his batting, which missed its usual thumping cadence. Not that he didn't have moments when the earthy reel of pulls and heaves was rejoined. He welted 80 against Derbyshire and slammed 140 against a Northamptonshire side whose bowlers looked less like an attack than a nervous reproach.

His best bowling came when it was most needed, against Lancashire in the Roses match. Set a modest total for victory, Albert Hornby's team might have expected to cruise to victory, but they reckoned without George Herbert, who bounded to the stumps and sent swerver after swerver flying on to muscle and timber. He finished with six for 23 as Yorkshire romped home by 65 runs. He bowled with similar verve against Middlesex at Headingley taking seven for 95 and finding the edge with such regularity Hunter took three catches off him behind the stumps.

While George limped and winced, Wilfred had a brilliant season with the bat, scoring more than 2,000 runs and hitting five centuries. He also took 141 wickets, including five in an innings a dozen times. He produced noteworthy moments for Yorkshire all summer. His best batting came against Sussex at Hove where he struck 199 and 84, his grittiest when making a century at Huddersfield trying – unsuccessfully – to stave off a Kent victory. He finished with 101, though he cheerfully admitted to being caught at the wicket when he was 16 and given not out by the umpire. Walking wasn't Wilfred's way.

He concluded his season with Yorkshire by striking 101 against MCC at Scarborough in a style that so suited the holiday mood of the seaside resort he might have been batting in a boater. Even *Wisden* was forced to acknowledge that Wilfred had become 'an exceptionally good batsman'.

Rhodes's reward for his form that season was eventually to be promoted to number three in the England batting order for the series against Monty Noble's Australians. For England it was another disastrous encounter. They were beaten for the second successive time. Many held the selectors responsible. There was a degree of blithering uncertainty among them that called to mind later generations. In all, though they used 26 players, most observers felt they still hadn't picked the right ones.

Hobbs made his home Test debut in the first Test at Edgbaston. England won thanks in the main to the bowling of George Herbert and Blythe. George Herbert showed what he was capable of at the highest level, taking four for 28 in the tourists' first innings and five for 58 in the second. One of those wickets came thanks to Arthur Jones of Nottinghamshire, who took a catch to dismiss Noble that Wilfred rated as the best he'd ever seen, sticking out his hand and holding on to a shot that was travelling like a comet. Unfortunately, George Herbert couldn't sustain his form and took only seven wickets in the next three Tests. He was dropped for the fifth encounter at The Oval. He would never play for his country again.

George Herbert's record in his 24 Test appearances was modest. He'd scored 790 runs at 22.57 and taken 59 wickets at a little over 30 apiece. The difference between first-class and international cricket was wide and many fine county players failed to bridge it, or were not given much of a chance to try. Tich Freeman, the great Kent leg-spinner who is second behind Wilfred in the all-time wicket-takers list with 3,776, played just 12 matches for England, his career ended in 1929 when he conceded 169 runs without claiming a single victim against South Africa at The Oval. Gloucestershire slow left-armer Charlie Parker (third on the list) got only one Test cap, against Australia in 1921. He took two wickets. More recently Mark Ramprakash finished his career with 114 first-class centuries and a batting average of 53.14. His average in Tests is 27.32.

As Wilfred noted, international cricket was more intense, the crowds more excitable and the atmosphere of expectancy imposed greater wear and tear on a player's nerves. There was also noticeably less camaraderie. When he was turning out for Yorkshire, George Herbert was shoulder-to-shoulder with pals; when he played in Tests he was mainly among strangers. The class divide was greater with England, too. At

Yorkshire there were generally only a couple of amateurs and often none at all. The line between gentlemen and players was blurred. Not so with England where it was so rigidly enforced visiting Australian Charlie Macartney observed that the opposition professionals were often 'treated like dogs'. Of the Triumvirate, Wilfred, the hard-shelled introspective loner, was the best equipped to deal with these differences. That he was arguably the most talented, diligent and ambitious member of the trio was also a help, of course.

For England a trail of woe followed the Birmingham victory. Australia skipper Monty Noble mimicked Jackson's feat by winning every toss. Players came and went as if through a revolving door. Only the captain and Lilley, the wicket-keeper, played in all five matches. Wilfred was a relative point of stability in the maelstrom, appearing in four games. He scored two half-centuries. His bowling was used sparingly, his best moment coming in Australia's first innings at Leeds when he took four for 38.

For the fourth Test at Old Trafford, Australia found themselves so short of bowlers they had to call in player-manager Frank Laver, now in his mid-thirties. It was perhaps a mark of England's disarray that he took eight wickets for 31 in the first innings. Charlie Macartney then saw off Barnes and Blythe with a display that combined obduracy and flair. Wilfred came on, slowed the run rate to a trickle and finished with five wickets for 83. The Test was drawn. But there was still bad news in it for England – Jessop had damaged his back throwing in from the boundary at Leeds, an injury that put him out of action for several months and from which, Wilfred believed, the great hitter never fully recovered.

On 4 August, the man who had encouraged Wilfred's

cricketing ambitions, his father Alfred, died aged 63. Alfred, the *Huddersfield Examiner* recorded, 'dedicated his son to cricket, and laid all his plans with that view. Mr Rhodes, sen., gave his son every opportunity in his power to learn our great summer game.' The same notice commented that Alfred had not allowed Wilfred to engage in work that would keep him away from cricket or impede his progress as a player. All Alfred's hopes for his youngest lad had been realised. As if to prove it, the day after his father's funeral, Wilfred travelled to London to join the England team for the fifth Test at The Oval.

He was, unsurprisingly below his best. Warren Bardsley scored a century in each innings – the first time anyone had done that in a Test match. The match was drawn.

Schof's season had got off to a rapid start. Against Essex in mid-May, he took seven for 32 in the first innings. At Old Trafford a fortnight later, he took a hat-trick and finished with match figures of nine for 36 as Yorkshire won a low-scoring game by 65 runs. He was picked to play in the second Test against Australia at Lord's that started on 14 June. Wilfred was missing. Haigh had not been Archie MacLaren's choice. The captain had wanted Thomas Jayes, a young fast bowler from Leicestershire, and made his annoyance known. It could hardly have helped Schof's fragile self-confidence. Haigh bowled 19 overs that were nice but insipid, Australia cruised to victory as if on casters, and he was dropped.

The match against Lancashire at Bradford was declared Schof's benefit. Haigh had a decent game taking three wickets in each innings, and his pal Wilfred ensured victory by taking 13 for 108. Schof was a popular man across the county and his benefit was a massive success, raising the tidy sum of £2,701 – worth close to half a million in today's terms. However, Schof didn't receive all of it. Under the rules Lord Hawke had introduced for benefit matches, the player only got a third of the money raised as a cash sum. The remainder was retained by Yorkshire, who invested it for the player and paid him interest annually. When he died, he could bequeath the sum to a relative, but they too were denied access to the cash, which it appeared Yorkshire were to retain in perpetuity.

His Lordship had introduced the system because he saw how many Yorkshire players from the past had ended up destitute. It was an example of Hawke's paternalism, designed to protect the players and their dependants from sharks and swindlers, and perhaps their own worst natures. All of which would have been well and good had those entrusted with looking after the money not treated those to whom it belonged with often lofty contempt.

After Haigh died, his widow, Lillian, wished to buy a cottage. She approached Yorkshire, who held close to £1,800 of her husband's money, which he had bequeathed to her on his death, and asked for £250. Instead of giving it to her from the capital sum, Yorkshire instead *loaned* her £250 and charged her interest on it. If the interest charged had been the same as that paid out on the capital sum, this action would have been pointless. If it had been lower, then it would have been senseless. The conclusion that many drew, therefore, was that the interest Yorkshire charged Lillian Haigh was higher than the interest they paid out. If that was the case, then it was indeed a Dickensian way to treat a widow. There were more and worse examples.

Hawke acknowledged the problems but seems to have done

little to correct them. Wilfred Rhodes, meanwhile, resented the whole system. His blood boiled when he thought of it. Though the scheme had been Hawke's idea, Rhodes had no doubt who lay behind the high-handed administration of it – Yorkshire's secretary, Frederick Toone. Wilfred's relationship with the ineffable Toone would be a bitter one. It would colour much of his final decades with the county.

Schof finished his benefit season with 120 wickets in all matches for Yorkshire. He topped the first-class averages once again. George Herbert's bowling had been slowly drained of snap as the season went on. He managed just 89 wickets for Yorkshire compared to the 156 he'd taken the season before. By the time the Scarborough Festival finished, George Herbert had entered his 40th year. He was balding, the ring of hair he still had was flecked with grey and his physique had grown more comfortably rotund. *Wisden* ran what appeared to be a valedictory article about his achievements, which suggested the editor, Sydney Pardon, thought the great all-rounder must be on the verge of retirement. If George Herbert read it that way, then he responded in typical fashion – hitching up his slacks, looking Father Time straight in the eye and saying, 'It's you or me.'

Wilfred was selected for Shrimp Leveson Gower's MCC tour to South Africa that winter. He attended a farewell dinner given by well-wishers in Huddersfield with George Herbert and Schof and afterwards they travelled with him to the station to wave him farewell. For Wilfred, this cheerful departure was perhaps his happiest moment for several months. His father's death weighed heavily on him and the tour was a disaster.

England seemed to have learned little from the previous

tour and were once again bewildered by the combination of leg-spin and matting. While acknowledging the difficulties, Wilfred was scathing about the tour party. The middle and lower order featured too many poor amateurs (including the ubiquitous ice-dancer Teddy Wynyard) and the bowling was so far below Test class that England's most effective wicket-taker was the eccentric George Simpson-Hayward of Worcestershire, who bowled underarm, spinning the ball with his thumb as you might a tennis ball. He took six wickets on his debut and another five-wicket haul in the third Test before the novelty wore off.

The South Africans, admittedly, were a formidable side, characterised by Aubrey Faulkner, a broad-chested, muscular giant of a man who looked capable of quite literally carrying the team on his shoulders. Wilfred considered him one of the greatest all-rounders he ever encountered. Faulkner hit hard and bowled leg-breaks and googlies that on the matting wickets fizzed like Alka-Seltzer and jumped like gerbils. Schof had noted that the matting was stretched tight at the start of play but gradually loosened as the day wore on, becoming more difficult to bat on. The ever-observant Wilfred took things a stage further – attributing the alarming bounce to the fact that when a ball landed it pushed the matting forward creating a slight hump which it then flew up as if it was a bicyclist springing from a ramp. Faced with these singular problems, England's batsmen adopted an assortment of eccentric counter-measures, none of which was effective.

In the first Test at Johannesburg, Wilfred opened the innings with Jack Hobbs and the pair put on 159. After that, things slid away and the home side won by 19 runs. In the second Test at Durban, Wilfred made 44, but South Africa dominated the latter stages to win comfortably. In the third Test, rain made the matting more benign. David Denton hit a century in the first innings and Hobbs, who had dropped down the order, scored 93 not out in the second as England scrambled home by three wickets.

At Cape Town, where the outfield was loose grass that took the sting out of even the most firmly struck shots, the matting wicket had been laid directly onto turf – normally it was laid on the soil from anthills – and was so somnolent the ball seemed to rise from it yawning as if from sleep. Timing shots was impossible even for the greatest stroke-players. Hobbs made one and nought, Denton nought and 10, and Wilfred nought and five. The South Africans coped better and clinched the series with a four-wicket win.

With the series lost, England finally brought Colin Blythe into the side. The Kentish man showed what had been missing from England's attack, picking up 10 wickets. Hobbs and Rhodes shared an opening stand of 221 in the first innings – a Test record – and England romped home by nine wickets. In the Tests, Wilfred had scored 226 runs at 25.11. He had taken just two wickets. In an attempt to make the best of the conditions he had tried to teach himself to bowl a googly, but for once his patience ran out and he gave up without ever using it. On the positive side, his opening partnership with Jack Hobbs had become an established feature of the England side. The two men had forged an understanding in the middle, their running between the wickets so quick and easy they seemed to be communicating telepathically.

After his troubled winter, Wilfred struggled for form. The 1910 season would be one of his poorest. Such things are relative, of course, and there were dozens of cricketers across the counties who'd have been punching the air in celebration if they'd scored a touch under 1,500 runs while taking 88 wickets. But it was the first time Wilfred had failed to take a hundred since he'd come into the Yorkshire team a dozen years earlier, the first time he'd failed to do the double since 1903.

When it came to bowling, it can be argued that Wilfred suffered as a result of his reputation. Yorkshire tended to bring him on when the opposition were scoring freely and somebody needed to apply the brakes, or winkle out a well-set batsman. He was still a great tormentor on turning tracks, though, as he showed against Derbyshire at Bradford when he took five wickets for five runs in 4.4 overs.

Wilfred's happiest memory of the season was scoring 88 not out against Surrey at Bradford. The Surrey attack was led by 'Razor' Smith, a lanky leg-spinner with a high action who cut the ball and made it pop savagely on soft wickets. Wilfred – who had taken 11 Surrey wickets for 72 – opened with Ederick Bates, Yorkshire needing 158 to win. After assessing the conditions, Wilfred decided attack was the best option. The pair put on 50 for the first wicket in half an hour, and when Bates fell, it was left to his senior partner to nurse the team to victory by five wickets.

The implication from some quarters that George Herbert was on the verge of retirement spurred him to greater efforts. In 1910 he was back to his best once more. His steadfast refusal ever to admit defeat was needed by his team more than it had ever been. Yorkshire endured their worst season for so long – losing seven matches – that many supporters felt it presaged the end of days. Cynics in the county (which accounted for about half the population) were given to saying that the only game they had truly enjoyed was the one abandoned because of the death of King Edward VII.

George Herbert at least gave the grumblers cause to crack a smile. He bowled so well that only Blythe and Razor Smith took more first-class wickets. His swerve was as remarkable as ever when conditions were right, as they were against Worcestershire at Headingley, where he took seven for 28 as the visitors, chasing 160 for victory, failed to make it into three figures.

Generally his batting retained its old blacksmith strength. He hit 90 against Hampshire at Bradford, bludgeoned 158 in 175 minutes against the students at Fenner's. He scored 103 and 88 at Huddersfield against Warwickshire and produced a brilliant second-innings century at Lord's to help Yorkshire score the 331 they needed for victory over Middlesex.

He also got the first pair of his career, against Northamptonshire of all sides, at Northampton in early May. He was clean bowled in both innings, first by Trinidad-born slow left-armer Sydney Smith and then by medium-pacer William Wells. George Herbert struck back, taking five wickets as Northants were bowled out for 61 in their first innings. Yorkshire won by 145 runs.

Yorkshire and George Herbert's best moments came against Lancashire. The Red Rose county batted first in May at Headingley, scoring 229 on the opening day. With the thunderous Brearley galloping to the wicket with such force it was a wonder clods didn't fly out behind him as he tore into the Yorkshire batting. Only Schof (who top-scored with 27), George Herbert and the amateur Everard Radcliffe – captain in the absence of Lord Hawke – put up any resistance and the innings closed with Yorkshire trailing by 77. If Lancashire thought this lead commanding, they had reckoned without

George Herbert. With the ball boomeranging, he clean bowled eight batsmen and had another caught in the slips. Schof chipped in, hitting top scorer MacLaren's stumps and Lancashire were all out for 61. Rain washed out the final day and the match was drawn.

Schof's season was a disappointing one. He took just 76 wickets in the Championship at a cost of 20.27. There were as ever some startling performances. Against Worcestershire at Leeds he took three for eight in the visitors' second innings to add to the six for 30 he'd taken in the first. He also showed his cunning against Hampshire, taking the final wicket by inducing Alex Bowell to hit his own wicket after gradually forcing him to retreat further and further back into his crease by shortening each delivery.

In November, Lord Hawke resigned after 28 years with the county. He was closing in on his 50th birthday. His contributions as a cricketer had been moderate (he'd only once scored more than 1,000 runs in a season) but his leadership, whatever its faults, had helped transform the club from a dissolute bunch of talented troublemakers into the most successful side in cricket history. He would remain as club president – a role he'd been awarded in 1898 – until his death and also serve in the same capacity at MCC.

George Herbert and Schof had both been happy under the autocratic reign of Lord Hawke. Indeed they were full of praise for the way he'd fought for better pay and conditions for 'his boys'. They enjoyed his company and admired the way he maintained his cool in both victory and defeat after the manner of a Rudyard Kipling hero. Schof spoke admiringly of his captaincy, reckoning His Lordship 'worth a place in the side for his generalship alone'.

Wilfred's relationship with Hawke was trickier to fathom. His Lordship had been firm and consistent in telling Wilfred to look after his bowling and let his batting look after itself – advice which Wilfred admitted he 'wilfully ignored' to his captain's evident annoyance. Rhodes undoubtedly had respect for Hawke and his powers as a captain, saying that 'he knew the game backwards' (others were less convinced; C. B. Fry for one – he claimed that Hawke's reputation for being a great captain was 'a myth'). Wilfred also acknowledged His Lordship's role in helping his professionals achieve financial stability, for establishing the ethos of the Yorkshire team and turning the county into the most formidable side in England. And yet . . .

In his memoir, Hawke speaks warmly and in detail about the characters of George Herbert, Schof, Hunter, Tunnicliffe, Brown and Denton. Often his words, however affectionate, have a slightly high tone, as if he is speaking of fondly remembered dogs, but there is a genuine warmth to it. About Wilfred – beyond praise for his abilities – he has surprisingly little to say. It suggests a coolness, which Wilfred perhaps reciprocated. Like Sydney Barnes, he was in outlook a more modern man than Schof or George Herbert, raised in a time of universal male suffrage, increasing trades unionism and a rising belief in working-class self-determination. Unlike his two pals who were happy with the status quo, Wilfred had aspirations. Lord Hawke's overbearing paternalism was a reminder of past times, of the beneficence of a feudal world.

Lord Hawke had been absent for large chunks of the 1909 and 1910 seasons and in his absence the captaincy had generally been taken by Everard Radcliffe. He was an amateur of moderate cricketing talents and, like Hawke, had been born outside the county, in his case in Tiverton, Devon. In 64 matches for Yorkshire, he'd score just over 800 runs, take two wickets and 21 catches. Actually, maybe moderate was an overestimate.

As captain, Radcliffe's position was compromised by the fact that he had to answer to Lord Hawke off the field, while trying to gain the respect of the seasoned pros on it. It was an awkward situation, one that might be compared to the role of leaders of the Conservative Party while Margaret Thatcher was still lurking in the background.

Wilfred watched Radcliffe and concluded coldly that he was a nervous man whose edginess prevented him from making the best of himself. Lord Hawke was even less impressed, criticising him not so much for losing matches but by doing so playing dull, negative cricket. After a series of dropped catches had cost Yorkshire dearly, His Lordship took it upon himself to write to the players and demand they do better. Poor Radcliffe must often have felt like a friendless man in a hostile world. Certainly, like many of the amateur captains who were to follow, he often appeared bewildered. It was a situation that would continue until the arrival of the tyrannical dictator Brian Sellers in 1932.

Radcliffe's situation was not helped by the struggles of the Yorkshire team. With David Hunter now in retirement, only Denton and the Triumvirate remained from the glory years at the start of the century. They had found some good support. Arthur Dolphin, a pugnacious-looking little wicketkeeper whose speed behind the stumps had an aggressive edge, had come in. So too had Major Booth (Major was his forename not his rank. When he served in the First World War, Booth would be a second lieutenant, the kind of *Catch-22* confusion he might have chuckled over later if he hadn't been killed on the Somme) a fast-ish medium-pacer who braced the lower reaches of the batting with his hitting. He was supported in Yorkshire's new-look attack by Alonzo Drake, who batted and bowled left-handed (the former must have annoyed Sir Arthur Conan Doyle, who had recently written an article calling for left-handed batsmen to be banned from competitive matches because the resetting of the field to them slowed the game up). A spinner whose deliveries curved through the air and broke both ways off the pitch and a cultured stroke-maker, Drake might have been an all-rounder in the great tradition of George Herbert and Wilfred – most agreed he had the talent. Sadly, he was beset with illness and was often overcome by a dark, almost Byronic, fatalism. This was not a trait shared by his mother. It was said that when he complained to her that Yorkshire had not given him his county cap, she'd replied matter-of-factly, 'Well, if they'll not give you one you'll just have to go and buy it yourself.'

The summer of 1911 was, for once, fine and dry. Yorkshire rose from eighth to seventh. George Herbert had another season filled with golden moments. Against Worcestershire, he took nine wickets in an innings and then hit a century. At Hastings against Sussex, he pulled, hooked and hoiked 34 boundaries and three sixes while making 218. He took 10 wickets against Nottinghamshire and five in an innings 14 times.

Against Lancashire at Old Trafford George Herbert bowled 35.4 overs, took six wickets and in Yorkshire's second innings took on the snorting Brearley on a hard, fast track, smashing the burly paceman over the leg-side boundary repeatedly as he raced to 156 in under four hours. Yorkshire won by 159 runs. His last ten-wicket haul for Yorkshire came at Leeds in

June against his favourite whipping boys, Leicestershire. He took 10 for 48 in the match.

Despite the sadness created by the death of his father John at the start of the year, Schof had a good season. When Yorkshire played the touring All India side, he took four for 19 in the Indians' second innings and hammered 111 as the home side emerged victorious. A watching Lord Hawke applauded, while guffawing at the amount of time the Indian players took over the drinks breaks.

Against Derbyshire in Sheffield, Schof took three wickets for four runs in 21 balls as Derbyshire collapsed in the first innings to 61 all out. Against Sussex at Leeds later in the summer, he picked up seven for 20 in the second innings. He came close to completing his second-ever double, falling just short with 906 runs and 97 wickets.

In the year of his benefit, Wilfred scored more than 2,000 runs and took 117 wickets. For the first time, he finished above George Herbert in the batting averages. His stroke-making shone all summer. He scored a century in Yorkshire's third match of the season at Sheffield and a century in both innings against MCC at Scarborough as the season drew to a close. His bowling remained dangerous when conditions were right. Against Derbyshire on a drying wicket at Chesterfield he reduced the home side from 70 for one to 111 all out with a spell of seven for 16.

Wilfred, it was noted, got through his overs at quite a clip once his field was set. One letter writer to the *Yorkshire Evening Post* who plainly made a study of such matters said that during Essex's second innings in the match at Dewsbury in 1923, Wilfred had bowled a maiden over in 57 seconds.

In his benefit match against Lancashire at Sheffield, Wilfred suffered a rare and unexpected clogging in Lancashire's second innings from Ken MacLeod, a giant Scottish rugby international, who hammered 121 in two hours before Schof finally put an end to his friend's misery by clean bowling him. Denton hit a beautifully judged century when Yorkshire batted last and the game was drawn.

Surprisingly the match, which had been played in sunny August weather, did not raise the kind of sum that might have been expected. In fact, the final total was embarrassingly low. Lord Hawke immediately launched an appeal to try to raise more through public donations and the sum was eventually settled at £2,202 1s. It was a considerable amount, but still lower than the sums received by George Herbert and Schof. Wilfred would later explain that part of the problem was the choice of venue – Sheffield had more cheap 'sixpenny' seats than Leeds, which reduced the gate receipts. That, alongside Yorkshire's poor season, was surely part of the reason, but there was more to it than that.

For all the great service he had given Yorkshire, Wilfred had never been as popular with the ordinary supporters as the other two members of the Triumvirate, or team-mates like Tunnicliffe and Hunter. The fact was noted in contemporary newspapers. 'His personality has never fired the public imagination,' noted the *Illustrated Sporting and Dramatic News*. Wilfred was taciturn. Silence was his default setting. He had neither the warmth nor self-deprecating charm of Schof and George Herbert, and completely lacked the latter's charisma. Perhaps also there was about him an air of self-sufficiency that some found off-putting. His confidence in his abilities and his honest appraisal of his own value was never voiced, but it was plain in his manner, the way he carried himself. To some, Wilfred's self-reliance may have looked like arrogance. He was celebrated for his greatness but never embraced. He was not a man for hugging.

Whatever the rights or wrongs of the benefit, Rhodes wisely invested the cash third in building what the *Leeds Mercury* called 'a pretty stone house' in Marsh, a smart Huddersfield suburb, close by the one that George Herbert, Emma and family had relocated to a few years earlier. The Rhodes family moved there from Kirkheaton as soon as it was ready. He and Sarah would remain there until her death 44 years later.

Yorkshire's poor performances over the past two seasons inevitably led to cries for a radical overhaul of the team. There was muttering that the Triumvirate had crested the hill and were accelerating rapidly down the back slope. Even the usually supportive *Huddersfield Weekly Examiner* noted in its 2 September edition: 'The great Huddersfield triumvirate of Hirst, Haigh and Rhodes have rendered exceptional service, but they cannot go on forever.'

Wilfred had been called in as a last-minute replacement for an injured Jack Hobbs in the England versus the Rest trial match at Lord's. He hit a chanceless century. As a result, he was picked for that winter's MCC tour of Australia. It would be a considerably happier experience than his previous two overseas winters. The side was strong in every department and included the men Wilfred rated as the greatest batsman and best bowler of all time: Jack Hobbs and Sydney Barnes.

Plum Warner was captain, but after hitting a spiffing hundred in his first match was struck down with illness and spent most of the rest of the tour convalescing in a nursing home. His place as skipper was taken by Johnny Douglas, a man who lacked Warner's easy charm, but compensated with square-jawed determination, courage and stamina — characteristics that won him respect rather than friendship and antagonised the top brass at Lord's.

Wilfred started the tour as he was to continue, with a couple of neat half-centuries against Victoria and Queensland. He and Hobbs had become England's regular opening pair in South Africa, but for the first Test at Sydney, Wilfred was dropped to number four in the order and Hobbs opened with Warwickshire's classically named Septimus Kinneir. Wilfred hit 41 in England's first innings, but the home side won easily thanks to a brilliant Trumper century and some extraordinary bowling from leg-spinner 'Ranji' Hordern, who'd learned his trade playing in the USA.

Wilfred was back at the top of the order for the second Test at Melbourne. Clem Hill won the toss and elected to bat. Conditions were perfect, but that didn't stop the England attack of Barnes and Frank Foster of Warwickshire, who dismissed them for 184. Foster was a rough-hewn but effective batsman who could drive the ball colossal distances and a match-winning bowler of left-arm swing. He was not truly fast, but he bowled what veteran cricketers call 'a heavy ball', or as Wilfred explained it, 'He knocked your bat back when you were defending.' Foster had the gentleman amateur's breezy self-confidence, too. He lived a fast life off the field, playing cards all night and turning up at Edgbaston for the start of play still wearing his tails. Late in the tour, he bet a team-mate he'd take five wickets in an innings at least once in the remaining three matches. He won the wager. Wilfred liked his attitude.

Though he was medium-paced with a habit of producing

nasty bounce, Barnes was actually a spinner. Using his long and immensely strong fingers, he could bowl off-spinners and leg-spinners with barely any change in his action (the keen-eyed Wilfred saw that the leg-spinner was usually delivered slightly slower). His accuracy was proverbial, so niggardly that in the Lancashire League, where he made his living, players celebrated hitting a boundary off him as if they'd scored a double hundred.

When England batted Hobbs fell early, but Wilfred made a steady 61, putting together a century partnership with J. W. 'Young Jack' Hearne of Middlesex. Wilfred admired Hearne's neatness and the way he never seemed to play a scoring shot yet somehow kept the scoreboard ticking like a clock. It was the kind of quiet, almost magical, craftsmanship that Wilfred appreciated. When Australia batted again Foster and Barnes worked their way through them. Wilfred and Hobbs put on 57 for the first wicket and England, with Hobbs – who made 126 – at his masterful best, strolled to victory.

At Adelaide in the third Test England again won easily. Barnes and Foster had a riot. Hobbs scored a beautiful 187 and with Wilfred, who hit 59, put on 147 for the first wicket. They did even better in the fourth Test at Melbourne. After the home side had been dismissed for 191, Wilfred and Hobbs batted them out of the match with a partnership of 323, an English Test record that would stand for 35 years, broken by another great opening pair, Len Hutton and Cyril Washbrook. Back home in the Broad Acres, the sub-editors at the *Yorkshire Post* broke out the exclamation marks. 'England 323 for One!' cried the headline, 'Australian Bowlers Collared and Demoralized'.

Hobbs made 178, Wilfred 179. Hobbs's batting was the

quicker and more polished, Wilfred the more obdurate. He was solid and consistent. He paid attention to tiny details. In Australia he used a bat weighing two pounds six ounces on slow wickets and one that was three ounces heavier on faster tracks, like the one at the MCG. The extra few ounces gave him the additional power he needed to strike the ball beyond the cover fielder. Cricket was a game of narrow margins. Calculation paid off.

Wilfred thoroughly enjoyed opening with Hobbs. 'It was always a pleasure to be in with Jack ... it was an education to watch him play.' The pair ran swiftly between the wickets, always looking for quick singles. This was a novelty for the times and a source of vexation to the Australian fielders, who could never relax when Wilfred and Hobbs were at the wicket. The understanding was based on a deep-rooted belief in each other, not only as cricketers, but as men. Both were professionals of considerable integrity As Hobbs said, 'You can always trust Wilfred.' The feeling was mutual.

Hobbs played shots that lived in the memory. Wilfred left his record on the scorecard. Well, usually that was true. In the game against New South Wales at Sydney, he scored an immaculate and typical 119 in the first innings and then in the second allowed himself a little frolic, striking a century filled with extravagant drives and whirling cut shots that had some observers recalling Trumper.

Foster and Barnes, supported by Douglas and Woolley, had been so devastating with the ball that Wilfred was rarely called on to bowl in the Tests and in fact didn't take a first-class wicket on the entire tour. He had become a batsman, and a rather good one. He'd finish the trip with 1,098 runs at an average of 54.90.

Poor Everard Radcliffe had stepped down at the end of the 1911 season. His replacement was Sir Archibald White. White was the first new Yorkshire captain to have been born in the county since Tom Emmett took the job in 1878. Educated at Wellington College and Cambridge, a baronet and coal mine owner, he was, if anything, even posher than Radcliffe and, more remarkably yet, an even worse cricketer. He'd finish his career with a batting average of 14.42, a highest score of just 55 and having bowled a meagre seven overs without taking a wicket. Unlike Radcliffe, however, Sir Archibald was popular with his team. Schof reckoned him 'keen and enthusiastic' and Wilfred would recall him as a grand sportsman and smile at the memory of his sitting waiting to bat puffing his pipe to soothe his nerves. He sought the advice of his veterans, got the best out of the players and turned Yorkshire back into a winning team.

The 1912 season was so wet it might have inspired ark building. The dismal summer dampened the spirits and the performances. Despite a persistent knee problem, George Herbert rose above it all, scoring 1,133 runs and taking 118 wickets, his 10th double on the trot. Only five other players achieved the feat. George Herbert's face was memorably described as being like the harvest moon in seasons of glory and plenty, and there was a wide grin across it when he took 10 Hampshire wickets for 138 at Southampton and topped that performance by taking 12 for 67 at Taunton against Somerset. His only century of the season came against Worcestershire after he'd been dropped in the deep before he'd got off the mark. Nobody begrudged the old Trojan such a slice of luck.

Stung by suggestions he might be finished, Schof came back fighting. The rain, as long as it fell outside the hours of play, was his firm friend. Nobody exploited a wet track better than he did. If there'd been cricket in the equatorial rainforests, he'd have signed up in a flash. In Somerset's first innings at Bradford he took five for 14; against Lancashire at Bradford towards the end of May he was instrumental in securing a heart-warming ten-wicket win by taking five for 25 in the visitors' second innings.

Against the Australians at Bradford in a match that began on 10 June, he was at his devastating best, taking five for 22 in the first innings and six for 14 in the second. A few days later against Gloucestershire at Leeds, he posted his best-ever figures in an innings, snapping up nine for 25 in the first knock. In the second, he added five more wickets to finish with match figures of 14 for 65. Against the same opponents at Bristol, Schof made 61 in the second innings after bagging six for 46 in the home side's first. Haigh finished with more than 100 wickets in first-class cricket for the season. Once again he topped the Yorkshire averages. He took 96 wickets for his county in the Championship at 11.46, taking five wickets in an innings on eight occasions and 10 in a match twice.

Under the captaincy of Sir Archibald White, Yorkshire won the title for the ninth time. Sir Archibald recognised his limitations. He leaned heavily on the Triumvirate for advice about tactics, declarations and field placings. Under this expert guidance, they lost just once and were in winning positions in many matches that had to be abandoned. Denton had a fabulous season with the bat at the age of 38 and the bowling of the Triumvirate was well backed up by Booth and Drake. The promising all-rounder Roy Kilner – the nephew of Irving Washington – was also beginning to emerge. He took four wickets in an innings and scored 83 not out in the game against Nottinghamshire at Trent Bridge.

The middle-order batting had been strengthened by Edgar Oldroyd from near Batley, base of the notorious stone-waller Louis Hall. Oldroyd inherited the Batley Giant's style. He was regarded by many pressmen – including John Arlott – as the best bad-wicket player in England. He had a long career, hitting 36 centuries for Yorkshire, but his batting had the same ungainly dour cast as his name. When he joined the equally intransigent Benny Wilson at the wicket, the crowd saw it as a chance to do a crossword, or take a nap.

Australia and South Africa both spent the summer in England to play in the Triangular Tournament, an early attempt to create a cricket World Cup. Wilfred would play in all six of England's matches.

At Lord's against South Africa, Barnes unleashed a newly perfected in-swinger against the South Africans, having revealed his intention to Wilfred in a taxi on the way to the ground. England won easily. They then drew with Australia at Lord's and beat the South Africans for a second time at Leeds. Wilfred had been in indifferent form in the early part of the summer. He had struggled to score on damp wickets and was averaging barely 20 for Yorkshire despite hitting a century in the Roses match in May. As he travelled on the train from Huddersfield to Manchester for the next encounter with the Australians his nerves jangled. He was aware that he was currently being picked on reputation rather than performance. His place in the England side was in jeopardy.

He walked out to bat with Hobbs almost as nervous as he'd been on his first appearance for Yorkshire 14 years earlier. He began shakily, but a few lucky escapes restored his usual equilibrium and he was soon batting freely again. He finished with 92, his highest Test score in England. It was enough to secure his place in the team for the rest of the summer. Recalling the innings later, C. B. Fry would comment that the wicket was so wet Wilfred had practically 'dug the runs out of the slush'. Unsurprisingly, Schof's performances for Yorkshire had caught the eye of the England selectors and he also played at Old Trafford. With most of the match washed out he bowled just six overs. It was to be his last Test cap.

After his morale-boosting knock in Manchester, Wilfred's form for Yorkshire improved too. And when he was available he batted consistently well, often in partnership with the dashing Denton. His best all-round performance came against Nottinghamshire at Harrogate, where he batted all day to score 176 and then took five for 68 to secure an easy victory. Most of the time, though, his bowling was now a secondary consideration. He was barely used by England and in 1912 took just 53 first-class wickets. The transformation Lord Hawke had fought so hard against appeared complete.

With South Africa indifferent, the final of the Triangular Tournament was contested between Australia and England at The Oval. The match was designated as 'timeless' to ensure a result. The weather made the provision utterly pointless. Rain turned the Surrey strip into treacherous gummy mess. England, for whom Fry and Woolley were in superb form, made 245 and 175 and Australia subsided to 65 all out in their second knock as England sealed a comfortable win. Wilfred was second in England's batting averages behind Hobbs. Though he could hardly have known it, world events would ensure he'd play just two more Tests in England.

There was no MCC tour that winter and for once the

Triumvirate found themselves spending the off season together in Yorkshire. They used the break from cricket to get reacquainted with their wives and to learn something of their children (George Herbert had a son, James, and two daughters, Annie and Molly; Schof the reverse, two sons, John and Reginald, and a daughter, Lillian; while Wilfred had his daughter, Muriel). With their winter pay from Yorkshire, accumulated 'talent money' from early and late season appearances for Kirkheaton and Armitage Bridge, and earnings from promotional activities (Wilfred had joined George Herbert in advertising a patent cure-all, in his case Guy's Tonic, which claimed to drive out everything from depression to flatulence via 'coated tongue'), the trio had no need to work. Nor did they make any particular effort to keep fit. In those days cricketers judged dog walks and spells of digging the garden quite sufficient to keep them in trim. When George Herbert was offered a free bicycle so he could get exercise during the off season, he rejected it outright. When asked how he intended to stay in shape he replied simply, 'Hunting.' All three great cricketers knew how to shoot. They had grown up in poor families. Knowing how to trap and kill game was a necessity. Rabbits, wood pigeons and the occasional rook were part of their regular diet.

When not out on the moors with guns and terriers, the three pals attended cricket club dinners across Yorkshire and occasionally even over the Pennines in Lancashire (though they never ventured west of Clitheroe). They handed out cups and medals at awards ceremonies in schools, opened church bazaars and charity fetes. None of them would ever be comfortable speaking in public but pitching in together they could provide enough entertainment with their self-deflating anecdotes to satisfy a home crowd.

The Triumvirate were always invited to events together. George Herbert and Wilfred had lived next door to each other in neat and well-tended cottages in Field Place, Kirkheaton. Now they were 50 yards apart in Marsh. Schof was a couple of miles away in Taylor Hill. The trio were so inseparable that Schof once joked, 'If you went looking for George Hirst, you'd also find me and Wilfred.' Their wives and children were close, too. They attended matches and social functions together. When Muriel married Thomas Burnley in 1924 one of her bridesmaids was Schof's daughter, Lillian.

As well as a profession, the three men had a common background and shared an outlook on life. Wilfred was a strict teetotaller, while George Herbert and Schof drank so sparingly that, by the standards of the place and time, they might as well have been. None of the trio hung around in pubs or gambled. When George Herbert was young he had been a brilliant player of knur and spell, the rough-hewn northern working-class form of golf. He had never played the game competitively, though, because knur and spell matches were made for cash stakes, the players backed by bookies and local members of what, in the Victorian age, was still known as 'the fancy'. Like prize fighting and horse racing, knur and spell had a disreputable edge and George Herbert wanted no part of that. He and his two chums were Anglicans who acted like Methodists. They were upstanding, temperate family men, determined on self-improvement; just the sort of steady, respectable fellows Lord Hawke had been seeking when he dumped Peate and Peel. When they appeared in public, the Three Musketeers were always well groomed, polite and smartly turned out. George Herbert and Schof wore dark, traditional three-piece suits of local worsted cloth. Wilfred was more dashing. He favoured pale grey chalk-stripes and jackets that were a fashionable cut. He liked to carry a Malacca cane and on sunny days might pop on a straw boater. Around the West Riding he was considered so dapper one Sheffield wag described him as 'the Beau Brummel of cricket' and claimed that he was more graceful in his movements than the Canadian dancer Maud Allan. Since Allan was notorious for performing the 'Dance of the Seven Veils' in Oscar Wilde's scandalous *Salome*, it's unlikely the austere Rhodes took this as a compliment.

At leisure, the trio played billiards together at the Huddersfield Liberal Club. They became fans of Northern Union, the professionalised form of rugby (now known as rugby league) that had been created in Huddersfield in 1895. The three were regulars on the terraces of Fartown where, along with 18,000 others, they cheered on the great claret-and-gold-shirted Huddersfield team of Harold Wagstaff, Albert Rosenfeld and Stan Moorhouse.

When the weather was fine, the Triumvirate sometimes played golf at smart local clubs at the invitation of various West Riding worthies. Observers noted that while George Herbert and Schof engaged in 'rollicking, light-hearted smiting', Wilfred played more studiously and had the makings of a decent golfer (he'd eventually play off a 12 handicap).

So it was that these winter breaks went by warmly, cheerfully and rapidly. Then came March and a return to Leeds where their team-mates gathered, muffled up in sweaters, blazers and scarves, and Schof invariably greeted them with a cry of 'Merry Christmas, lads!'

It was the time of year Wilfred disliked most, the period when a muscle or a ligament in a stiff limb was most apt to pop. He approached it with caution, stretching himself gradually into his work, mindful of how a cold wind could chill even a warmed through body and cause the sort of pull or strain that would blight a season.

Admittedly, things were now more comfortable than when Wilfred had first joined Yorkshire. In his early days the pre-spring practice sessions had taken place out of doors, the players swaddled in wool and frequently driven into the pavilion by snow and sleet. Then, in 1909, Lord Hawke had bulldozed aside the objections of the committee and spent £600 on building an indoor nursery at Headingley with nets and matting wickets. The Shed, as it was known, was unheated. The players could still see their breath in the icy morning air, but at least they were no longer trying to bowl in pelting hail.

As it transpired, in 1913, the sun shone all summer. Barely a minute of play was lost to the weather. Wilfred was Yorkshire's best all-rounder, scoring more runs than George Herbert and taking only slightly fewer wickets. He hit four hundreds including 152 against Leicestershire. He came close to several more, but as in previous seasons often got out when within a dozen runs of three figures. If Wilfred hadn't been a byword for practicality and pragmatism, people might have suspected nerves. His bowling was consistent if unspectacular, though on a gloriously damp afternoon against Kent at Tunbridge Wells he took five for 42 in 14 overs.

Despite a series of niggling injuries, George Herbert topped Yorkshire's batting averages and was third behind Booth and Drake in the bowling. He did the double again. His best performances came in low-scoring games. Against Gloucestershire, he made a half-century and took six wickets;

against Somerset he scored 58, the highest innings of the match. George Herbert hit three centuries. Against Kent – the eventual champions – at Park Avenue, in the second innings he came in with Yorkshire at 41 for four in pursuit of over 300. On a worn track in dimming light, he attacked Blythe, Woolley and Arthur Fielder with merciless precision and strength to score 102 not out and salvage a draw.

Against Sussex at Hastings, George Herbert arrived in another crisis – Yorkshire three wickets down and only 20 on the board. After a brief survey of the field and the wicket, he clubbed 166 not out in just over five hours. It was Schof's last match in the County Championship. The final day was washed out by rain. The little man bowled just five overs and scored 30. Struggling for form and fitness, Schof managed to take just 38 wickets – his lowest tally since he had first broken into the Yorkshire side close to 20 years before. There were no match-winning heroics. He missed several matches after the car in which he'd travelled to a match dropped him off and then reversed over his foot. It seemed symptomatic of his decline.

Schof made his final first-class appearance against MCC at Scarborough. He was still injured and produced barely a handful of overs, his final victim: Shrimp Leveson Gower, clean bowled. By now his decision to leave first-class cricket to take up a post as coach at Winchester School had been made public. At lunch on the final day of his final match, Schof was presented with a silver ink stand by the Earl of Londesborough. Shrimp Leveson Gower spoke of the tinge of regret that Schof's retirement brought to the festival and praised him as a genial companion whose cheerfulness was maintained even during the greatest adversity. Schof had been taken by surprise. It was a day of high emotion and public speaking always made him nervous. His response was, by all reports, 'suitable', but unrecorded.

During his career he'd won the County Championship eight times, topped the national bowling averages four times and the Yorkshire bowling averages eight times. For his county, he had taken 1,876 wickets, scored 10,993 runs and pouched 277 catches. His laughter and his wisecracks had made him friends all over England. There was sadness at the news that his wide grin and sparkling eyes would be seen no more around the county grounds. 'As a sportsman,' said the *Huddersfield Weekly Examiner*, 'there is no one more cheery and great-hearted.'

His team-mates would miss his chaff and his quirks. He had a habit of going out and inspecting the pitch with great care before each day's play. They could tell how the pitch would play by the expression on his face. After inspecting what was plainly a raging turner, he'd amuse them by observing mildly, 'I reckon it may deviate somewhat.'

David Hunter compared Schof favourably to the great Aussie medium-pacer Charles 'the Terror' Turner, whose 106 wickets in an Australian season is still a record. 'Haigh was the worst bowler on earth – for batsman and wicketkeeper. With wickets to help him his break-back was tremendous, and all the time he could disguise what he was going to do.' In his first half-dozen seasons, the wicketkeeper had found Schof baffling and the bowler didn't help. 'I never had any signal with Schofield,' Hunter reported, before adding ruefully, 'or any other Yorkshire bowler for that matter.'

Yorkshire would be able to replace Schof's wickets, but never his personality. He was, A. W. Pullin observed in the

Yorkshire Evening Post, 'the shine of the team'. With his departure some of the gloss was gone from Yorkshire, leaving a rough surface that would grow increasingly abrasive as the decades went by.

CHAPTER NINE

Tours and Tragedy

The final overseas tour before the world descended into chaos took MCC and Wilfred to South Africa. The previous two visits had been disastrous; this one proved to be a doddle. Wilfred considered it the easiest tour he ever went on. Faulkner, Vogler, Schwartz and White, the players who had created such havoc on the matting wickets, had retired and South Africa had found nobody even halfway capable of replacing them. The only player of true class in the side was the captain, Herbie Taylor.

If the leg-spinners had baffled England on their previous visit, this time it was an Englishman who would be doing the bamboozling. Sydney Barnes was on the loftiest peak of form that winter. With his high action, he got vicious lift off the matting and made the ball move both ways with his finger spin. Only Taylor – who averaged over 50 in the series – had any idea how to play him. The other home batsmen hopped and sprang about as if attached to a battery by jumper cables. Chances were snicked into the slip cordon so frequently when

South Africa batted it felt like an extended fielding practice. By the end of the tour, the South African cricket authorities were so concerned about the loss of revenue from games ending early they delayed the starts until after the players had eaten lunch.

With Barnes imperious, England won the series comfortably. The first Test at Durban saw England establish total superiority, winning by an innings and 157 runs, with Taylor scoring more than half of the home side's runs in the first innings. Wilfred had watched Barnes bowl in England and Australia and now South Africa with equal effect. There wasn't a wicket on earth that didn't seem to suit him. His accuracy was unflagging. If the batsmen waited for the bad ball to hit, they waited all day. 'He always bowled as much with his head as with his arm,' he said, admiring qualities in his England team-mate that were recognisable in himself.

If Barnes was Wilfred's perfect bowler, Hobbs was his batting equivalent. A master of all conditions with perfect judgement and wonderful execution, he had mastered a bewildering array of shots and knew just when to play them. He didn't hit a century in the series but batted so consistently he averaged over 60.

In the second Test, Barnes took 17 wickets. Wilfred compiled a painstaking 152, taking his time on the matting wicket, even when the crowd barracked him for slow scoring. Barnes got eight more wickets in the third Test and another 14 in the fourth Test. He was rested for the fifth but even without him England romped home by 10 wickets. Wilfred returned home in good spirits after his second invigorating winter in a row. He had scored 731 runs on the tour and taken 31 wickets in first-class matches.

Wilfred had barely arrived back in England before it was time to report to Headingley for pre-season nets in the Shed. Touring during the glory days of the Triumvirate was long and arduous and resulted in close to 12 months of continual cricket. 'Yes. I have had a good rest on the ship,' George Herbert said when he returned from Australia in 1905 and was asked by Yorkshire pressmen if he was ready for the new season. George Herbert never complained about his work-load, neither did Schof or Wilfred. After all, most of the folk who paid to watch him from the sixpenny seats at Leeds and Sheffield worked 66 hours a week, risking limbs and lungs in mills, coal mines, blast furnaces and foundries for a fraction of the money they were paid. That didn't mean it wasn't tough, however.

Trips to South Africa and Australia saw the players leaving home in late autumn and returning home in early spring. In 1903-04 MCC arrived in Australia on 5 November and left for home on 16 March. They played 20 matches in 11 cities and towns. In South Africa in 1905-06, Warner's side played 26 games spread across 16 grounds, from Cape Town to Middelburg. The 1907-08 Ashes tour lasted a day over 20 weeks, not including the journey. Leveson Gower's trip to South Africa in 1909-10 featured 65 scheduled days of cricket in 15 weeks with dozens of 800-mile train rides wedged in between. With his appetite for cricket and rail travel apparently still unsated, Shrimp then took an unofficial party off for a few matches in Rhodesia. Wilfred, wisely, decided to return to Yorkshire instead.

Each tour began with a long sea voyage, at least 21 days from Southampton to Cape Town and nearer 40 to Melbourne, usually with a few days' break in what was then Ceylon. Since it was the middle of winter this was not always a pleasant experience. When Schof set off for South Africa with Warner's side they hit storms almost the moment they left Southampton. In the Bay of Biscay their ship, the *Kinfauns Castle*, was struck by such high and violent waves they stove in some of the portholes. MCC baggage man 'Toby' Brown was almost drowned in his cabin. Later there was a fire in an engine room. None of this appeared to have bothered Schof all that much. Warner recalled later with astonishment that while many players refused to leave their bunks, or ate only dried toast until they docked at Madeira, the Yorkshireman would be found sitting in the forward saloon merrily tucking into a mighty roast dinner as the floor rose and fell beneath him.

Wilfred, too, was a good sailor, but George Herbert had to take to his bed as soon as the sea began to move. On the 1903-04 trip, on a particularly rough stretch from Colombo (where the players had visited a former Boer POW camp) to Fremantle, his team-mates joked that Hirst had added to the records he'd set for batting and bowling, by establishing a new high mark for throwing up.

When the seas were calm enough the players amused themselves with games of deck cricket. The roll of the ship presented problems and every so often when it increased during a game a bowler might put more than the ball on a good length, but it passed the time and kept the players in reasonable trim.

Once on shore the travel barely stopped. In Australia and South Africa the players moved around by train. The journeys were long and tiring. The trip from Sydney to Brisbane took 29 hours and, Bernard Bosanquet reported, sleep was impossible due to the tooting of the engine whistle and the squeal of the brakes. The players' discomfort was increased by the heat – Bosanquet likened one trip to travelling in a 'mobile Turkish bath' – and the fact that at every station great crowds gathered and peered in through the windows, shouting and pointing at the England players until they felt – as Warner put it – like 'a new cage of monkeys bound for the zoo'. To liven things up, Wilfred joined Johnny Tyldesley, Tom Hayward and Ted Arnold in a singing quartet that provided a moderate onboard entertainment.

In Australia meals were not served on the trains but had to be taken in a 20-minute break at a designated station. According to Bosanquet the only man capable of bolting down a three-course lunch in this short time was George Herbert, who went to his table from the train as swiftly as he did when pursuing a ball from mid-off and gobbled down steaming hot soup as if his mouth and throat were lined with tin. Afterwards he was so full he had to be prised from his chair.

The players generally stayed in decent hotels, but in South Africa they were occasionally billeted with the local British garrison. In return for the Army's hospitality they'd play an extra, one-day game against a regimental side. At Roberts Heights in 1905 Schof took four wickets in four balls, each clean bowled, against a team of Cameron Highlanders.

When they weren't playing matches, the players attended functions given by local and visiting dignitaries. In Australia in 1903 George Herbert and Wilfred met Lord and Lady Tennyson and took tea with the Countess of Darnley, who, in her younger days as plain Florence Morphy, had been one of the Melbourne ladies credited with creating the Ashes urn.

At other times the players were hosted by ex-patriots

from their home counties. In Durban in 1905 Schof and David Denton were looked after by an immigrant from Huddersfield who, after getting Schof fixed up with a new pair of boots that gave him proper ankle support, took them on a rickshaw ride, then on a trip to the coast where they 'walked across the Indian Ocean sands' and scanned the sea for the fins of great white sharks (they didn't spot any). In Johannesburg, Schof was one of the guests of honour at a dinner given by the Yorkshire and Lancashire Association after which he was presented with a silver-inlaid pipe with his name engraved on it. He'd be spotted puffing away at it on the boundary at Yorkshire matches for years afterwards. When asked about the pipe, he'd joke that he'd picked it up in South Africa but, like most things you got there, it was 'likely made in Birmingham'.

On rest days, the players were taken on excursions. In Maritzburg, Schof watched the blasting operations at a De Beers diamond mine and afterwards was taken to a sorting room where he was allowed to handle gems 'said to be worth £1,300'. A trip down an Australian gold mine near Bendigo was less glamorous, Bosanquet recording that 'not a scrap of precious metal was seen' while the heat below ground was infernal and the mineshaft as dirty and dismal as the English coal pits Wilfred's father had worked down. The Middlesex bowler was similarly unimpressed by a shooting party the players were taken on in New South Wales at which 'the bag was not very large: one swan, two larks and a sparrow compromising the greater part of it'. Things livened up later when a pigeon shooting contest was organised, Ted Arnold emerging victorious after killing seven birds in a row.

Christmas Day was celebrated far from home and family

with the players at least enjoying the novelty of eating fresh strawberries in December. In South Africa, Schof enjoyed his plum pudding and iced drinks with his old Yorkshire team-mate Frank Mitchell, now settled in Johannesburg. For George Herbert and Wilfred in 1904 the meal was no sooner eaten in Melbourne than they were back on an overnight train bound across country for another match.

There was interest in the changing landscape and the exotic wildlife and in the differences between life in Britain and in her colonies but ultimately George Herbert and Wilfred both shared the sentiments of Schof, who told a reporter from the *Sheffield Telegraph* the day after he returned from his second trip to the Cape, 'Africa's alright, but it's good old Huddersfield for me!'

Nineteen-fourteen was Yorkshire's first season without the full Triumvirate since 1898. If people in the Broad Acres were concerned about what that might mean, by the end of the summer they had more serious things to fret about. There was little sign that they were missing Schof in May when they won three matches by an innings – against Northamptonshire, MCC and Essex. The batting in all these matches was excellent and the bowling exceptional.

George Herbert had a number of injuries that limited his appearances and hampered his performances. He failed to do the double for the first time since 1903 and managed barely half the overs he'd got through in previous seasons. When he got to the wicket, his batting was still as punchy as ever. He hit three hundreds, among them a couple of knocks against Northamptonshire at Huddersfield and Somerset at Bramall Lane that had a carnival jollity to them. The latter innings, struck at better than a run a minute, came on 27 July.

The county season carried on despite the declaration of war in August, though three matches were abandoned. Against Surrey at Bradford, Wilfred scored 89 in the first innings and took 11 wickets in the match, but Yorkshire lost by 28 runs. In a remarkable game against Derbyshire at Chesterfield, the home side totalled just 68 in the second innings. Fifty of them were made by opening bat Arthur Morton. There were eight extras. The other 10 batsmen contributed 10 between them. The last six wickets fell in eight deliveries. The mercurial Drake took five for six in 18 balls, including four wickets in four balls. Wilfred took a relative tanning, finishing with four for 12.

The game against Middlesex at Sheffield was at first declared off because of the rumbling threat of war. The Middlesex team then reconsidered and the match started. George Herbert captained Yorkshire. They won in a tense finish by two wickets against superb bowling from 'Young Jack' Hearne – just the sort of match George Herbert relished.

By the time Yorkshire travelled to London to play Surrey on 13 August, The Oval was under the control of the Army and the match was played instead at Lord's. There was an attempt by the government to use cricket as a means to show the public that the war wouldn't interrupt ordinary life, but the crowds stayed away and the players performed in a desultory fashion. Certainly Yorkshire seemed uninterested in the outcome and lost by an innings and 30 runs – one of their worst performances of the century so far.

Yorkshire's next match was against Sussex at Bradford. Wilfred hit a hundred and Yorkshire won by an innings. A game at Harrogate against an England XI the following day was cancelled and the Scarborough Festival was also scrapped. Yorkshire went down to the West Country. Against Gloucestershire, Drake and Booth bowled unchanged throughout both innings, taking all the wickets that fell. It was the first time a pair of Yorkshire bowlers had performed such a feat since George Herbert and Schof in 1910.

In their next outing, against Somerset, the pair took five wickets each in the first Somerset innings and in the next Drake did something no Yorkshire bowler had done before – took all 10 wickets. The pitch, it should be noted, had recently been relaid by a local clergyman who must have been a bowler himself.

By now, the seriousness of the situation was apparent to all the players. Shortly after a game against Sussex at Hove, Major Booth, Roy Kilner and Arthur Dolphin volunteered and joined the Leeds Pals battalion of Lord Kitchener's Army. They immediately went off to Colsterdale Camp to train. Drake tried to sign up, too, but despite being both a professional cricketer and a professional footballer, he was ruled unfit for military service because of the lung problems that would eventually kill him.

With war approaching, the Rhodes family moved to their new house in Grove Road, Marsh – an affluent suburb of Huddersfield. The new home was close to that of George Hirst and his brood. The future was uncertain. Friends needed to stick together. The Triumvirate were too old for active service – Wilfred, the youngster, was 37.

The trio signed up to work at the national shell factory in Huddersfield. Wilfred worked on a lathe. He had little experience with machinery but soon acquired a knack for it. He rectified 18-pounder field gun shells and became so good at it he was promoted to charge-hand overseeing a workforce of 12 women. Eventually, he was made output manager of the factory and worked from 6 a.m. until 5.30 p.m. during the week and a half-day on Saturday. The factory produced about 1,600 shells per week. It seems that Wilfred took easily and happily to the work, while the older Schof and George Herbert did it as a duty, but skedaddled as soon as they could when the finish bell rang.

Working in the munitions plant, the three men earned £2 a week, a considerable drop from their cricket pay. Yorkshire were kept financially stable by the generous donations of members, who contributed £5,560 during the course of the war for the upkeep of grounds and to pay allowances to players who were expected to turn out – service permitting – in charity matches. George Herbert and Wilfred were each paid £17 10s a year by the county in return for playing 20 one-day matches on Saturday afternoons.

George Herbert, Wilfred and Schof also turned out regularly for an assortment of club sides. On 26 June 1915, for example, a huge crowd turned up to see George Herbert play for Otley against Horsforth Hall Park. He did not disappoint them, smashing 122 in under two hours and plonking one massive six over square leg and out of the ground. On the same day, Wilfred scored a less explosive 93 not out to help Chickenley beat Heckmondwike – a fixture of almost peak Yorkiedom – by three wickets. Not to be outdone, Schof made his presence felt for Silsden, taking nine wickets for 10 runs as they beat Yeadon. The trio picked up cash payments for playing in these games, money slipped in a pocket or a shoe by the club captain. It was usually two guineas a game, though George Herbert was known to negotiate the fee down, if he thought the club were strapped financially.

As well as his war work and service in the GR Volunteers (the First World War's answer to the Home Guard), Wilfred also found a new hobby – photography. He made a darkroom in the house in Marsh and drove Sarah mad with the stink of his chemicals and his yells not to turn the lights on.

As the war rolled on, George Herbert's son James joined the West Riding Regiment. Schof's boy John, a promising player who'd scored runs freely for Armitage Bridge in the Huddersfield and District League, was working as a clerk for a Huddersfield wool merchant (coincidentally called George Hirst). He signed up as a private in the Royal Flying Corps in the winter of 1917. He'd rise to the rank of second lieutenant, serving in the 24th Squadron, Royal Air Force. James came back safely. John was not so lucky. On a training flight in an S. E. 5 fighter on 15 August 1918, he got into difficulties and crashed fatally. John was buried at Vignacourt Cemetery. He was 19. His death shattered Schofield Haigh, driving the sparkle from his eyes and wiping the smile from his face. Those who met him in the months following the November armistice worried that he had shrunk. His effervescence had made him seem bigger than he was; now the bubbles had gone out of him.

CHAPTER TEN

Bed and Cricket

Wilfred would sometimes wonder how Yorkshire would have fared if the First World War hadn't interrupted cricket. Major Booth had been killed at the Somme, James Rothery had also died from combat wounds, while Alonzo Drake had succumbed to disease shortly after the conflict had ended. But idle speculation was not really part of Wilfred's character and he offered no conclusion.

The return to spring nets at Headingley in 1919 was a melancholy day. As well as Booth and Drake, Roy Kilner was also missing, recuperating from a wrist injury sustained on the Western Front. The offices in the pavilion had been taken over by the military and used as the headquarters of the West Riding Volunteers. Lord Hawke had served there as the county adjutant, yet despite his presence the ground still had the look of somewhere ransacked and abandoned. It was plain, too, that a new team would have to be built on some sturdy old foundations. Of the old guard, George Herbert, Wilfred and David Denton were present and correct. Roy

Kilner would return. Percy Holmes, an opening batsman from Huddersfield who'd played a few games before the war, was also present. So too was Tommy Birtles, a genial all-rounder who was valued as much for his comedic personality as his abilities as a cricketer. His most celebrated utterance came after two opposition batsmen had carted him all over the field: 'Don't take me off now, skipper, I've just got them nibbling.'

Yorkshire had a new captain: Cecil Burton, who hailed from Bridlington. A Cambridge Blue, he'd made his Yorkshire debut back in 1907 when he was still a student. He'd make two centuries and a dozen fifties in first-class cricket, which marked him as a class above his two immediate predecessors. His brother Claude also played a few games for Yorkshire in 1914, while his uncle, Arthur Trollope, had made himself a footnote in cricket history during his time at Cambridge when he missed the Varsity match after being badly injured by 'the catapult', an erratic early form of bowling machine. Burton, like his uncle, was prepared to risk life and limb while batting and in his first season would be knocked unconscious by Jack Gregory when Yorkshire met the Australian Imperial Forces.

The untried captain could lean on the veterans and keep his fingers crossed about the performances of a number of promising younger players, among them a recently de-mobbed Army captain from over by Pudsey, Herbert Sutcliffe.

To add to Burton's burden, the season that was about to start was being played to a singular new formula. Fearing that an increase in admission charges caused by the imposition of an amusement tax might lead to thin crowds and mindful that the players were unfit after five years of enforced lay-off, the cricket board introduced a dramatic change to the format of the County Championship – games would last just two days with play scheduled from 11.30 till 7.30. Yorkshire, in the formidable form of Lord Hawke, opposed the idea but it went through by a majority in the vote.

By the middle of the season, it was plain the new format was not a success. The last hour of most days was played to empty stands, the spectators having left to go home for tea. Attempts to persuade them to stay by offering a post-close 'supper' were a singular failure, especially in the north of England, where eating a meal after 6 p.m. was considered a certain recipe for nightmares and indigestion. The players, meanwhile, spent so much time travelling they rarely settled in one spot for longer than a wasp, criss-crossing the country with little time for anything but playing, travelling and sleeping. Wilfred would remember it as a summer of 'bed and cricket'.

A cursory look at the players at practice told George Herbert that the side was soft in the batting, weak in the bowling and needed some sharpening up with the fielding. He wasn't captain, but he'd have to lead. Closing in on 50, stiff-kneed and white-haired though he was, he still had his old dash and charisma. He exuded belief in himself, in others, but most of all in Yorkshire cricket. The younger players such Holmes, Sutcliffe, Kilner and the left-arm quick bowler Abe Waddington found his presence reassuring. He gave them confidence and his brilliance as a player seemed undimmed by the passing of time and the five-year interruption. In the first months of the season, he seemed to be carrying Yorkshire forward single-handedly. For Yorkshire against MCC he reacted to a crisis – his side 368 behind on first innings and three wickets down and still close to 200 adrift – with typical gusto, blasting 180 not out with a mix of bludgeoning pulls and smashing off drives.

He followed this with a lightning 80 at Fenner's, a century against Essex that helped Yorkshire avoid the follow-on and saved the match, caned 120 against Warwickshire and 88 against the Australian Imperial Forces. It was mid-June. He couldn't keep it up, naturally, but that early-season gallop was a cheering spectacle for all who loved cricket and it galvanised his side.

Wilfred, too, led by example. The weakness of the county's attack meant he was pressed back into service with the ball. He became a top-class bowler once again, while his batting remained resolute. In what was his first county match for five years, against Gloucestershire, he opened the batting and hit 72 then took seven wickets. When Gloucestershire followed on, Wilfred was brought on first change and recorded the remarkable figures of four for 5. His spell lasted 21 deliveries. He scored a hard-hitting hundred against Hampshire, took 10 Northamptonshire wickets at Northampton and another eight when Northants came to Sheffield. He took eight in the match with Warwickshire and 10 against Middlesex.

The years had taken their toll and Wilfred felt it. 'I found I could not spin or flight the ball as much as before the war . . . and could not get as much body into my bowling.' Instead, he had to rely on length, line and his matchless ability to get inside the minds of opposition batsmen, or perhaps simply to make them think he had got inside their minds, because batsmen feared Wilfred and he knew it and took advantage. For dozens of years he'd worked to make his reputation, now it was time for his reputation to work for him.

His action remained a thing of simple beauty – three steps to the wicket and an easy swing of the arm. It was as practical and solidly beautiful as a Robert Thompson trestle. As Plum Warner noted, 'It seemed literally to be part of himself.'

In his glory days, Wilfred had bowled the standard line of the slow left-armer, pitching the ball on or a fraction outside the right-hander's off stump, tempting him to drive and snick to Hunter behind the wicket or Tunnicliffe at first slip. Now that his fingers could no longer induce the ball to turn, he focused instead on the zone between leg and middle. He would keep up the pressure, evenly but remorselessly, pinning batsmen down, limiting their scoring and tempting them into rashness.

Wilfred had a mental catalogue of batsmen's quirks. Frank Woolley, for example, cut across the ball when he drove so that it curved away late in its flight. As a consequence when bowling to the Kent left-hander, long-off had to be moved wider. He set his field to block the batsman's favourite shots, forcing him to hit towards other points of the ground that were not so natural to him. He made them uncomfortable.

Wilfred had made a study of the psychology of batting and turned it to his advantage. The first ball he bowled to a new batsman was often a half-volley. He reasoned that the newcomer would be unlikely to drive hard at his opening delivery, but having failed to accept such an easy chance to get off the mark, would be more likely to dash at the next ball, which Wilfred would bowl slightly shorter, inducing an edge to slip or a catch at long-off. In his first season deploying the new method, he took 164 wickets at 14.42. In the next 11 seasons, he'd fail to take 100 wickets just twice and average over 20 on a single occasion.

The turning point in Yorkshire's campaign came at the end of June, when Sutcliffe was pushed up from number six to open the batting with Holmes. The decision was taken by Burton after a long chat with George Herbert. Having returned to being a strike bowler, Wilfred felt he couldn't continue as the regular opener. The captain was uncertain who should replace him. It was George Herbert who spoke up for Sutcliffe.

The man who would become one of England's greatest ever batsmen (his Test average of 60.7 suggests he has some claim to have been *the* greatest) had first been invited to attend practices at Headingley in the early summer of 1912. By now an invitation to the Yorkshire spring nets was likely to turn a teenager momentarily into a local celebrity, with his picture splashed across the sports pages of the evening paper along with a few quotes from his parents. It increased the pressure on the boys, ensuring that a failure to impress became public knowledge. Sutcliffe arrived feeling awkward and nervous, unsettled by the great names and the unfamiliarity of the surroundings. George Herbert spotted him, walked over and patted him on the arm, saying, 'I've heard a lot about you. Don't be nervous, make yourself at home. You ought to feel at home because we're all cricketers here. Play your own game and you'll be quite all right.' This short speech had the desired effect. Sutcliffe impressed enough to be invited back. He received expert tuition from George Herbert and second team coach, Steve Doughty. George Herbert emphasised the importance of pad play, especially against the swinging delivery, which was now a feature of county cricket. 'Nobody these days can play with their bat alone,' he told Sutcliffe.

After that, George Herbert kept a benign proprietary eye on the youngster, revelling in his success. When Holmes and Sutcliffe batted brilliantly in an opening partnership against Northamptonshire that raised 279, George Herbert, watching from the pavilion as Sutcliffe hit a series of boundaries to reach 94 and close in on his maiden county hundred, turned to his team-mates and said, 'He ought to hit a six now.' A couple of balls later Sutcliffe smashed Ted Freeman into the stands just as George Herbert had suggested. When Sutcliffe learned of George Herbert's comment later, he shook his head. There was something about Hirst. He understood the game so well he seemed to be able to read minds.

Holmes and Sutcliffe made their first appearance as openers together against Kent at Headingley on 30 June. By the end of the season, they'd posted five century opening partnerships and scored five hundreds apiece.

Burton was generous in his praise of George Herbert. 'His experience repeatedly stood me in good stead; I learnt a great deal from him and benefited greatly by taking his advice on many occasions. He was in short a great friend to me – a friend to all, in fact, and especially encouraging to young players.'

When Burton was flattened by Gregory, George Herbert took charge of the side for several matches. It was he who brought Abe Waddington into the team after watching him play for Laisterdyke in his native Bradford. Waddington was a left-arm fast-medium bowler with an easy action. His stock delivery swerved into the right-hander, but he could also make it go away off the wicket, which made him very dangerous in the right conditions. He was a match-winner in the style of Schof, though instead of geniality he displayed a brand of brooding insolence, which combined with his brutish physique and dark hair, might have made him the love interest in a novel by a Brontë sister. To add a dash of grim northern comedy, Waddington's family owned a fat-rendering business.

The menacing Waddington took 100 wickets between July and the close of the season. He was soon opening the bowling with another newcomer, Emmott Robinson, who could swing the ball in the air and move it off the pitch. As a youngster, Robinson had an avuncular, quizzical look, like a man awaiting the punchline of a shaggy dog story. He was a bright spark in the side, a tough customer who fielded so close at silly midwicket batsmen often expressed fear for his safety. 'Never mind me, you just get on with playing' was Robinson's characteristic response. He and Wilfred would become as close as George Herbert and Schof had been, though their influence on the Yorkshire team was not entirely so benign.

Wilfred's bowling had caught the attention of cricket writers, many of whom found his return to the top of the averages the biggest surprise of the season. He didn't neglect his batting either. He hit one century and six half-centuries. In the game with Hampshire at Dewsbury, Wilfred scored 135 and put on 254 with Burton, who made 142 not out coming in at eight. It was a Yorkshire record for the seventh wicket.

Since the counties had agreed to set their own schedules, the Championship was decided by win percentage – a system that effectively penalised teams when a match was lost to bad weather. Despite their grumbling, Yorkshire won the title by a narrow margin, playing close to twice as many games as second-placed Kent, who lost out thanks to a late defeat to Middlesex.

At the conclusion of the season, the Scarborough Festival drew huge, happy crowds. Many thought it might be their last chance to see George Herbert. The 40 he struck for the Players against the Gentlemen was applauded as if it had won the Ashes. Once again, the farewells proved to be premature, though it would turn out that the 120 George Herbert had struck against Warwickshire during his great early-season streak would be his last of the 56 centuries he'd score in first-class cricket.

George Herbert had taken up the position of cricket coach at Eton College and would be available to play for Yorkshire only after the annual match between his new team and Harrow School. For the first time in his life, Wilfred was on his own. It didn't seem to bother him much. He was buoyed no doubt by the fact the hated two-day format had been scrapped. Three-day games returned and with them the big novelty of the season: Saturday starts.

Against poor Derbyshire at Bramall Lane, Wilfred bowled eight overs (six of them maidens) and took four wickets for two runs. In the return fixture, he bowled 17 overs (seven maidens) and took seven for 24, including his first first-class hat-trick. He'd been on a hat-trick three times before, the closest he'd come to securing one had been against Kent when paceman Charley Bradley had skied the ball towards long-on, who dropped the catch.

He completed his 11th season double in the match with Hampshire in which he scored a not out fifty to set alongside an 11-wicket haul. It was the end of August. When congratulated on his achievement, Wilfred remarked gruffly, 'Fancy scratching for it until this time of year!' In truth there had been little scratching. Wilfred had blazed through the season with a series of headline-grabbing all-round displays. Against Essex at Dewsbury he'd scored 66 in Yorkshire's second innings and taken eight for 47 in the match; against Hampshire at Portsmouth he scored 63 not out in Yorkshire's only innings and then took 11 for 129 as Yorkshire won by an innings and 235 runs. There were ten-wicket hauls against Surrey and Middlesex and the highest score of his summer, 167 not out, came against Nottinghamshire.

He did not have everything his own way. For Surrey at Sheffield, Percy Fender scored 56 in 20 minutes and flayed Wilfred for 21 in a single over – the kind of scenes that presaged a biblical cataclysm. In this case it was a 204-run defeat for the home side.

George Herbert returned from Eton for Yorkshire's final few games, battering the Surrey attack at The Oval, where he was denied a final century when an acrobatic catch by wicketkeeper Strudwick saw him depart for 81.

Yorkshire didn't lose until they were battered by Surrey at Sheffield towards the end of June. They fell away after that shock and ended up fourth behind Middlesex, Lancashire and Surrey, but they played entertainingly all season and gate receipts for their home matches had soared. At the end of the season, George Herbert and Denton announced that they would not return in 1921. Wilfred would now be the last survivor of the glorious side of the early 1900s and his county's senior professional.

Winchester cricket master Rockley Wilson, aged 41, had such a remarkable season with the ball during his summer holiday with Yorkshire, he was picked to go on the MCC tour of Australia under Johnny Douglas. Wilfred, Waddington and Arthur Dolphin joined him. It was said of Wilson that he was 'equally capable of snubbing a bishop or soothing a fretful baby'. Whether he got a chance to do either in Australia is not recorded.

Of all the tours Wilfred went on, this was the one that pained him most. In later years he could barely be prevailed on to speak of it at all. It was eight years since England had last toured Australia, but it might have been a century, so changed were the times. The Australians had pushed for the tour – they'd actually wanted it a year earlier – but many in England considered it unwise. The country had barely returned to a semblance of normality after the end of the First World War, many players had been killed or wounded and those who had come in to replace them were inexperienced and untested. The same held true for the Australians, of course. Tibby Cotter had died fighting in Palestine. But on the home front they had not suffered the same privations. The Australian players were young, bouncingly fit and aggressive, filled with that bristling self-confidence that was to become all too familiar.

The team selected to oppose them, by contrast, appeared elderly and out of date, the fielding so clownishly bumbling the barrackers in the crowds howled with derisive laughter. Wilfred's role in the side seems to have been ill-defined. Sometimes he opened the batting with Hobbs, at others he was dropped into the middle order where he was now batting for Yorkshire. His bowling was used so sparingly – he bowled just 85 overs in five Tests – he could not build up any rhythm and his return was poor – four wickets at a cost of over 60 each. Douglas admired Wilfred and sought his advice out so constantly on the field one wag yelled out, 'Christ, Douglas, can't you do anything without asking that fella first?'

Douglas led from the front with his usual pugnacity and Jack Hobbs batted superbly, but on hard, fast wickets, the combination of pacemen Jack Gregory and Ted McDonald, bouncy fast-medium bowler Charlie Kelleway and the wrist-spinner Arthur Mailey, who gave the ball such a massive tweak he could have extracted turn from a ballroom floor, proved too much for the rest. The home side won the first Test by 377 runs, the second by an innings and 91, the third by 119 runs and the fourth and fifth by eight and nine wickets. It was the biggest hiding in England's history.

Wilfred performed no better or worse than most of his fellow tourists. He made 730 first-class runs on the trip thanks mainly to two massive innings – 162 in sweltering Brisbane heat against Queensland and 210 against South Australia at Adelaide in the last match before setting off for home. His bowling was generally as ordinary as it had been on his visit under the unlucky Arthur Jones. The one highlight was a six-wicket haul on a Melbourne sticky dog. In the Tests his batting fell short of his usual standards, his best being a courageous 73 in the fourth match of the series.

If Wilfred had thought things couldn't get any worse, he was wrong. During the final Test in Sydney, the team received the news that Schofield Haigh had died. He was just 49. Schof had carried on coaching at Winchester after the war had ended. He was successful and popular. *The Times* noted that he had done 'wonderful things' at the school and was 'always one to encourage not to depress his pupils'.

In 1919 he had been fit enough to pro for Keighley and had taken enjoyment in seeing one of his ex-students, Claude Ashton, hit 92 against Yorkshire for Cambridge University. But in the summer of 1920 his health failed. After watching his pupils comfortably defeat George Herbert's Eton College, he'd played a game for Hampshire Rovers against United Services and afterwards returned to Huddersfield with the intention of turning out for D. C. F Burton's XI in charity matches. It never happened. No sooner was he back in

Yorkshire than he was bedridden with heart trouble. When he appeared to have recovered from that he was struck down by tonsillitis.

Those who saw him at that year's Scarborough Festival, where he umpired in his usual eccentric manner (he'd once given John Tunnicliffe out for 'looking guilty'), were shocked by the changes in him. Though Schof still smiled and joked, his face was gaunt and his skin pale. He'd been bedridden for much of the winter and finally gave out on 27 February. A condition known as 'athlete's heart' (an enlargement of the left side of the heart more usually associated with endurance athletes such as cross-country skiers and marathon runners) was held responsible, though several papers mentioned the death of his son, John, and the awful toll it had taken on him. There was some adversity that even Schof's genial nature was not resistant to.

His death was quietly mourned. Rockley Wilson, who had played alongside him for Yorkshire and worked with him at Winchester, called him 'one of the most popular crick-eters who ever played', while the England captain, Johnny Douglas, said he was one of the finest sportsmen he'd ever met. George Herbert and Wilfred made no public comment. The newspapermen discreetly left them to private grief.

Schof was buried in Armitage Bridge Church on 2 March. The pall-bearers included George Herbert, David Denton, Irving Washington, Billy Ringrose, Roy Kilner, Percy Holmes and Herbert Sutcliffe. A wreath was laid by Lord Hawke. Wilfred would have been there too, but he was trav-elling through the New South Wales bush on his way to an up-country match against an Albury XV.

CHAPTER ELEVEN

The Trouble with Mr Toone

Mr Frederick Toone was balding, moustachioed, with dark eyes and a smooth, round face and unctuous expression that suggested a senior cleric or successful funeral director. Mr Toone was the secretary of Yorkshire County Cricket Club.

Yorkshire's first secretary had been Joseph Wostinholm, the man to whom George Herbert had asserted his intentions of making a place in the first team his own. Wostinholm was a Sheffield solicitor. He had helped found Sheffield United Football Club – effectively serving as the club's manager for several years – and it was through his industry that Bramall Lane had become the best cricket ground in Yorkshire. Wostinholm had done a commendable job in running Yorkshire CCC. In 1892, the club had just 200 members. By the time Wostinholm resigned in 1902 that number had risen to 3,000.

The vacancy created by Wostinholm's departure was a coveted one. Not only were Yorkshire the best-supported and most successful cricket county, the salary on offer was £350 a year, dwarfing that paid anywhere else. Unsurprisingly there were dozens of applicants. Eventually the candidates were whittled down to just two. One was the dashing Essex batsman Edward Sewell; the other Frederick Toone. Sewell had a better knowledge of the game (he'd hit a century while batting with W. G. and played for the first All India XI) and the richer antecedents – his grandfather had been a major general who'd served under the Duke of Wellington. Toone had the greater experience of sports administration. Having begun his professional life managing a printworks, Toone – a keen rugby player and runner – had been appointed secretary of Leicestershire in 1897. In five years, he'd raised county membership from 500 to 1,800 while displaying what A. W. Pullin described as 'driving moral force and enthusiasm'.

After interviews in Leeds, Toone was appointed. Sewell immediately applied for his old post at Leicestershire, but missed out on that, too. Like many people thwarted in their original ambitions he was forced to take to writing.

Toone would serve as Yorkshire's secretary from 1903 until his death in 1930. During that time, club membership would double. Toone carried out massive reforms of the organisation of the cricket club that improved it financially and structurally. Before his arrival, county matches had been organised, financed and managed by the clubs that owned the grounds on which they were played. Toone took this responsibility and risk away from them. Yorkshire CCC shouldered the financial burden, administered the games and collected the revenues. The clubs that hosted matches received a percentage of gate receipts and bonuses based on end-of-season profits. The gamble of volunteering to stage matches was removed, the revenue of the clubs was increased and playing facilities around the county improved.

Yorkshire also organised any Test matches that were played in the county.

Before Toone's arrival there had been a long-standing and often bitter dispute between Sheffield and Leeds over where the true centre of Yorkshire cricket lay. Toone settled it by moving into a large detached house in the smart Leeds suburb of Horsforth. Yorkshire's captain and president, Lord Hawke, lived a few miles away. All power had now been centralised into the county office, which was at Headingley. Sheffield had lost.

Toone was an indefatigable worker who carried all this through pretty much on his own (his only member of staff was an office boy). Yorkshire's committee, evidently dazzled by Toone's energy and expertise, agreed to whatever he decided – 'my committee' he called them.

Through his role at Yorkshire and his mastery of administrative diplomacy, Toone built up ties with MCC. He was chosen as tour manager on the Ashes trips of 1920-21, 1924-25 and 1928-29 and praised when he returned for helping forge closer ties between Britain and Australia.

It was not only Lord's that was impressed with Frederick Toone. After the chaotic scenes at the 1923 FA Cup final, at which it seemed only the intervention of a police officer on a white horse had prevented disaster, the government organised a crowds committee to look into public safety at football and cricket grounds. Toone was one of the first men appointed to it.

Toone was a gentleman of tact and subtlety who moved silently through the corridors of power as if on well-oiled casters. In 1929, he became only the second person to be knighted for cricket-related activities. The first was Francis

Eden Lacey, a man perhaps even more forgotten now than Frederick Toone.

Writing of Toone in his memoirs, Lord Hawke praised the Yorkshire secretary for 'his unfailing tact and courtesy'. Toone was, His Lordship affirmed, 'without exaggeration, the best friend to all the players'. Furthermore, 'I am not going too far when I emphatically state that Toone is Yorkshire cricket to the backbone.'

Hawke's emphasis in this final flourish written in 1924 suggests it was a riposte to some unheard complaint from the back of the room. That is not without possibility. For, despite Lord Hawke's comments and the support of some of English cricket's, and indeed English society's, most powerful men, Frederick Toone was not universally admired. There were some who actively detested him and one of those people was Wilfred Rhodes.

It is possible there was a political element to the animosity. Frederick Toone was a member of the British Fascists. So too was Sussex and England captain Arthur Gilligan. Toone and Gilligan were friends and it has been suggested that they used MCC's tour of Australia in 1924–25 to establish ties with fascist groups in the Antipodes. Certainly, there is evidence that British intelligence officers were keeping an eye on their activities.

The British Fascists are not to be confused with Oswald Mosley's later British Union of Fascists. Some historians have said they were little more than an adult version of the Boy Scouts, misguided paternalists who felt that British working-class men needed firm leadership, discipline and plenty of fresh air to prevent them from falling into the clutches of vice, or worse still, socialism. Yet while the British Fascists certainly seem to have posed no direct threat to parliamentary democracy, they were not without a nasty edge. At meetings, Gilligan and Toone would have found themselves exchanging pleasantries with fellow members who included the future Lord Haw-Haw, William Joyce, the virulently anti-Semitic Neil Francis Hawkins and Arnold Leese, a veterinarian who filled his spare time by publishing pamphlets claiming that the Jewish Passover celebrations included the sacrifice of Christian children. If these were Boy Scouts, they were the sort who would happily burn a cross on a lawn. The symbol of the British Fascists was, coincidentally, a white rose.

Fascism, like all extreme political doctrines, was riven with factions and arguments. One thing that all fascists could agree on, however, was that organised labour was something that had to be crushed. Save perhaps for the fact that his father was a Yorkshire pitman (the Miners' Federation of Great Britain, led by left-wing firebrand Arthur Cook, was arguably Britain's best organised and most radical trades union), there is nothing to suggest Wilfred had leanings towards political radicalism of any kind, but the very fact that he sometimes refused to salute his leaders with sufficient enthusiasm may have been enough to mark him out as just the sort of truculent bolshie Toone and his marching men were pledged to eradicate.

As senior professional at Yorkshire, Wilfred was the man designated to present the grievances of the dressing room to those who ran the club. He was, effectively, the shop steward of the professionals. Frederick Toone came to regard him less as the deliverer of complaints than the instigator of them. To him, Wilfred was potentially the Arthur Cook of Headingley. He needed to be put in his place, and kept there.

Wilfred's troubles with Frederick Toone had begun

perhaps before he even realised it. At the end of the 1914 season, Yorkshire had dispensed with the services of batsman Benny Wilson. The Scarborough-born right-hander had been Wilfred's regular opening partner for several years. He'd hit 14 centuries and 35 fifties for the county. Wilfred liked and respected Wilson, but the general perception among Yorkshire members was that he was too apt to treat a half-volley as if it were a hand-grenade. Edgar Oldroyd was also the target of criticism for scoring so slowly some said you could tell which direction north was by checking where the moss grew on his bat, but Oldroyd scored far more runs than Wilson. There wasn't room for both of them, not if you wanted to win in three days, so Wilson was sacked. To Wilfred the pragmatist, the decision was born of an ignorance of the realities and finer points of the game. It was Toone and his committee's sop to public opinion, of which Wilfred generally had a low regard. He believed that nobody at Yorkshire had been better placed to judge Wilson's 'solid usefulness' than he was. Yet before deciding to get rid of Wilson, the committee had not bothered to seek his opinion. It would not be the last time Toone chose to ignore him.

The next sign of trouble came in the autumn of 1919. Wilfred had been approached by Haslingden of the Lancashire League, who offered him an attractive deal and a three-year contract. This was a guarantee of employment Wilfred had never enjoyed before because, incredibly, Yorkshire professionals in those days had no contracts at all. Instead, at the end of each season, the committee reviewed the professionals' performances and, well into the autumn, informed them whether they were being retained, or not. Even great players were only a couple of bad years away from being terminated.

The uncertainty of county cricket when compared to the leagues was such that when Hedley Verity was offered terms by Yorkshire while playing as a pro for Middleton in the Central Lancashire League, his father advised him to stay where he was.

Wilfred was friends with Sydney Barnes, who spent most of his career in the leagues, so he knew the great bowler's view on things. To Barnes the choice between the grind of county cricket and the leagues was really no choice at all. In the leagues the professional was respected rather than treated as a second-class citizen. He, not some public school dimwit, called the shots. The work rate for the league pro was much lower – he played on Saturday afternoons and occasionally on Wednesday evenings – and the money was excellent. When the all-rounder Cec Parkin left Lancashire to play for Rochdale in 1919, he was paid £15 a week, plus a signing-on bonus of £20 and a guaranteed benefit of £100, earning him £420 for the season, plus the cash collections that were gathered from the crowd when a player scored a half-century or took five wickets. Although these came in coppers and sixpences, they often totted up to £20 and over the course of a season a good all-rounder might expect to live off them and bank his pay.

Between 1913 and 1919, the retail price index had doubled. Yorkshire had increased admission prices and membership subscriptions substantially, but the wages of the professionals stayed at pre-war levels. There was even talk at some counties of abolishing winter pay, or playing more amateurs.

Wilfred considered his options. After consulting Sarah – as he did before making any big decision – he signed to play for Haslingden starting in the spring of 1920. The rumours of what was afoot were reported – in suitably shocked tones – in the Yorkshire press. As the *Haslingden Gazette* put it, the story had caused 'a flutter in the Yorkshire dovecote'. Wilfred was called in to a meeting at Headingley with Lord Hawke and Frederick Toone. Shortly afterwards, relieved articles announcing that Wilfred was not leaving Yorkshire after all appeared across the Broad Acres.

The whole affair unsettled Wilfred deeply and for once the great all-rounder lost his cool. Aware that reneging on his deal with Haslingden would create negative publicity in Lancashire, Wilfred wrote two letters on the same day to the influential Manchester-based sports journalist James Catton, the first apparently urging the reporter to put Rhodes' side of the story to the public west of the Pennines and the second asking him to keep quiet about the whole business. Catton later wrote: 'Only once have I ever known [Rhodes] disturbed about an incident in his career. And then, as usual, he refused to talk about the matter.' Leaving Yorkshire had proved harder than Wilfred thought. Had he been a different man you might have suspected sentiment.

What had been offered to persuade Wilfred to stay went unrecorded, but from 1920 Yorkshire dramatically increased the players' pay to £11 for home matches (up from £5) and £15 for away games (up from £8). The threat of league cricket to the county game – Wilfred was not the only Yorkshire player to be tapped up and, had he left, others would likely have followed him – had forced the hand of the administrators. To Toone, it must have looked like Wilfred had used the Haslingden offer to leverage the extra money for himself and his fellow pros.

Everything looked good until the 1920 season got under

way. As soon as this happened, the Yorkshire professionals discovered that other counties had upped their pay rates to the same level. Yorkshire's players had once been the best rewarded in the County Championship. That was no longer the case, yet the side they played for was still the wealthiest and most profitable. To add to the sense of grievance, Toone had also decided that the pay rise would only cover county matches – the annual away fixtures with MCC and Oxford and Cambridge Universities would be paid at the old rate of £8.

It quickly became apparent that Yorkshire were the only one operating in this cheese-paring manner. With Wilfred to the fore, the players made their feelings known to captain Cecil Burton. He wrote to Toone laying out their complaints. Toone responded saying that he would look into the matter. He then let it drop, apparently telling other members of 'his committee' that the trouble had been instigated by Wilfred and that the other players would soon forget about it. Wilfred came to believe he had also discussed the matter with MCC and that it affected his future as an England player.

The evasive response to Burton's letter was, to Wilfred's mind, typical of Toone. The secretary had developed a manner and style of expressing himself that often left Yorkshire cricketers baffled. When a young Bill Bowes was trying to decide whether to accept a playing position with MCC, Toone wrote to him with what might have been an offer of a place at Yorkshire, or might not. After studying Toone's words for a considerable time and becoming ever more infuriated by his inability to understand what they meant, Bowes opted to pledge himself to Lord's. 'As a specimen of evasive letter writing I consider it a masterpiece,' Bowes would note in his autobiography. This was Toone the bureaucrat, a Leeds Sir

Humphrey Appleby, couching utterances in so many evasive clauses and sub-clauses as to render words meaningless.
Eventually Bowes would join Yorkshire and Toone would
award him a county cap, though with such strict provisions
about what that did and didn't mean that Bowes described
them sarcastically as 'quaint'.

Wilfred was a man who valued plain speaking. He liked
Johnny Douglas because he was direct and told people what
he thought and wanted. Toone's coy and evasive language
struck him as deceitful. He was a man who spoke, as they say
in Yorkshire, out the side of his mouth. Or as Wilfred himself
said more than once, 'Toone was not straight.'

A perfect demonstration of Toone's nefariousness came
during the disastrous Ashes tour of 1920-21. Toone was the
tour manager, Johnny Douglas the captain. The appointment of the Essex all-rounder was met with dismay by some
influential figures at Lord's. Not everyone shared Wilfred's
appreciation of Douglas's straightforwardness or his pugnacity. As Sir Derek Birley noted, the England captain had
'aggression and a win-at-all-costs attitude that jarred with
the nobler minds at headquarters'. The fruity Old Etonian Sir
Home Gordon took it a step further, claiming Douglas was
'not only bad, but brutal, almost incredibly ruthless'.

Perhaps taking his lead from these dissenting elements,
Toone attempted to organise a coup after the first couple of
Tests had been lost. He canvassed senior players – including
Jack Hobbs and Frank Woolley – about having Douglas
removed and replaced by Percy Fender. After receiving mur-
mured support for the idea, Toone went to Douglas and asked
him to stand down. The England captain refused point blank
and, since he had once told one of his Essex spinners after a

poor spell, 'If you ever bowl tripe like that again I shall punch you in the head', it was likely a message he delivered with some force. Wisely, Toone dropped the matter.

Significantly Wilfred was not one of the players Toone had consulted about the plan to dump Douglas and only learned of it later from the other pros. Since he was close to Douglas, that makes sense. But there is a little more to it than that. Because also on that tour Abe Waddington would allege that Toone had told him 'Wilfred's finished'. Perhaps as well as ousting the captain, Toone had a mind to get rid of his senior professional as well. Did Toone mean Wilfred was finished with England or finished as a cricketer more generally? It seems it may have been the latter, but he was taking it one step at a time.

Back in England, the arrival of the Australians caused more trouble. Wilfred was called up to play in the first Test. The tourists proved that their winter triumph was not simply down to mastery of local conditions by swiping England aside, bowling them out for 112 and 147, to win by 10 wickets. Wilfred scored 19 and 10 and took two for 33, which was hardly the worst performance in the team, yet he was summarily dropped for the rest of the summer. Indeed, he would not play for England again until 1926. Some believed the dropping of the ageing Wilfred was justified against the ferocious Australian pace attack. Yet earlier in the season for Yorkshire, he'd made 63 runs and taken five for 87 against the same opponents.

While Wilfred had no evidence, he saw the behind-the-scenes influence of Toone in the decision. 'Wilfred's finished!' He proved what rubbish that was by using his time during the second Test at Lord's to pile up 267 not out against

Leicestershire at Headingley. It was the highest score of his career. He batted for five hours and hit 30 boundaries. That he was 43 years old was a mark of his enduring stamina and remarkable levels of concentration. Little wonder that the *Huddersfield Examiner* would later comment that Rhodes had 'a considerable streak of radium in his combination' and hint at some secret elixir that maintained his youth (presumably not Guy's Tonic).

Adding to Wilfred's rankling ill feeling was the benefit situation. Frederick Toone had taken control of administering the retained two-thirds of the benefit fund that was supposed to secure a player's future. It was Toone who loaned what was effectively her own money to the widowed Lillian Haigh.

She was not the only one to suffer at his hands. Toone took a high-handed attitude to requests for financial help from old professionals. When Bates, the Kirkheaton batsman, wrote asking the finance committee to advance him £56 of his benefit money to settle debts, Toone turned him down simply because he didn't like the tone of the letter. If Bates wanted aid, he wrote, he should learn some manners. Others received similar treatment.

You didn't need to be a Leninist to see the injustice in it, especially when you looked at how Toone himself was rewarded by the club. By 1920, he was being paid an annual salary of £600. That same year, the club gave him a new car valued at £400. A testimonial raised £3,500 for him shortly afterwards (when Wostinholm retired he'd been given a cheque for £200). Did the club retain two-thirds of it? Of course not. When Toone fell terminally ill in 1930, Yorkshire covered his medical expenses and the cost of his funeral. Yet a few months later, when Roy Kilner's widow asked Yorkshire for money from her husband's benefit fund to cover the cost of the education of her second child, she was turned down flat.

Wilfred's anger smouldered like an autumn bonfire. When Toone was knighted in 1927 and returned to Headingley to celebrate with champagne in the pavilion, George Herbert suggested to Wilfred they might call in and congratulate him. Wilfred refused. 'No,' he replied. 'I don't like him and if I wished him well I'd be telling a lie. So I'm saying nowt.'

Things would reach another crisis in 1927 when Major Lupton's resignation as Yorkshire captain precipitated one of those uncivil wars for which Yorkshire would later become so infamous.

The whole affair began in predictably furtive and Machiavellian fashion when Toone called Wilfred into his office shortly before the start of the season. He told Wilfred that he was concerned about the strains cricket was placing on him. He was now in his late forties, still a frontline bowler and a pillar of the middle order, but it was surely time for him to take things a little more easily. This could be achieved, Toone suggested, by Wilfred resigning from the role of senior professional. Free of this burdensome responsibility, Wilfred would be able simply to focus on his game again. He asked Wilfred to write a letter to the Yorkshire committee to that effect – he could do it right now at this very desk if he liked.

Wilfred considered. He replied that he would need to discuss the matter with his wife first. Sarah Rhodes had bobbed hair and circular glasses that gave her an owlish look. The *Leeds Mercury* described her as 'a typical Yorkshirewoman of charming disposition'. Wilfred admired her sound practical sense and thriftiness. She was very good with money and he'd later comment ruefully that he wished he'd let her look after his business affairs as she'd have done a far better job of it than he had. When he laid out the facts to the shrewd Sarah, who had followed the goings on at Yorkshire for 30-odd years, she immediately suspected something shifty. Heeding her advice to keep an eye out, Wilfred wrote to Toone and told him that he would not be resigning. He owed Yorkshire everything, he said. To step down for the benefit of his own game would be contrary to everything he believed in. The team came first, as it always had and always must. While there's little doubt that this sincerely reflected Wilfred's beliefs, there was undoubtedly an edge of cunning in it, too.

It seems likely that Toone, bolstered by Lord Hawke, had been trying to clear the path for the future captain they had in mind: Herbert Sutcliffe. Like Wilfred, Sutcliffe was a working-class professional, but he looked and carried himself like a gentleman, his hair so famously suave and immaculate it looked like it was applied with a paint brush. During the First World War, Sutcliffe had been commissioned into the Green Howards as a second lieutenant. As an Army reservist, he'd rise to the rank of major. He was smart and intelligent and had invested his pay from Yorkshire so cleverly – initially in a sports shop – he could afford to drive to matches in his own car.

Sutcliffe was his own man. In a world in which the professionals addressed the amateurs – even those half their age – as 'sir' or 'mister' – Sutcliffe called them by their first names. He was self-confident, courageous and had an unshakeable sense of decency. He was also one of the world's greatest batsmen. No wonder the younger Yorkshire professionals thought the world of him. 'He was our representative all the time and never let us down,' Bill Bowes said.

There were two giant obstacles standing in the way of Sutcliffe's appointment. One was the obsession with amateur captaincy. The other was Wilfred Rhodes. This was where the letter Toone had asked him to write came in. Because if Wilfred had admitted to finding the role of senior professional too onerous, he could hardly have then kicked up a fuss about being passed over for the captaincy.

Despite the fact that Wilfred had dodged Toone's trap, in November 1927 the Yorkshire committee voted to appoint Sutcliffe as Yorkshire captain for the 1928 season. When he received the news, Sutcliffe was on a ship bound for South Africa with the MCC touring party. He told the Press Association that this was the greatest honour of his career and that he would attempt to emulate 'the greatest of all Yorkshire captains, Lord Hawke'.

Sutcliffe's standing among his fellow Yorkshire professionals was so good that, even though Wilfred and Percy Holmes were senior to him, the players supported the appointment. In other parts of Yorkshire, the news was not so warmly welcomed.

Charles Crane, president of Yorkshire supporters' group, the Craven Gentlemen, spoke for many when he talked of the potential jealousy within the dressing room the appointment of Sutcliffe might create. Inevitably eyes swivelled towards Huddersfield. Wilfred told the press that he had not been consulted about the appointment. The first he knew of it was when he read about it in the newspapers, he said. The decision had been taken over his head. Some newspapers reported that Wilfred had told the Yorkshire committee he was planning to retire and did not want the captaincy. This, he said, was untrue. 'I have not announced my retirement from cricket and that could not have been the reason the captaincy was not offered to me.' Whatever he thought of Sutcliffe, Wilfred's pride had been pricked and he doubtless saw the hand of Toone in the way the newspapers jumped on the idea of him retiring. 'Wilfred's finished.' Not yet he wasn't.

Speaking to the press Wilfred speculated on the wisdom of the decision and concluded with a slight note of self-pity. 'One cannot help thinking that after playing so long the committee would have given me first refusal of the captaincy. It almost looks as if my services are not appreciated.' When asked if he'd be prepared to serve under Sutcliffe he was non-committal, commenting that he had only a few seasons of his career remaining.

Across Yorkshire people chipped in with support either for Rhodes or Sutcliffe, or for the amateur ideal. In December, a Yorkshire supporter named Sid Grimshaw polled 7,000 members for their opinion on whether Sutcliffe or Rhodes should be captain 'if it is not possible to secure a suitable amateur'. Close to 3,000 responded. More than 2,000 preferred an amateur captain to a professional, and twice as many voters thought Rhodes a better choice than Sutcliffe.

When the results of Grimshaw's intervention were published, the Yorkshire committee panicked. They telegrammed Sutcliffe in South Africa and asked him if he might – in light of the upheavals – withdraw his acceptance of the captaincy. Backed into a corner, Sutcliffe agreed. Lord Hawke congratulated the player on his loyalty and swiftly set about finding a suitable gentleman for the job.

After all the back-stabbing, the furore in high places and the discord in the dressing room, Yorkshire ended up back where they had started. In place of Sutcliffe or Rhodes, they appointed Captain William Worsley from Hovingham Hall. In terms of his cricketing skills, Worsley was an improvement on Lupton. He'd hit a half-century against Hampshire and finished with a first-class average of 15.69. Wilfred remained as senior professional. When another Lancashire League club came offering him a fortune to cross the Pennines in 1928, he turned them down flat. He was staying at Yorkshire. He'd still be there when Frederick Toone died. For all his vaunted skills as a schemer and diplomat, Yorkshire's fascist secretary had failed either to outwit Wilfred or outlast him.

CHAPTER TWELVE

The Birth of Grim

Yorkshire's transformation from the jolly, smiling, popular team of George Herbert, Schof, Hunter, Denton, Brown, Tunnicliffe and the ruddy-cheeked Wilfred into the dour, surly face-like-a-bulldog-licking-piss-off-a-nettle brood that would dominate public perception for most of the modern era arguably began in 1921. It was the year Schof died, George Herbert retired from first-class cricket, Wilfred adopted the two-eyed batting stance and Cecil Burton stepped down as Yorkshire captain to be replaced by the ineffectual Geoffrey Wilson.

George Herbert spent the summer coaching at Eton and returned in August to play in the Scarborough Festival, his bank balance swelled by £700 raised by Yorkshire in testimonials for him. His final hurrah came in the last match of the Scarborough Festival for the Players against the Gentlemen. George Herbert was made captain of the professionals. It wasn't his finest match, but he struck a belligerent 37 in the second innings and took the last two wickets when the Gentlemen batted last to secure his team a 198-run victory.

Afterwards, a vast crowd surrounded the pavilion calling for George Herbert. He came out and delivered a speech of moving simplicity. 'I thank you for your kindness to me. A person always knows his limitations and I'm not such a good man as you make me out to be.' Cricket, George Herbert said, was the best game of all. 'What can you have better than a nice green field, with the wickets set up, and to go out and do your best for your side? I leave first-class cricket to those who have got to come. I hope they'll have the pleasure in it that I have had.' There was no wonder everybody loved him.

All great sportspeople have apocryphal stories attached to them, tales that come with vague attributions and which, even if they are entirely fictitious, contain the kernel of a wider truth: George Best's high living, Fred Trueman's rudeness. Those that were appended to George Herbert attest entirely to his kindness and decency. There is the small boy who writes to him for an autograph and receives by return of post two autographs with a note advising that one is to keep and the other 'for swaps'. There is the army bandsman from Yorkshire whom George Herbert locates in the bustling crowd at Lord's after an impassioned plea from the soldier's father: 'His regiment have been ordered to depart for active service unexpectedly. Please find him for me, Mr Hirst, or they'll mark my lad as a deserter!'

There are many more on similar lines. Most have the whiff of fiction and the strength of true feeling, for this is how people regarded George Herbert Hirst. He was both a muscular hero and everyone's favourite uncle; Hercules and Eric Morecambe combined. There is perhaps only one sporting figure from more recent times who has attracted as much public goodwill as George Herbert did during his long career – the racehorse Red Rum.

The season had not been a great one for Yorkshire, who finished third in the Championship. It had been an even worse one for England, who had been roundly thrashed by Warwick Armstrong's Australia. The selectors ran through 30 players in an attempt not so much to beat them as to slow down the speed of their victories. The final two Tests were drawn, largely, or so it seemed, because Australia had lost interest – an attitude graphically demonstrated by their skipper in the final Test at The Oval, where he spent several minutes when he was fielding in the deep leaning on a fence and reading a newspaper.

Wilfred played in the first Test at Nottingham. Rain fell on a hard Trent Bridge wicket, creating conditions the fearsome pace duo of Gregory and McDonald would have paid to bowl in. The ball spat and kicked dangerously. Wilfred batted stoutly and courageously in the first innings, making 19, despite being hit on the head by McDonald and gloving Gregory over the heads of the slip cordon. England were hopelessly overmatched and lost by 10 wickets. Wilfred was dropped. He did not imagine he would play Test cricket again, lamenting that 'I had ended my Test career with a sound thrashing'.

To combat the pace of Gregory and McDonald, Wilfred had adopted a two-eyed stance that saw him facing down the pitch. It gave him an awkward and crab-like appearance and severely limited the shots he could play on the off-side. As a batsman, Wilfred had always been more craftsman than artist; now he appeared to some to have transformed himself into a day labourer.

Wilfred's new position – his feet pointing at the bowler, his waist twisted and left shoulder pointing towards mid-on – was not particularly successful against the raw speed of the Aussie duo, but he persisted with it. He felt it stopped him edging into the slips and made it easier to use his pads against the increasing number of bowlers who attacked from outside leg stump. Other batsmen began to modify their own stances. It seemed to the Yorkshireman's critics that the master of calculation was creating a fashion for pragmatic ugliness. They wondered if the cover drive might go the way of the passenger pigeon. Asked how he would play a cut shot from his new cramped position, Wilfred replied grumpily, 'The cut isn't a business stroke.' The aesthetes rolled their eyes and tutted.

When it came to batting, Wilfred was methodical. He minimised risk. He came to the crease like a bookkeeper, neat and precise. His runs were accrued through prudence. It was not a scene anyone would spend their money to watch, but it was effective, and to Wilfred that was all that mattered.

The new stance seemed to mark another stage in the great all-rounder's trajectory towards the utilitarian ideal. He had begun by bowling the sort of classical, slow, looping deliveries that brought joy to purists, only to become a spinner who pushed them through fast and flat. Now he had taken another step towards trimming all romantic frills out of his game. To the southern gentlemen he appeared the very epitome of the northern roundhead.

Yorkshire's new captain Geoffrey Wilson had captained Harrow before the war, served in the Royal Marines and played for Cambridge University in 1920 and 1921. He'd scored a century for Yorkshire Seconds in 1921, but otherwise seemed ill-equipped for the role. He was a smart, decent gentleman who struggled to maintain discipline rather after the manner of his namesake Sergeant Wilson from *Dad's*

Army. Wilfred was irritated by his skipper's inability to close the gap between his bat and front pad that led to him being clean bowled by in-swinger after in-swinger. It spoke to the great all-rounder of a lack of application, of a man who did not take things seriously.

Whatever the criticism of his style and methods, Wilfred had a fine season in 1922. He finished top of the first-class bowling averages and averaged nearly 40 with the bat. Only Herbert Sutcliffe headed him for Yorkshire.

Wilfred was now batting at five or six. He made four centuries. They were workmanlike affairs. Rhodes's conservative approach to batting often drew complaints from the paying customers at away grounds, but he didn't feel obligated to provide entertainment. If folk wanted that, they could go to a circus. His bowling was similarly efficient and unfussy. He took four wickets for six runs with this approach against Northamptonshire and five for 12 when Yorkshire met Warwickshire.

By now, Wilfred was part of a formidable attack built around the brooding, belligerent Waddington supported by Emmott Robinson and George Macaulay. Robinson and Macaulay were both no more than medium pace.

Macaulay, who would end up a place below Schof on the list of wicket-takers for Yorkshire, was the son of a wealthy Thirsk publican and had been educated at Barnard Castle School. He had a cherubic face and the manner of a James Cagney gangster. Pelham Warner wrote that Macaulay was too 'apt to become depressed or upset when things go wrong', which was a polite way of putting it.

Robinson's character is hard to discern, because nearly everything we know of him comes from the pen of Neville

Cardus ('I reckon Mr Cardus invented me,' Robinson would comment glumly). The great cricket writer of the *Manchester Guardian* loved Robinson and turned him into a figure of both wisdom and comedy, a dishevelled, bandy-legged cricketing sage. It was an entertaining and much-loved portrait and there was a good deal of truth in it. However, there was also a sharper edge to the scruffy little all-rounder.

Robinson had not begun playing for Yorkshire full-time until 1919, when he was 35 years old. He had honed his cricketing skills in the Lancashire League, playing pro for Ramsbottom. In the Lancashire League bitter local rivalries were fought out on the field (and often more literally in the stands). Unfettered by the Corinthian ideals imposed from Lord's, matches here were short, intense and sometimes nasty. When the great West Indian Learie Constantine first played for Nelson in the Lancashire League in 1929 the players of Rawtenstall tried to unsettle him when he came out to bat with an orchestrated barrage of racial abuse. When Nelson fielded, Constantine, not unreasonably we might judge, retaliated by sending down a barrage of bouncers so ferocious the umpires feared someone might be killed. This was the hard school in which Emmott Robinson had learned his cricket and he brought some of its sharpness with him. Robinson and Macaulay bowled military medium pace and Waddington was not much quicker. Since they could not intimidate batsmen with bounce or speed, they did it by shrieked appeals, glowering and insults. They burned with fury and bowled so aggressively that if either of them had been as quick as Ted McDonald they'd likely have killed someone.

With this attacking trio, the spin of Wilfred and Roy Kilner, the batting of Holmes, Sutcliffe and the obdurate

Edgar Oldroyd, Yorkshire won the Championship easily. They gained few friends, however. The cricket they played was too aggressive, and their refusal to lose to anyone, which when George Herbert had been playing was characterised by a kind of doughty glee, was now more negative.

Robinson, who had emerged as Wilfred's main lieutenant, was a cautious cricketer. Like his new best pal he was a studious, almost obsessive, observer of the game, keeping a notebook in which he jotted details of opponents and pitches. Robinson seemed paralysed by the fear of losing and was always the man to voice an objection when a declaration was proposed by the skipper. Wilfred shared his circumspect approach and, as senior professional, he set the tone. George Herbert did not like to lose either, of course, but if he had to get beaten, he would go down in a blaze of glory. The new Yorkshire preferred instead to grind their way tediously to a draw.

Yorkshire's new attitude was epitomised by that season's Roses match at Old Trafford, which ended like one of those drunken pub fights where the adversaries end up wrestling futilely on the floor while the barman mops around them. Yorkshire were set 132 to win. Wickets fell quickly. Wilfred came in at five. Runs came in drips. Another batsman was out, then another.

The sky began to darken. Yorkshire's captain, Geoffrey Wilson, was laid up in a hospital bed having been struck down by appendicitis on the opening day. Yorkshire were a man short. Rockley Wilson coming in at 10 was Yorkshire's final batsman. Six runs were needed for victory and six overs left to bowl. In the first five of them, Wilfred and Wilson scored just three runs. Wilfred played the final over with grim circumspection, patting every delivery away. The last ball came. Spectators craned forward. Surely now the great all-rounder would try to crash a boundary and win the match? The ball pitched outside off stump and broke slightly away. Wilfred ignored it completely, shouldered his bat and walked off the field. Later it would emerge that during the final hour the players' behaviour had become so foul-tempered the umpires had had to intervene.

Kilner would later say of the Roses match that the Yorkshire team shook hands with the Lancashire players before the start of play and didn't speak to them again for three days. 'It's fair cheating and no umpires you want for that match,' he'd say.

It seems Kilner and his team-mates had gradually begun to extend this glowering attitude to other key fixtures in the calendar, too. The Lancashire players understood and gave as good as they got, but those at other counties were not so empathetic. Yorkshire's new abrasiveness rubbed a lot of people up the wrong way. There was muttering in the pavilions of the south about gamesmanship and time-wasting. It was said that Macaulay, for one, was a ball-tamperer who deliberately scuffed up the wicket in his follow through.

Aside from the Roses match, Yorkshire's other great grudge fixture was against Middlesex. Partly it was a North v South, Roundheads v Cavaliers thing, the inter-war cricketing equivalent of Leeds United against Chelsea in the 1970s, though its origins lay in what many had come to see as Yorkshire's growing arrogance and sense of entitlement.

In 1920 at Bradford, Yorkshire had needed four runs to beat Middlesex with their last pair of Rockley Wilson and Abe Waddington at the wicket. Greville Stevens bowled a half-volley. Waddington drove it powerfully for what might have been the winning hit. But the drive was too straight, it zipped past the bowler and straight into the stumps at the non-striker's end. No run. A couple of balls later, Waddington misjudged a Stevens leg-break and was bowled. He left the field fuming at the southerners' good luck and his own misfortune. A festering sense of grievance attached itself to the incident as if Waddington's drive into the stumps was somehow representative of wider social injustice, a sign from providence that the posh boys from London were blessed with advantages. Combined with the fact that an element among Yorkshire's team and its supporters had, in the words of the club's official historian Derek Hodgson, 'a growing conviction . . . that success was an inherent right and failure a blasphemy against God and nature', this proved an unhappy mix. Yorkshire talked of playing hard and tough, but when they lost were often overcome by diva-ish petulance.

Captain Wilson seemed aware of the problems, but was powerless to do anything to stop them. He sounded increasingly like a student RE teacher confronted by an unruly class of 15 year olds. 'I feel personally that any match, however serious it might be, and however much may depend upon the result, should be played in the most friendly spirit. The result should be second in importance.' As to the dullness of his team's batting, 'Our county batsmen have been subject to various criticisms owing to slow play, and I feel bound to agree that at times such criticisms have been merited.'

His appeal to his team's better natures having evidently failed, Wilson seems more or less to have given up. If their own captain found some of his players hard to like, it is unsurprising that others outside the county found it even more difficult. When George Herbert was playing, Yorkshire had been popular wherever they went (well, maybe in Manchester not so much). Now they rapidly became the most reviled club in the Championship.

The players were one element of it, another was the crowd at Bramall Lane. Sheffield was notorious for its vocal supporters who were well informed but opinionated, and fervent in their support for their team.

In late May of 1924, Yorkshire arrived at Lord's to do battle with their main rivals Middlesex in poor shape. Robbed of several first choices, they handed debuts to three men – Spencer Allen, Frank Turner and Harry Taylor – who would play just 15 games for the county between them, and brought in John Drake for his third and, as it turned out, final appearance.

Wilson won the toss and elected to bat. The pitch was hard and flat as a billiard table. But Yorkshire batted carelessly and were all out for 192. Middlesex showed how it should be done, piling up 465. Frank Mann, the captain, was particularly dazzling, clubbing Wilfred for four sixes in an over, including two that smashed into the shingles on the pavilion roof. Schof would likely have guffawed with laughter, and teased Wilfred about it afterwards, but the new Yorkshire did not go in for self-mockery. They scowled at Mann like wise guys who had just seen their don disrespected. Things got worse when Middlesex declared. Yorkshire needed to bat for more than a day to save the match. Instead, they swished about like farmhands clearing nettles and were bowled out for 121 to lose by an innings. It was the team's first defeat in over a year. They took it very badly indeed.

Things got worse. For the Roses match at Headingley, Wilson was absent and Wilfred was made captain. It was a disaster. Yorkshire bowled well enough, dismissing

Lancashire for 113 and 74. The home side batted last needing just 57 to win on the final day. Rain fell overnight. A wicket that had been tricky from the start now turned evil. Dick Tyldesley and Cec Parkin skittled Yorkshire out for 33, with only Kilner, who made 13 not out, offering any resistance. The pitch was a mudslide, the bowling excellent, but even so, Wilfred could offer no excuse for the performance. It was the most shameful moment of his career and he still grimaced at the mention of it decades later. Yorkshire for once seemed to panic. Last man Dolphin danced down the wicket and was stumped. He might have received a withering recrimination from his captain, but Wilfred himself had been out in mortifying fashion – slashing at a ball outside off stump and edging straight to Harry Makepeace in the slips. In all his time with Yorkshire they'd only been bowled out for one lower total – by Surrey in 1909.

After such humiliations it was little surprise that when Yorkshire met Middlesex at Bramall Lane in the return match they were bristling for revenge against the visitors and the world at large. This time the full team were available and the pitch was damp as a Saturday night bar towel. Wilson won the toss and took Wilfred with him to inspect the wicket. He opted to bowl first. It proved a mistake. The sun hid behind clouds, the pitch dried slowly and gave no help to the bowlers. Later Wilson would comment of his period in charge of Yorkshire, 'One of the chief difficulties is to make a decision that is considered the correct one in the opinion of the majority of the team, not only in the judgement of one's "chief adviser".' His chief adviser was Wilfred. Perhaps this was one of the moments he had in mind.

As the captain's mistake became apparent, things got out of

hand. Inevitably Waddington was involved. The left-armer was not quite the force he had once been. The previous season against Leicestershire at Huddersfield he'd slipped, dislocating the shoulder of his bowling arm. He never fully recovered. Struggling for form he'd become increasingly irascible, burning with such rage it was a wonder his hair didn't catch light.

Waddington was bowling to his nemesis, Greville Stevens, when he had an lbw appeal turned down by umpire Harry Butt, a former England wicketkeeper. The crowd went into such an uproar over it that play had to be suspended. When the noise had died down, Waddington promptly had a plainly distracted Stevens caught. Horace Dales was lbw to the first ball of the next over, bowled by Roy Kilner, before Waddington struck again taking the wicket of 'Young Jack' Hearne, who swung at the ball with a suicidal air. Later, it was alleged that Waddington had tripped Hearne while he was running between the wickets and then stood on his hand. Patsy Hendren and Clarence Bruce brought things back under control calmly, adding 174. Waddington did not take any more wickets. Macaulay, too, was thwarted and yelled 'Owzat!' so often the umpire Bill Reeves, who'd had a long career with Essex, would comment that he made as many appeals as Dr Barnardo. Robinson also let his feelings known. The crowd were just as vociferous, bellowing and howling incessantly.

Middlesex were eventually all out for 358. Looking on, the *Yorkshire Post*'s great cricket correspondent J. M. Kilburn shook his head sadly. It was, he said, 'A sorry exhibition of ill-feeling and bad manners.' Some of the spectators took a different view. One gentleman who had attended all three days wrote to the *Sheffield Daily Telegraph* contending that the trouble was all the fault of the officials. 'Some of the decisions were so unsatisfactory to my mind that both players and spectators could be excused for getting excited and annoyed.'

The second day was watched by 11,000 spectators. Yorkshire battled to establish a first-innings lead. They made a decent start but when Robinson, Macaulay and Waddington were all given out lbw in quick succession, the crowd were outraged and the umpires were subject to a raging torrent of abuse. *The Times* thought the crowd's behaviour made 'the task of umpiring almost unbearable' and the *Yorkshire Post* agreed. The *Sheffield Daily Telegraph* noted that many of the supporters bawling that the lbw decisions were wrong sat in parts of the ground which made any such judgement impossible. Arthur Dolphin and Maurice Leyland, batting with the slow caution of men walking through a dark tunnel behind enemy lines, took Yorkshire through to the finish. They were nine down and still 24 runs behind. On the final day, with the pitch getting ever more benign, the match fizzled out.

Off the field, it was a different story. As soon as stumps were drawn, the umpires lodged a complaint to MCC about Waddington's belligerence and the way he had incited the crowd against them. The Yorkshire committee interviewed Wilson and Waddington about the matter. Evidently unwilling to take unilateral action, they invited MCC to conduct a full inquiry and listen to all sides. Before MCC could respond, Middlesex announced that they would not play Yorkshire in the 1925 season – a match that had already been announced as Roy Kilner's benefit.

The fall-out continued. Although he was arguably the best medium-pacer in the country, Macaulay was left out of the team to tour Australia. Plum Warner remarked more pointedly now on the bowler's 'lack of self-control' and Lord Hawke also spoke out: 'It is a pity [Macaulay] is not with the team in Australia. It is – and I am bound to say it – entirely his own fault ... Still I am hoping that with experience his temperament will improve and that the distinction to which his performance has entitled him, will in due course come to him.' His Lordship made it sound like Macaulay was a teenager. In fact he was 27 years old and appeared as likely to mellow with age as a Tasmanian devil, something that was confirmed in 1933 when, at The Oval, he was involved in an incident that made even the saintly Jack Hobbs lose his temper.

Macaulay would play for Yorkshire until 1934 before finishing his career in the Lancashire League. He'd die on active service with the RAF during the Second World War. Waddington, meanwhile, would retire in 1927 as a result of the shoulder injury. Controversy would continue to dog him. He'd end up in court for everything from drunk driving to assaulting a policeman. Charmless and splenetic, Waddington made Bobby Peel look like Cliff Richard. It was easy to blame Wilson and the senior pros for Yorkshire's surly arrogance, but the lack of leadership higher up also contributed. When he was captain, Hawke had hoofed out Peate and Peel. Now as club president he sat on his hands while Waddington and Macaulay did 10 times more damage to Yorkshire's reputation than the two Victorian spinners had ever done.

Writing in the 1925 edition of *Wisden*, the editor, Sydney Pardon, noted that the scenes in Sheffield had 'disturbed the usual cheery atmosphere of our cricket'. He added, 'The trouble in Yorkshire cricket seems to be confined to a minority of players – from what I have been told not more than four.' Macaulay and Waddington were surely two of them, so who were the others? Ruling out Leyland, who was a universally popular joker after the style of Schof (late in his career he'd miss a Test match in the West Indies with a back injury sustained when one of his punchlines had so entertained a listening sailor, he'd clapped the batsman on the shoulder and knocked him off his chair), Holmes and Sutcliffe – both diligent and well-mannered – leaves us with a handful of candidates of whom the most likely are Robinson and Rhodes. While it seems unlikely the laconic and insular Wilfred was involved directly in any of the various spats, his failure to intervene may have been taken by some as tacit approval of what was happening.

The other question is, who was the source of Pardon's information? No doubt, if you were Wilfred, you'd have pictured Frederick Toone whispering behind his hand in the Lord's Long Room.

Whether he was one of Pardon's evil foursome or not, as senior professional and – on the field at least – one of the most powerful figures at the club, Wilfred was clearly implicated in the trouble. Wilfred, as Neville Cardus noted, was 'not a man given to affability'. An introvert, he had been jollied into sociability by George Herbert and Schof, but in their absence settled into an enveloping quietness that became increasingly brooding and dyspeptic. Perhaps he couldn't have stopped Waddington and Macaulay's surly displays of dissent even if he'd wanted to – he was no natural leader, after all. And maybe a little bit of him enjoyed the fuss it created behind the scenes and the trouble it stirred for the smooth *éminence grise* of Headingley.

Eventually, Yorkshire announced they would take action to stop the unruly behaviour of the crowd at Sheffield and issued a warning to Waddington, who wrote a short letter of apology for his behaviour to MCC. It was enough. Middlesex reversed their decision over the 1925 season and matches between the two counties would be played in future in a more muted atmosphere. The damage to Yorkshire's reputation had been done, however.

Reviewing the situation in *Wisden*, Pardon commented, 'For all these difficulties arising from ill-temper and lack of discipline there is one unfailing remedy – the assertion of the authority of the captain.' Lord Hawke seemed to agree. The ineffective Wilson stepped down. His replacement was a 46-year-old former Army major, Arthur William Lupton. Lupton had played one match for Yorkshire back in 1908 and was even less of a cricketer than the men who'd preceded him. He did not bowl and batted number 10. He left cricket matters to Wilfred and Robinson. His job was not to make runs or set fields, but to try to discipline the wilder elements of the side. Even carrying the deadweight of the skipper, Yorkshire were still far too powerful for the rest of the counties and won their fourth successive title in 1925. Lupton played in 32 matches and contributed 186 runs and eight catches. Little wonder that Maurice Leyland would remark to John Arlott, 'I don't count the captain in the Yorkshire side, we do it with ten.'

Yorkshire finished second the following year and third in 1927. Lupton seems to have been popular with the hard-bitten pros, but has gone down in history as a comedy figure – the epitome of the hapless amateur stooge. Various tales, mostly apocryphal and many emanating from Neville Cardus, show the major being amusingly patronised by Wilfred. In one story, Lupton is batting with Arthur Dolphin.

He hits the ball and begins to run only to hear the bell in the pavilion sounding. 'No need to bother, Major,' Dolphin tells him, 'Wilfred has declared.' In another tale, a series of furious foul-mouthed outbursts from Macaulay leads to the intervention of the umpires. Asked later why Major Lupton did not intervene, one Yorkshire player replies, 'How could he? Wilfred had sent him down to third man to spare his embarrassment.' Whether the stories were true or not, they illustrated a point. By now Wilfred ran things on the field. He stood where he wanted and, so his fellow spinners noted bitterly, kept himself in reserve until the pitch started turning, at which point he'd seize the ball and refuse to relinquish it whether he was taking wickets or not.

Under Lupton, discipline returned, though complaints about Yorkshire's negative play continued. Wilfred blamed his side's cautious approach on the improved pitches that had resulted from the introduction of heavier mechanised rollers and the practice of top-dressing wickets with marl. Since bowlers could no longer exploit the wicket so easily, he noted, more and more of them had opted to bowl in-swing ('Swerve bowling is easier to master than spin,' Wilfred observed flatly). Before the First World War, the main point of attack had been the area on or outside off stump. The bowling had been full length. Batsmen were deliberately tempted to drive, so they would edge to the slips or hole out in the deep. The results had been exciting, attacking cricket.

After the war, thwarted by the easy-paced strips, bowlers began to focus on leg stump, the ball swinging in towards it. They bowled shorter to prevent the drive, packed the leg-side field and tried to tuck batsmen up. The mindset of the players changed as a result. They stopped attacking. Cricket became a battle of attrition. It was no longer about winning, but about not losing. Wilfred did not endorse this approach, but he didn't repudiate it either. He was not a romantic, he was a professional. He did what needed to be done as circumstance dictated. When the crowd jeered him for slow scoring, or opposing amateur captains complained that Yorkshire were too fixated on avoiding defeat, Wilfred ignored them. Cricket wasn't for fun.

As for Yorkshire's gamesmanship, he remained unrepentant. 'We were accused of being too keen and there was all sorts of criticism of us,' he'd recall after he retired, 'but it mattered little. We were keen to win; what would be the use of playing the game if you were not?' It was an answer that dodged the issues in a manner that would have drawn an approving nod from Frederick Toone.

CHAPTER THIRTEEN

The Fading of the Light

Amid the controversy on the field and the back-stabbing off it, Wilfred continued to play outstanding cricket. In 1922 he took nine for 59 in the match against Warwickshire, scored a century and took seven for 86 in the match against Essex at Harrogate, and six for 43 in Sussex's first knock at Hull, a match Yorkshire won by an innings despite being bowled out for 125. In the return match at Hove, he took six for 13 in six overs in the second innings to help his side to victory by 92 runs.

In 1923, he drew level with George Herbert by completing the double for the 14th time. Against Essex at his happy hunting ground of Leyton, he took five for eight in 41 deliveries; against Nottinghamshire at Trent Bridge six for 23. Despite flurries of snow blowing in off the hills, he hit a century and took five for 29 against Middlesex at Bradford, made 88 and took eight wickets against Sussex at Headingley, and made a fifty and took eight more wickets against Glamorgan at Sheffield. Yet his most startling bowling came in Bristol, where he took the last four Gloucestershire wickets in four overs for one run. The home side's young batsmen were so mesmerised by his wizardry they staggered dizzily back to the pavilion. Wilfred's 120 wickets in the County Championship at 11.27 placed him at the top of the averages. He was as accurate as ever and so hard to score from he was like a mute button to batting.

Wilfred, however, was not impressed. Applying his usual unemotional logic, he told people his status simply showed how poor the bowling in England had become and how shoddy the batsmanship. His view was shared by another veteran pro, Fred Root of Derbyshire, the master of in-swinging leg-theory, who claimed there were players in the England team in the 1920s who'd have struggled to get in the starting XI of even the weakest county before the war.

Wilfred ploughed on regardless. The following season, he passed George Herbert by taking his 15th double. His best all-round performance of 1924 came against Somerset at Weston-super-Mare, where he scored a hundred and took nine for 77 in the match.

In 1925, Yorkshire won the title for the fourth consecutive time, though Wilfred rated them less highly than the team of the early 1900s. Nobody in the side was as good as George Herbert and the opposition were weaker. In a hot summer, he contributed manfully with the bat, hitting two centuries and nine fifties in the Championship to finish the season with the best first-class batting average in England of his lengthy career. It compensated for a poor season with the ball, the worst he'd had since the days when he was opening the batting.

Wilfred did the double for the final time in 1926 and

topped the English bowling averages for the fifth time since the war. He scored 132 against Essex and took 14 Somerset wickets for just 77 runs. Wilfred's performances created an interesting problem for the England selectors, not least because he was now one of them. He'd been added to the selection panel along with Jack Hobbs at the start of the summer to pick the side to face Australia.

The tourists lacked the firepower of the early '20s, but it was still a strong side with an attack built around the brilliance of wrist-spinners Clarrie Grimmett and Arthur Mailey, and the batting resting on the solid foundations of Warren Bardsley and Bill Woodfull, and the dazzling brilliance of Charlie Macartney.

The weather was poor that summer and rain clouds seemed to stalk the visitors around the country. The first Test at Trent Bridge saw the players on the field for less than an hour. The second at Lord's was played in a rare burst of sunshine. The batsmen took full advantage and more than 1,000 runs were scored for 17 wickets lost. England easily salvaged a draw despite following on at Headingley and at Old Trafford the weather closed in and only one innings was completed.

Sitting on the selection panel, even with England undefeated, was no picnic. According to Leveson Gower, the selection committee received dozens of anonymous poison-pen letters from angry supporters of various counties who felt their favourites were being ignorantly and purposefully ignored. He had been receiving them at a rate of one per day. Wilfred Rhodes, he reported, first looked to see if any letter he received was signed and if it was not threw it immediately into the fire. Shrimp concluded this was the only tactic to adopt if a man wanted to retain his sanity.

One of the players some of the letter writers felt was being wrongly ignored was a veteran all-rounder from Yorkshire. Wilfred's form with the ball certainly merited a recall. Before he travelled down to London for the final selection panel meeting of the summer, he stayed in Leicester with his wife, Sarah, and daughter, Muriel. The newspapers were full of speculation about Wilfred 'picking himself' for the Oval Test.

Sarah and Muriel both knew that Wilfred would not put himself forward, but what would he do, they asked, if the other members of the committee offered him a place in the team. Wilfred didn't hesitate. He would turn them down, he said. His wife and daughter were horrified. They insisted that if he was picked he must play. Having received his orders, Wilfred travelled to Lord's. Sure enough, he was picked to play and – though he kicked himself for doing it – followed the advice of the two women in his life and agreed.

As he drove away from London, he bitterly regretted saying 'Yes'. Every mile he travelled along the Great North Road brought greater conviction that this return would prove an even bigger humiliation than his last appearance at Trent Bridge. He was nearly 49. What had he been thinking of when he agreed?

He travelled down to The Oval with a sense of dread. He was fearful of letting his team-mates down. He had more than 50 caps and had been playing Test cricket before many of his team-mates were born. The captain, Percy Chapman, had the sort of rosy cheeks that might have been made especially for a maiden aunt to pinch and a face so boyish he made Wilfred feel like Methuselah.

Wilfred tried to steady his nerves. On the second morning with Australia on 84, Chapman called Wilfred into the attack.

He started with two maidens, which settled him down. The fifth delivery of his third over was quicker, short and slightly wide. Bill Woodfull cut at it but misjudged the bounce and chopped it on to his stumps. It might have seemed like a fluke, but Wilfred had dismissed Woodfull exactly the same way when Yorkshire played the tourists at Bramall Lane. A second wicket, with a real stroke of fortune to it, followed shortly afterwards, Arthur Richardson driving hard and straight to mid-off, where George Geary caught the sizzler brilliantly. Wilfred bowled a tidy 25 overs giving away just 35 runs.

Hobbs, who'd been out to a Mailey full toss in the first innings, and Sutcliffe batted superbly in England's second innings on a drying wicket to set up a thrilling final day. On a suspect batting track, Australia needed to score 415 to win and retain the Ashes. Harold Larwood soon had the ball flying round the Australian batsmen's ears. At Wilfred's suggestion, Chapman brought Geary in as an extra slip. Woodfull and Charlie Macartney both edged lightning quick Larwood deliveries straight to him.

Hobbs approached Chapman and offered the view that Wilfred should be brought on at the Pavilion End to provide a steady counterpoint to the Nottinghamshire paceman. Chapman was a captain who listened to his senior pros. He did so now. Bowling with his customary tightness, Wilfred quickly had Bill Ponsford caught by Larwood at second slip. A few overs later, Woolley snapped up a Herbie Collins edge and then caught Bardsley in the same position. Wilfred ended his final spell in a Test in England by getting Richardson in one of his cunningly baited traps. A looping half-volley was dispatched to the boundary. The next delivery looked exactly the same. Richardson attacked it exactly as he had the previous one, only to find it pitching shorter and coming in at him with the arm. His drive missed and he was bowled. Shortly afterwards Geary knocked over Arthur Mailey and England had regained the Ashes. Thanks to the intervention of his wife and daughter, Wilfred had ended his Test career on home soil in fitting style.

Wilfred played for four more seasons in county cricket. He seemed untroubled by the passage of time, commenting on his 50th birthday that the only reminder he had of his age was 'a slight stiffness in my right leg'. He didn't do the double again, but he remained good for 500 runs and 80 wickets and his expertise was priceless. As Emmott Robinson said, 'What he doesn't know of this game is hardly worth knowing.'

There were bumps along the way. Roy Kilner died unexpectedly from gastric typhoid picked up while visiting India – a blow to Wilfred, who had nurtured the slow left-armer as a youngster and bowled effectively with him in tandem for hour after hour (though he sometimes was irritated by Kilner's cavalier approach to field placings). There was annoyance, too, when Yorkshire decided to dispense with the services of veteran wicketkeeper Arthur Dolphin against Wilfred's wishes. Dolphin was in his forties and suffering from sciatica. He had been remarkable in his consistency and so robust that his only serious injury had come about in comical circumstances – in 1921 he fell off a chair in the dressing room while reaching round for his clothes and broke his wrist.

Dolphin had once told Wilfred that his bowling was so accurate and he was so used to it that he regarded keeping wicket to him as 'a little rest'. 'I could take your bowling in my sleep, Wilfred,' he once told Rhodes. Shortly afterwards, a delivery from Rhodes spat alarmingly out of the bowler's footmarks and struck Dolphin in the face, opening up a gash above an eye that needed stitches. 'Better stay awake in future, Arthur,' his team-mates joked.

At the start of the 1929 season, Wilfred took 12 wickets for 80 runs against Essex at Leyton. His performance against Nottinghamshire at Trent Bridge, where he took 11 for 85 in the match at the age of 51, provoked comments about the fountain of eternal youth perhaps being located over by Holmfirth.

He was Yorkshire's best bowler again, taking 85 wickets for the county in the Championship at 17.22. Batting at number eight, his reduced footwork and failing eye was replaced by increased stubbornness. He helped Sutcliffe bat Yorkshire to victory against Warwickshire at Harrogate when he came in with six wickets down and 37 runs needed, making just eight runs in that time.

Bill Bowes had by now started his career with Yorkshire and watched Wilfred with awe, fascination and a little dread. Wilfred was terse and gruff. He did not mince his words. When a young centurion returned grinning to the pavilion, it would be Wilfred who'd wipe the smile off his face by barking, 'Fancy making a hundred and getting out to a shot like that!' After taking seven for 26 against Hampshire, Hedley Verity was likewise rewarded with a detailed lecture about his field placings which had allowed Arthur Judd to hit an unnecessary boundary.

When Wilfred spoke of cricket, his knowledge was so deep it was often baffling even to the expert. Watching him, though, was an education in the precision of the game at its loftiest peak. Wilfred had studied cricket as a financier does the stock market. 'If he suggested a fieldsman at a particular position or that a bowler should adapt this or that manoeuvre,' Bowes noted, 'his opinion was accepted and acted upon without question.'

Bowes soon found out why. In a game against Essex, the young fast bowler was fielding at mid-on. Wilfred told him to move back a bit. Bowes took a couple of steps back. 'Too far,' Wilfred called. Bowes took a step forward. Wilfred nodded, 'Now a bit to your right ... no, not that far ... in a bit, no ...' Eventually, Wilfred came over and marked a cross in the turf where Bowes was to stand. Three balls later, Laurie Eastman struck a drive hard and fast and straight into the paceman's midriff. 'Had I been a foot on either side of the mark, I should never have seen the ball. As it was, I had either to catch it, or it would have gone clean through me. I caught it.' The episode, Bowes recalled, 'made more impression on me than almost anything else in my cricket career.'

Playing for MCC against Yorkshire at the Scarborough Festival, Bowes saw 'how well Rhodes could flight the ball'. Batting against the great man, he watched him toss the ball high into the air and thought he would dance down the wicket and smash him for six. 'I set off down the wicket to catch the ball on the half-volley, but, to my amazement, it dropped much shorter than I expected, and I had an awful job trying to stop it, never mind hit it.' The next ball was another seemingly innocuous delivery looping into the seaside sky. Again Bowes charged out to what he assumed was the pitch of it, only to find himself mysteriously 3ft short. The resulting drive flew into the air and into the hands of Frank Greenwood. Wilfred reacted with a small grunt of satisfaction.

Amazingly, Wilfred was not quite done with England. He

was selected to tour the Caribbean in 1929–30 for what would be the West Indies' inaugural home Test series. MCC were decidedly understrength – England were also playing a Test series in New Zealand, while Tate, Larwood and Hammond had opted to stay in England. The composition of the team suggested it was designed to make the 52-year-old Wilfred feel like a man in the prime of life. The tourists were captained by 37-year-old Freddie Calthorpe of Warwickshire and had a prune-ish look. George Gunn, recently turned 50, hadn't won an England cap since 1912, while 42-year-old Nigel Haig had been absent from Test cricket for eight years. Ewart Astill was 41, Andy Sandham 39, Ronald Stanyforth 38. Forty-year-old Patsy Hendren was at least still an England regular. He had played in all five Tests in England's 4-1 Ashes triumph the previous winter. Jack O'Connor was 32. Wilfred would describe it as 'an old crocks' team. The idea put about by Sandham and others was that the veterans had been selected for the benefit of the hosts, who would be able to watch and learn from the great men. It was the sort of patronising attitude that seemed bound to backfire and indeed the Test series was characterised by some fearsome short bowling by Learie Constantine that led to an appeal for calm.

The weather was exceptional, even for the Caribbean, and the wickets were hard, flat and true, except when they were matting. It was a series for batsmen and fast bowlers, yet despite that handicap Wilfred finished the tour as MCC's second highest wicket-taker behind Bill Voce, whose fierce pace and bounce was infinitely more suited to the conditions. He bowled more than 500 overs on the tour and took 39 wickets at 24 apiece, a fine effort on pitches that offered as much encouragement to spin as a frozen pond.

His appetite for bowling was now of almost Hirstian proportions. In one tour match, Wilfred shored up one end while the pacemen rotated at the other. In the third Test he bowled 40 overs in the first innings and 51 in the second. Later he'd recall himself, not unreasonably, as being 'the donkey of the team'.

For all his apparent hefted-to-the-Yorkshire-fells grumpiness, Wilfred loved travelling. The crowds in the West Indies were knowledgeable and vocal, and Wilfred took a great and unexpected delight in their antics. On rest days he'd happily wander about on his own in the markets or on the quaysides, or simply sit on a bench watching the scene in Kingston or Bridgetown playing out around him. He liked studying people and fathoming out what they were about. His spirit of enquiry and appetite for observation was undimmed by time.

On his return from the West Indies, Wilfred announced that the 1930 season, his 30th in first-class cricket, would be his last. It was the right decision. Over the course of the season his powers at last began to fade. He scored 478 runs (22.76) and took 73 wickets (19.10) for Yorkshire. His best bowling came against the striplings of Cambridge when he collected seven for 35.

He said his farewell against the Australians at Scarborough, playing for Leveson Gower's XI. The wicket was drying in the sunlight after a rain shower. The Australians were struggling in their first innings. Wilfred had bowled to W. G. Grace in his first game and now he bowled to Don Bradman in his last. He did not get the Don's wicket, though he came close three times. Five other Australians were not so lucky. The last of them, Tim Wall, knocked up a catch to Bob Wyatt that ended the innings. Rain cut off any chance of the Australians batting again. It was Wilfred's last wicket in first-class cricket, his 4,187th in all. He walked from the field for the final time, warm applause ringing around North Marine Road. It didn't quite match the rousing reception George Herbert or even Schof had received, but then, as Bowes noted, 'Wilfred was never popular in the accepted meaning of the word.'

The following season Yorkshire would win a 15th title. It was the first time they had won a Championship without at least one of the Triumvirate in the side.

CHAPTER FOURTEEN

On Towards Twilight

In the autumn of 1921 George Herbert and Wilfred travelled to Marseille, boarded a P&O ship for Bombay, then took the thousand-mile train journey north to the Punjabi city of Patiala. Wilfred had his camera with him and soon a cluster of his photographs were covering an entire page of the *Leeds Mercury*. The photographs showed George Herbert sitting in an elaborate horse-drawn coach before a sightseeing tour of Patiala. He was wearing a solar topee and had his pipe clamped between his teeth. Next to him sat the former Warwickshire skipper Jack Parsons, wearing a spiffy striped blazer and Panama hat. Alongside snaps of the 'Fairy Palace' of Moti Bagh, the *Mercury*'s readers also got to see George Herbert standing in front of a gateway in a rather heavy-looking three-piece suit and in cricket whites and a trilby hat. Other photos featured a tall and imposing Sikh. In one, he was batting in the nets, in another reclining on a sofa in his whites next to the scorer's table. He was evidently watching a match in progress.

The *Leeds Mercury* informed its public that the princely gentleman in Wilfred's photos was Sir Jagatjit Singh Sahib Bahadur, the Sikh ruler of the state of Kapurthala, who had recently built himself a splendid new home, Jagatjit Palace, which was modelled on Versailles. Sir Jagatjit – who'd serve as India's representative at the League of Nations – was a globetrotter, a committed Francophile and, his marital record would suggest, something of a playboy. He was married six times. Among his wives was a Spanish flamenco dancer and a Czech actress.

As it transpired, the *Leeds Mercury* had got its Sikh maharajahs muddled. Because while Sir Jagatjit's daughter by the Spanish flamenco dancer would go on to captain the girls' cricket XI at Sherborne School, her father had no interest in the game whatsoever. The maharajah in Rhodes's photos was in fact the pioneering Indian cricket patron and player, the Maharajah of Patiala. The two great Yorkshiremen were there to coach his two sons and also his officers and personal staff. The Patiala team at that time was captained by General Tara Chund, commander of the Patiala State Army, and also featured Colonel Mistre, Guardian of the Royal Children and a noted player of polo, who had toured England with the Patiala Tigers.

Long before the Indian Premier League came to dominate world cricket, highly paid professional cricketers from across the globe had been imported to the subcontinent by wealthy men eager to use the sport as a means of besting their rivals. Rajendra Singh, the Maharajah of Patiala, educated at Cambridge and said to be second only to Ranjitsinhji among Indian cricketers, was the leader of the trend. A crack shot, an expert at billiards and a fine polo player, the first man in

India to own a motor car and the husband to more than 300 women (at least one of whom – the *New York Times* reported in his obituary – was Irish), Rajendra Singh had built a cricket ground and now needed a team to play on it. To that end, he secured the services of 'Old Jack' Hearne and Bill Brockwell, England team-mates of George Herbert and Wilfred, and brought them over to his vast estates surrounding the Moti Bagh Palace.

When Rajendra Singh died in a riding accident in 1900, his son Bhupinder Singh succeeded him. The new maharajah was even more extravagant than his father – he used to proceed about the country in a motorcade of 20 Rolls-Royce cars, and often batted wearing pearl earrings valued at several thousand pounds – and just as committed to cricket.

Arguably the maharajah's most successful early import was Frank Tarrant, who played against the Triumvirate for Middlesex. Tarrant was particularly successful in India. His most notable performance came in 1917 when he took five for nine and seven for 36 as the Maharajah of Cooch Behar's XI defeated the Bengal Governor's XI by an innings in front of packed stands at Eden Gardens, Calcutta. The Australian seems to have taken to life in India and, as well as playing and coaching, also umpired matches and took his share of groundsman's duties, laying one of the country's first grass wickets at the maharajah's ground at Amritsar. Eventually, the maharajah's great rival, Sir Nripendra Narayan, the Maharajah of Cooch Behar, cheekily lured Tarrant away from Patiala to play for his team in Bengal.

George Herbert and Wilfred were given accommodation in the pavilion at the Patiala cricket ground and a Greek servant to cook and clean for them. The ground was as big as Headingley, with views across to the snowy peaks of the Himalayas. The wicket was true and so hard the new ball left polish marks on it. The surface was trimmed daily by a gang of boys armed with sharp knives, while the fast, even outfield was regularly flattened using an immense heavy roller pulled by an elephant. A team of local bowlers of what Wilfred considered a reasonable standard was permanently on site to provide batting practice for anyone who turned up.

The maharajah himself was hugely welcoming to his Yorkshire visitors. A giant of a man who stood over 6ft tall and weighed 18 stone, he could hit the ball with prodigious power, though his technique meant he often missed it completely. Bowling he left to others and fielding he felt slightly beneath him. George Herbert and Wilfred enjoyed his company immensely, his habit of pulling out a rifle as they sped along in one of his chauffeur-driven Rolls-Royces and loosing off a few rounds at passing game lived long in their memories. The maharajah was an excellent shot, it should be said. The locals still spoke in wonder of the time before the war when he had appeared in his Rolls and gunned down a mad camel that was running amok in the city's market.

After a period of acclimatisation, George Herbert and Wilfred caught the mail train and travelled 36 hours to Bombay to play for the Europeans in the annual Quadrangular Tournament at the Gymkhana ground. The Europeans that season were something of an all-star XI, with Jack Parsons and C. B. Fry opening the batting. In the match against the Hindus, Fry managed to get run out for a duck, but Parsons hit a century and Wilfred batted resolutely to score 156.

A Hindu batting line-up that featured the hard-hitting C. K. Nayudu found Wilfred too much to handle on a wicket that had begun falling apart on the first evening. He bowled 27.3 overs, conceded just 26 runs and took seven wickets. When the Hindus followed on, George Herbert worked up some of his old fire and took six wickets as the Europeans won by an innings.

In the final, the Europeans met the Parsees. Wilfred was again superb, hitting 183. George Herbert came in late to join him and hammered a rapid 62. When the Parsees batted, the two Yorkshiremen rolled them over, Wilfred taking five wickets and George Herbert three. Batting again on the sort of dusty track that would later bring a twinkle to the eyes of Bishan Bedi, Anil Kumble, Harbhajan Singh and their colleagues in tweak, the Parsees collapsed to the wizardry of Wilfred, who took seven for 33 in 13 overs. Wilfred had enjoyed himself, but at the celebrations that followed the match he'd hear mutterings that the presence of the Yorkshire duo had spoiled the tournament as a spectacle.

Back in Patiala, there were various local matches to play in and organise. The ground was massive, but George Herbert cunningly pulled in the boundary rope so it was easier for the maharajah to hit the sixes he delighted in. His sons had inherited his fondness for smashing the ball, and though Wilfred and George Herbert did their best to teach them the basics of defence, Wilfred soon concluded it was a waste of time. 'They were only interested in seeing how far they could hit the ball.' Despite that tendency, one of the sons, Yuvraj, went on to play Test cricket, hitting a half-century against England at Madras during the 1933–34 series.

As the winter wore on and the pleasures of partridge shooting from the back of an elephant began to pale, George Herbert seems to have grown slightly restless at the lack of any real cricket. Wilfred, meanwhile, was busy with his camera taking photos of the visit of the Prince of Wales to Patiala and selling them to the *Leeds Mercury*.

The pair arrived back in Huddersfield in late March. George Herbert had generally enjoyed his trip. He felt the Indian bowlers were poor, but he was impressed with the fielding and the enthusiasm for the game of the youngsters he had encountered. 'The Indian boys generally like cricket and if there were facilities they would likely do well at it,' he commented.

The following winter, Wilfred returned to Patiala, this time in the company of Roy Kilner. Perhaps mindful of upsetting the balance as much as he had done the previous winter, Wilfred was relatively subdued in both the Quadrangular Tournament and newly conceived Lahore Tournament. His best performance came at Lawrence Gardens against the Hindus where he hit 71 in the first innings and then took three wickets for six runs in the Hindus' first innings. At the Gymkhana in Bombay his best bowling was a modest three for 51 in 15 overs. Not that it halted the progress of the Europeans, for whom an Irishman named Fred Shaw caused carnage with the ball.

Wilfred would spend five winters in Patiala, always accompanied by one or two of his Yorkshire team-mates. They coached and shot ducks. They did their own shopping in the bazaar. Beef was banned in Patiala and so the players found themselves dining on antelope, which they found lean and stringy. They played against local sides, amused themselves with billiard tournaments, were occasionally startled by a Scottish ghillie who told tales of venomous pythons and man-eating tigers, and attended the annual Patiala dog show, which showed off the maharajah's collection of Alsatian police dogs and English setters.

The maharajah's team played on Saturdays and Sundays, often against college sides from Lahore, Bombay and other cities. Large crowds turned up to watch the matches, which were accompanied by the military marches of the Patiala army band. Emmott Robinson enjoyed the music and the delighted shrieks of the crowd when a ball was struck high in the air.

Maurice Leyland recalled the maharajah telling him before the start of one match that he wouldn't be able to get there till 1 p.m. and that Leyland and Wilfred should open at 11 and hold the fort till he arrived. Sure enough, shortly before 1, the dust clouds that announced the arrival of the maharajah and his fleet of Rolls-Royces were seen in the distance. A few minutes later, the maharajah's car pulled to a halt by the boundary rope and he jumped out wearing his pads and gloves and brandishing his bat. After a brief chat, Wilfred volunteered to retire and the maharajah marched to the wicket and commenced walloping the ball with all his might.

In February 1927, Patiala played a two-day match against Arthur Gilligan's touring MCC side. Wilfred, Leyland and Dolphin all played, as did the ageing Frank Tarrant. The home side won the toss and batted. The star of the innings was Wazir Ali. Against an MCC attack led by Maurice Tate and John Mercer, the opener struck 149 in four and a half hours. Wilfred made 13 not out before the maharajah declared. He dismissed Parsons, Ewart Astill and Guy Earle for 73 runs as the game fizzled out to a draw. The match drew 8,000 spectators.

Like George Herbert, Leyland was impressed with the

cricket he'd seen in India. He thought the locals decent players, though lacking in stamina – a deficiency he attributed to
the heat, which did not allow them to train all through the
day as players did in England.

Wilfred held a different view, one that fell in line with
prevailing colonialist opinions. He concluded that the Indians
were not temperamentally suited to cricket. They were over-
excitable and lacked the ability to fight their way out of a
tight spot. It was the common view among Englishmen of the
time, but in the end the kinder assessment of George Herbert
would be proved correct. Gradually, the facilities across the
country would develop and the enthusiasm George Herbert
had recognised in the population would be harnessed.
Though they could not have known it at the time, he and
Wilfred had played a small part in helping India on its way
to becoming the greatest powerhouse in the game.

George Herbert's winter with the maharajah was solid
preparation for what was to be his first full season serving at
another bastion of class privilege, Eton College. A number of
his former team-mates had taken up coaching posts at public
schools: Tom Emmett at Rugby, Louis Hall at Uppingham,
Joe Mounsey at Charterhouse, Bobby Moorhouse at Sedbergh.
John Tunnicliffe was coach at Clifton and Schof had coached
first at Clongowes Wood College in County Kildare, the
boarding school where James Joyce had learned to play the
game, before going to Winchester where'd he'd been a great
success during his cruelly truncated spell.

That appointment had come via Winchester's cricket
master, the Yorkshire amateur all-rounder Rockley Wilson.
Wilson was an amiable, self-deprecating man who kept a
newspaper cutting in his cigarette case showing the first-class

batting averages on the one day of his career that he'd topped them. Wilson and Schof both coached future England captain Douglas Jardine. When Jardine was appointed to lead the England party to Australia in 1932–33, Wilson was asked by a journalist for his opinion and replied, 'He might well win us the Ashes, but he might lose us a Dominion,' which proved as accurate as one of Haigh's yorkers.

George Herbert's first day of umpiring at the Upper Club ground at Eton drew a crowd of journalists and photographers, who took delight in the contrast between the sturdy old Yorkshireman in his neat, well-worn whites and county cap, puffing on his plump brown pipe and passing comment in his broad accent, and the elegant pupils in their billowing shirts and brightly coloured caps. Hirst confessed to finding the whole set-up rather different from anything he had previously encountered. But he got on well with the boys (though they were puzzled by his habit of wearing a singlet under his shirt no matter how hot the day) and within a month was as firmly established in the life of the college as the school clock, and as familiar to staff and pupils as the chapel.

George Herbert was no world-renowned thinker, but his first words to the boys at Eton College carried echoes of those of Albert Camus when he spoke of football. 'You may learn all about philosophy in school,' Hirst told them, 'but you have got to practise it on the cricket field.'

George Herbert was at leisure in the mornings, but his afternoons and evenings were busy throughout the summer term. Nets were held on Mondays, Wednesdays and Fridays from three until eight, with a short break for tea. He was there for every session, bowling long spells. Matches were played on Tuesday, Thursday and Saturday afternoons.

George Herbert stood as umpire in every game from first ball to last. His dedication was so complete that one afternoon when he nipped away for an hour to meet a friend in Reading it caused a ripple of speculation through the school.

George Herbert was revered and loved by his charges. Newspaper cartoons depicted him as a kindly uncle to an admiring brood of boys, which may not have been far from the truth. Hirst's analysis of the game and his hints and criticism were always delivered in a kindly way, often accompanied by an anecdote drawn from his own early years as a cricketer. He interspersed practical advice – how to grip the seam, the position of the fingers when taking a catch – with far-ranging insights into the psychology of the game – 'Never let yourself be bluffed', 'No matter the provocation do not lose your temper'. His advice to Eton's batsmen mirrored his own approach to the game. 'Keep your wicket up by all means – but do not forget to hit *hard*. Don't think only of keeping the ball out of the wicket – think of what part of the field you are going to put it.' At times, he'd simply gather the boys in a circle around him and tell them stories from his own career. He had a massive store of them, each one well-polished and carefully wrought, so that every fable concluded with the point he wanted to make.

He was kind and encouraging even in difficult circumstances. After a mauling at the hands of Winchester, a young man who had finished with no wickets for 86 runs asked the coach what he had done wrong. After a moment's consideration, George Herbert replied, 'Aye, you see, what it was, was that you bowled too badly and too long.'

George Herbert never tried to force the boys into orthodoxy, allowing the high-scoring curly-haired Eton skipper

Wilfred Hill-Wood — elder brother of future Arsenal chairman Denis — to persist with the slightly Jessop-like crouching stance he'd adopted to stop himself backing away from the ball. He knew that each player developed the technique that best suited him and worked to improve that.

George Herbert's progress was keenly followed in Yorkshire, and when Eton defeated Harrow at Lord's in his first season, the *Leeds Mercury* carried a match report under the headline 'George Hirst's Boys Win'.

When his duties at Eton finished at the end of the summer term, George Herbert returned to Kirkheaton, played for Scarborough in the Yorkshire Council and ran coaching courses around the county, pitching up for several days at a time in Hull, Halifax, Harrogate, Middlesbrough and other outposts, with cricket school for under-14s in the afternoons and sessions for older boys and school masters in the evenings.

His influence at Yorkshire continued to be felt. He made minor adjustments to George Macaulay's action that turned him into one of the best medium-pacers in England. Later, when Hedley Verity arrived from playing in the Central Lancashire League, where the small boundaries and one-innings matches tended to make spinners push the ball through fast and flat, it was George Herbert who took him aside and advised him to employ less pace and more air. When Bill Bowes felt that he had no future at Yorkshire, it was George Herbert who supported him. 'He helped and encouraged me all he could; I never hope to meet a better coach or a better man.'

When George Herbert was asked about his coaching style, he'd call back an anecdote about his younger days when old Tom Emmett had sat beside him and said he ought to 'lean on the forward strokes more, without bending the legs much and smell the ball'. It was, George Herbert said, what the thing was all about, 'sound advice without any fancy trimmings'.

During his 18 seasons at Eton, George Herbert would coach a number of youngsters who'd go on to have an impact in the first-class game. Fast bowler Gubby Allen, Eddie Dawson, who'd hit 14 first-class hundreds for Leicestershire and play in five Tests, and Ronnie Aird, who played for Hampshire and served MCC for nearly 60 years, starting as assistant secretary in 1926 and finishing as president. He would never lose a match against Harrow and his side lost just once to their other great rivals, Winchester. When he retired in 1938, in appreciation of the all-rounder's long and faithful service, Eton College rewarded him with a cheque and a reading lamp, perhaps so he could study it more easily.

Wilfred's appointment as the cricket coach of Eton's arch-rivals Harrow was announced by headmaster Dr Cyril Norwood, whose spell as a teacher at Leeds Grammar School before the First World War might have given him some familiarity with Yorkshire cricket. There were some in the school who would claim it was made hastily and without consultation with the other cricket staff; others said the business had been forced through at the urging of F. S. Jackson, an Old Harrovian. It was clear from the start that there was resentment.

Wilfred arrived on the first Saturday in May 1931. His salary was said to be £300 for the term. It was considerably more than George Herbert was getting and double the money Schof had been paid by Winchester 10 years earlier. Harrow had not defeated Eton for 23 years. Like most 'marquee signings' in sport, this one smacked of either intent or desperation.

The Yorkshire papers followed the opening fixture between George Herbert and Wilfred with an interest they had never before taken in the Eton College v Harrow School match. The game was the last social event of the London season. It attracted 16,000 spectators to Lord's, many of whom arrived in horse-drawn carriages, and was considered the greatest sporting fashion parade in the capital. It was a long way from Kirkheaton v Heckmondwike. Journalists from the Broad Acres reported breathlessly that the game looked 'like an extension of a Buckingham Palace Garden Party' and giddily reported sightings of the Duke of Devonshire, Lord Salisbury and Lord Hailsham among the top hats in a crowd dressed largely in dark blue and black and described by one gossip columnist as 'funereal yet fashionable'.

It quickly became clear that, despite Wilfred's assurance of sharply focused training for the game, Harrow were not going to break their cycle of failure. George Herbert's lads piled up a record stand for the first wicket. Wilfred's boys batted like they were lost in a fog. They lost by an innings.

In most of the five subsequent encounters, Harrow had the better of things, but could never press home their advantage over the two days. In 1935, they ran out of time needing just four more wickets for a comprehensive victory and in 1936 they went in as favourites only to see the game interrupted by a massive thunderstorm that flooded the Lord's pavilion and reduced the game to what one weekly magazine described as 'an abbreviated battle in the mud'.

Despite that first defeat, Wilfred initially seemed happy at Harrow. He got on well with the head groundsman and cricket coach, Stan Haywood, and lived in a comfortable fur-nished room. In that first summer, his only major complaint seemed to be that Harrow's Yorkshire puddings were made with too many eggs.

In the second summer, things began to turn against Wilfred. When it came to interacting with Harrow's pupils, he was plainly unsuccessful. It was said that part of the issue was Wilfred's broad Yorkshire accent that rendered him comically incomprehensible to the boys. Given the success of other working-class Yorkshire cricketers – including George Herbert and Schof – in public schools this seems unlikely to have been the main problem. The trouble seems to have been Wilfred's own intractable attitude to the business of cricket. He was a craftsman, cricket was his trade. Though he took quiet pleasure in exercising his skills, the notion that cricket might be a pleasure was as alien to him as the concept of minimalism to a Renaissance Pope.

Wilfred tried to instil in the young amateur gentlemen of southern England the style and pragmatism of the northern pro. Defence and safety first were the cornerstones of his method, but he was teaching privileged young men who had grown up on tales of the dazzling stroke-play of Old Harrovians such as Archie MacLaren and F. S. Jackson. Wilfred's insistence they get on the back foot and jab the ball away was anathema to them. For Wilfred, cricket was work; for them it was play.

Wilfred found himself in conflict with the Harrow masters and fathers – many of them former pupils – who would come to watch matches and call from beyond the boundary ropes for the batsman to get on the front foot, to come down the track, to attack, for pity's sake. To Wilfred, who had spent a lifetime trying to lure batsmen into committing such acts of folly, these cries were as baffling as they were annoying.

Perhaps Wilfred simply knew too much and cared too much about the game. Pupils spoke of his constant advice, of his microscopic analysis of their faults. In the nets, he bowled to them as if he was playing in a county match, never giving them easy balls to hit and plotting their downfall as he would have in his playing days. As a result, the players learned little except that they weren't good enough to bat against one of the greatest spinners England had ever seen. While George Herbert was noted for building up his students' confidence, Wilfred seemed actively to be demoralising his. He wanted to toughen them up, but simply left them with confidence battered and self-belief so flat it could slide under a duck.

The contrast between the two coaches of these great rival schools inevitably told against Wilfred. The extrovert and genial George Herbert was beloved by the boys, masters and parents and his teams played better, more successful cricket. That Wilfred was being paid £100 a season more than Hirst was a further mark against him.

When Eton and Harrow met in the annual match at Lord's during this period, the games generally ended in draws. The blame for this was implicitly put down to the coaching of Wilfred and his defensive 'win or draw – but never lose' mentality. He was blamed for cramping the batsmen's style, of paralysing them with his defensive approach and of forcing them to adapt his own awkward two-eyed stance.

That Wilfred had appointed his old Yorkshire opening partner Benny Wilson as his assistant hardly helped his case. Wilson would go on to become a well-respected coach at Yorkshire (it was he who in legend taught young Jim Laker to spin the ball), but he had effectively been sacked by his county for slow scoring. Those looking for signs of Wilfred's negativity had something else to point at.

Though the criticism of dull play in Harrow's annual tussle with their arch-rivals might have felt like it was directed at

Wilfred, that was not always the case. In a waspish article in society magazine *The Bystander*, the BBC's principal sports commentator, Howard Marshall, wondered whether coaching was responsible for creating a dull spectacle at the 1932 match and singled out George Herbert's Eton as the main culprits. 'I doubt whether there were a dozen off-drives or square cuts in both Eton innings,' he wrote, while noting that batsmen on both sides seemed to have been gripped by 'general paralysis'. The insistence on teaching the boys how to play, he believed, was turning them into mere automata. His ideas would find echoes across the country and the notion that the natural cavalier spirit of English sportsmen and women was being crushed out of them by 'over coaching' was one that would persist for generations, even as our national teams were being humiliated by those who were better taught and organised.

Whatever the truth of the accusations of negativity, Wilfred's problems were certainly exacerbated by the fact that, although he was senior coach, the running of cricket in the school ultimately fell to the cricket master, Cyril Browne, a Cambridge Blue who had played a handful of games for Sussex. It was Browne who selected the team to play in the all-important match with Eton, not Rhodes, and the selection process was based on a series of considerations that lay outside Wilfred's domain. The two men do not seem to have had a happy relationship.

Never a man to bow, even before the inevitable, Wilfred let his opinions on this process be known. At Yorkshire when he had spoken out, he had been listened to, partly because – as the captaincy fiasco had shown – he had the public on his side and also because he was too valuable to lose. At Harrow, he had failed to establish himself as a vital influence. Quite the opposite, indeed. Among many Old Harrovians he was viewed as a failure. That the school had not beaten Eton in 30 years mattered little. Wilfred had been brought in at huge expense to win the match and he had failed. One morning in the summer of 1936, shortly before the first XI played a fixture against Harrow Town, he was sacked. He had been in the job six seasons.

The year after Wilfred was fired, Eton won comfortably by seven wickets. George Herbert had extra motivation after the treatment of 'Young Wilfred'.

At the close of the 1936 season Schof's old club, Perthshire, announced that they would not be renewing the contract of their long-serving pro, Bert Marshall. The rumour in Scottish cricket was that the Big County were in talks with someone at Nottinghamshire. Then on 2 November came an announcement from North Inch that may have been the most dramatic in the history of Scottish club cricket – they had signed Wilfred Rhodes. It was a surprise. The great all-rounder had just turned 59, an age at which, in those days, even great men were considered ancient. Indeed, many of the professionals Wilfred had played alongside at Yorkshire had not even made it that far. Schof, Jack Brown, Irving Washington, Roy Kilner and Alonzo Drake had gone before they reached a half-century. Ted Wainwright and Bobby Moorhouse had both died aged 54.

Wilfred would later claim he was reluctant to go to Scotland, but Perth had sent men to his house to persuade him to sign and they refused to leave until he did. The once mighty Perthshire had been struggling for some years and they believed that Wilfred's 'wealth of experience and colourful personality will do much to restore the playing fortunes of the club'. The news that Perthshire were employing one of the greatest players in the history of the game caused a deal of excitement in Scotland, though it was tempered by the knowledge that Wilfred was a grandfather.

Any thoughts that the Yorkshireman would be playing in slippers with a mug of Horlicks in one hand were put aside after his debut on 1 May at Lochlands, home of Arbroath United, the club he'd made his highest score against while at Galashiels. This time he batted at number 11. Not that he was needed. Still bowling with artistry on a wicket that might have been prepared in his honour, Wilfred took six for 35 as Arbroath collapsed to 92 all out. The following Saturday he was back at it, knocking over five Stenhousemuir batsmen for just 15 runs. His bowling bewildered the Scots all season. In his final game against Brechin on the first Saturday of September, he took seven for 27 and scored three not out as Perthshire sneaked home by a single wicket. Then he boarded the train and headed south to Huddersfield.

Even the great Rhodes had been unable to shake the sleeping giant from its torpor. Perthshire had played 23 matches and won just five of them. He had done his best, of course, topping the Scottish bowling averages with 88 wickets at 8.76 apiece. Of the 345 overs he'd bowled, close to 100 had been maidens. This was remarkable enough in a man entering his seventh decade. What made it even more extraordinary was that it came at a time when Wilfred could barely see.

Wilfred had always had a fixation with sight. In interviews, he would speak of how the trees that fringed the Melbourne Cricket Ground made catching high balls difficult, or how the glare in Australia and South Africa interfered with the judging of distance. He noted that in the southern hemisphere, the blue sky made 'the strain on the eyes very trying'. At Adelaide, he thought the striped effect created by the white palings and the dark gaps between them created a kind of strobing effect so that at times the fences seemed to 'be moving up and down'. Though this may have just been Wilfred the observer talking, it does suggest that the problems with his eyesight had begun much earlier than anyone knew. It was at Harrow that others first wondered if Wilfred's vison was fading. One evening in a casual game with some of the pupils, Wilfred was clean bowled by one of the boys with a ball he played at and missed by a foot.

When he arrived in Perth, the problem became more obvious. Things appeared fine in net practice, but in that first game at Arbroath he attempted to catch a ball above his head that had actually gone past him on the ground. After that, he fielded little and batted rarely.

The season after leaving Perth, Wilfred spent the summer watching the Ashes series and writing a ghost-written column for the *Yorkshire Post*. He could see well enough to praise Stan McCabe, predict a bright future for Lindsay Hassett and become irritated by the havoc Bill O'Reilly and Chuck Fleetwood-Smith caused among the England batsmen, exhorting his countrymen to 'play the ball not the action'. The message failed to get through, the two leg-spinners picking up 36 wickets between them.

By the time the 1939 season came to a premature close, Wilfred's eyesight had deteriorated noticeably. His approach to the situation mirrored that of many men of his generation – he tried to ignore it and when questioned, simply blamed it on all the days of fielding in the hot sun that had had caused his eyes to 'wear out'. The handicap seemed minor. He still went to the Conservative Club every evening and played golf at Crosland Heath in the afternoons. He mowed his lawn, kept his hedge trimmed and his rose bushes pruned.

When the Second World War ended, he was still able to read a newspaper, if the light was good and he was wearing strong spectacles. Finally, he consulted a specialist. He had glaucoma. For reasons that are unclear, no operation was offered. The darkness descended more rapidly now. Wilfred attended cricket matches, but the players flitted across his vision like moths in a forest. By 1946 he could no longer read the newspaper, though he carried on trying to play golf, getting his directions from his friends. In 1951, Wilfred visited a Harley Street specialist. He recommended immediate surgery. It was too late. A year later Wilfred was blind.

He continued to attend cricket matches, often in the company of Sydney Barnes. His infirmity seemed to make him more human and people began to warm to him as they had never done before. Whether he could follow the game by sound quite as well as my father and others believed is open to question. But that was hardly the point. Frail and sightless, Wilfred exuded an ascetic monkish wisdom. People wanted him to be able to tell them from the sound of leather on turf whether a ball was turning, or seaming, or from the *pock* of a stroke if it was a defensive push or a pull to midwicket. They willed it to be so and as Wilfred said, 'If they think it's spinning, it's spinning.'

George Herbert looked robust but he had his health scares. He underwent an operation to 'correct internal problems' in 1922, was bed-ridden with jaundice in the summer of 1933 and with pleurisy during the autumn of 1938. In the summers, when he came back from Eton, he played for Scarborough, runs and wickets still piling up. George Herbert's final appearance for Yorkshire came against MCC at Scarborough in 1929. Bowes bowled him with a beautiful away-swinger when he had made 1. 'That would have been too good for me when I was good,' George Herbert told him as he walked from the wicket for the final time.

George Herbert wound his cricket down, but he still turned out in charity matches. He was as genial as ever and full of jokey tricks. In a benefit match at Thorp Arch, a young bowler who'd delivered a couple of tidy overs to him asked what he thought of his bowling. 'Very good, but you need to pitch them up by about a foot,' Hirst replied. In his next over the young bowler followed this wise advice. George Herbert hit him for a four and three sixes, laughed and said, 'Aye, that's more like it, lad.'

George Herbert and Wilfred were still regulars at Kirkheaton. The club had built a new stone pavilion and named it in their honour. On 23 March 1954, George Herbert and Wilfred were due to appear at Huddersfield Town Hall at an official function to honour the Triumvirate. George Herbert was in a nursing home. Emma had died the year before. His stamina had left him, his health failed and his son, James, had to go in his stead, watching with Wilfred as officials from the Huddersfield and District League presented the town's mayor with three commemorative silver plates. Six weeks later George Herbert was dead. He was 82. He had told the thousands of young players he'd coached, 'You can never give anything to cricket – it is loaned. Cricket is the one game in the world where everything is returned with interest.' He had tested that to the limit and proved it. Tributes came in from across the world, telegrams by the bucketload. The shortest and the best was from Bill Bowes. George Herbert he said was 'loved as a player, worshipped as a coach, revered as a man'.

Wilfred's wife, Sarah, died shortly after George Herbert. He left the house he'd built in Marsh and went to live with daughter Muriel and her husband, Tom, in Derbyshire. He went with them when they moved to Bournemouth. When Muriel died in 1970, Wilfred lived with Tom and when Tom died in 1973, he went into a nursing home in Broadstone, Dorset. He died a few months later, aged 95. His obituaries said he had taken 4,184 first-class wickets. Since then statisticians have gone back through the scorecards. Today Wilfred is credited with 4,204 first-class wickets. That he was snaring fresh victims even after death will surprise none of his admirers.

I was 12 when the last of the Triumvirate passed away. I don't recall much fuss being made over it. And if there had been, I wouldn't have paid attention. In 1968, the rules on the signing of overseas players in the County Championship had been relaxed. Garry Sobers had signed for Nottinghamshire, Barry Richards for Hampshire and Mike Procter for Gloucestershire. County cricket had gone technicolour and Wilfred belonged to a black and white world. In 1969, the county game was restructured. Since then only two players – Richard Hadlee and Franklyn Stephenson – have done the double.

Throughout my adolescence Wilfred's name and that of George Herbert still came up regularly, not just in our house but anywhere in Yorkshire where people talked of cricket. Over the years the name of Schofield Haigh had disappeared into the giant shadow cast by his two great pals. I first came across it while watching Armitage Bridge play Lascelles Hall on a soft early summer afternoon a decade ago. After that, it seemed he popped up more often and gradually I found that when I saw his name I smiled. He was funny and good-hearted and never let his anxieties cloud his disposition. 'He seemed to bubble over with chuckles,' A. W. Pullin wrote. Of the three great cricketers, I grew fondest of Schof – the forgotten one.

STATISTICS

compiled by Ian Marshall

YORKSHIRE RECORDS

ALL-TIME LEADING RUNSCORERS

	M	I	NO	HS	Runs	Avge	100	50
1. H.Sutcliffe	602	864	96	313	38558	50.20	112	167
2. D.Denton	677	1058	61	221	33282	33.38	61	173
3. G.Boycott	414	674	111	260*	32570	57.85	103	157
4. G.H.Hirst	717	1051	129	341	32035	34.74	56	175
5. W.Rhodes	883	1196	161	267*	31098	30.04	46	155
6. P.Holmes	485	699	74	315*	26220	41.95	60	115
7. M.Leyland	548	720	82	263	26181	41.03	62	123
8. L.Hutton	341	527	62	280*	24807	53.34	85	98
9. D.B.Close	536	811	102	198	22650	31.94	33	110
10. J.H.Hampshire	456	724	89	183*	21979	34.61	34	121
35. S.Haigh	513	687	110	159	10993	19.05	4	44

ALL-TIME LEADING WICKET-TAKERS

	Runs	Wkts	Avge	Best	5wI	10wM
1. W.Rhodes	57634	3597	16.02	9- 28	252	61
2. G.H.Hirst	44624	2477	18.01	9- 23	174	40
3. S.Haigh	29289	1876	15.61	9- 25	127	28
4. G.G.Macaulay	30555	1774	17.22	8- 21	125	31
5. F.S.Trueman	29890	1745	17.12	8- 28	97	20
6. H.Verity	21353	1558	13.70	10- 10	141	48
7. J.H.Wardle	27917	1539	18.13	9- 25	117	25
8. R.Illingworth	26806	1431	18.73	9- 42	79	11
9. W.E.Bowes	21227	1351	15.71	9-121	103	25
10. R.Peel	20891	1330	15.70	9- 22	100	28

Schofield Haigh won the County Championship eight times: 1896, 1898, 1900, 1901, 1902, 1905, 1908, 1912.

George Hirst won the County Championship ten times: 1893, 1896, 1898, 1900, 1901, 1902, 1905, 1908, 1912, 1919.

Wilfred Rhodes won the County Championship twelve times: 1898, 1900, 1901, 1902, 1905, 1908, 1912, 1919, 1922, 1923, 1924, 1925.

SCHOFIELD HAIGH CAREER STATISTICS

Schofield Haigh, born Berry Brow, Huddersfield, Yorkshire 19 March 1871; died Taylor Hill, Huddersfield, Yorkshire 27 February 1921.

Right-hand bat; right arm fast-medium.

Wisden Cricketer of the Year 1901.

Yorkshire 1895 to 1913; benefit 1909.

Also played for: Players (1898 to 1910), Lord Hawke's XI (1898–99), C. I. Thornton's XI (1902 to 1907), Lancashire & Yorkshire (1903 to 1909), North (1904 to 1908), MCC (1905–06), The Rest (1906) and Lord Londesborough's XI (1908 to 1912).

TEST MATCH CAREER RECORD

Batting and fielding	M	I	NO	HS	Runs	Avge	100	50	Ct
1898–99 to 1912	11	18	3	25	113	7.53	–	–	8

Bowling	Balls	Mdns	Runs	Wkts	Avge	Best	5wI	10wM
1898–99 to 1912	1294	61	622	24	25.91	6–11	1	–

Match list

Opponent/Date	Venue	1st Inns	2nd Inns	1st Inns	2nd Inns	Result
S Africa 14/02/99	Johannesburg	2 NO	1 Ct	3–101	2–20	W
S Africa 01/04/99	Cape Town	0 Ct	25 Ct	3– 88	6–11	W
Australia 15/06/05	Lord's	14 B	DNB	2– 40	DNB	D
Australia 03/07/05	Leeds	11 Ct	DNB	1– 19	1–36	D
S Africa 02/01/06	Johannesburg	23 B	0 LBW	DNB	0– 9	L
S Africa 06/03/06	Johannesburg	3 Ct	0 NO	4– 64	DNB	L
S Africa 10/03/06	Johannesburg	0 Ct	16 Ct	0– 50	1– 72	L
S Africa 24/03/06	Cape Town	0 Ct	DNB	1– 38	0– 12	W

Opponent/Date	Venue	1st Inns	2nd Inns	1st Inns	2nd Inns	Result
S Africa 30/03/06	Cape Town	1 Ct	2 Ct	0- 18	DNB	L
Australia 14/06/09	Lord's	1 NO	5 RO	0- 41	DNB	L
Australia 29/07/12	Manchester	9 Ct	DNB	0- 3	DNB	D

FIRST-CLASS CAREER RECORD

YORKSHIRE – BATTING AND FIELDING

Debut v Derbyshire, at Derby, on 8-10 July 1895, scoring 25 and 36, and taking 5-73 and 2-30.

Final game v MCC, at Scarborough, on 1-3 September 1913, scoring 6 and 3, and taking 1-6 and 0-5.

Year	M	I	NO	HS	Runs	Avge	100	50	Ct
1895	2	4	–	36	79	19.75	–	–	1
1896	15	23	5	32*	165	9.16	–	–	8
1897	27	37	10	34*	324	12.00	–	–	11
1898	30	37	5	85	501	15.65	–	2	15
1899	31	44	6	71	793	20.86	–	4	15
1900	32	41	1	73	719	17.97	–	4	19
1901	22	27	4	159	607	26.39	1	2	13
1902	31	38	6	85	653	20.40	–	4	14
1903	31	41	5	44	550	15.27	–	–	18
1904	32	42	4	138	1031	27.13	2	6	14
1905	32	45	3	78	847	20.16	–	5	20
1906	32	45	6	75*	670	17.17	–	2	14
1907	23	30	5	40	382	15.28	–	–	13
1908	25	26	5	31	252	12.00	–	–	8
1909	29	38	14	46*	376	15.66	–	–	28
1910	31	46	9	87*	851	23.00	–	4	13
1911	31	48	11	111	906	24.48	1	4	23
1912	33	42	10	62*	577	18.03	–	2	16
1913	24	33	1	92	710	22.18	–	5	14

YORKSHIRE – BOWLING

Year	Balls	Mdns	Runs	Wkts	Avge	Best	5wI	10wM
1895	225	8	147	8	18.37	5-73	1	–
1896	2933	201	1289	84	15.34	8-35	8	3
1897	3933	259	1713	91	18.82	7-17	6	2

Year	Balls	Mdns	Runs	Wkts	Avge	Best	5wI	10wM
1898	4160	291	1795	100	17.95	8–21	5	1
1899	3935	261	1693	79	21.43	8–33	2	1
1900	5633	262	2331	160	14.56	7–33	12	1
1901	2505	87	1199	56	21.41	6–48	4	–
1902	4374	210	1770	154	11.49	7–38	14	3
1903	4388	219	1706	102	16.72	6–22	6	1
1904	5179	225	2301	118	19.50	7–56	8	2
1905	4447	200	1715	118	14.53	6–21	8	2
1906	5292	199	2196	161	13.63	7–35	11	3
1907	3341	143	1182	96	12.31	7–13	8	1
1908	3212	157	1132	93	12.17	7–23	8	2
1909	4796	196	1601	120	13.34	7–25	8	3
1910	3603	125	1536	76	20.21	7–65	4	–
1911	4047	124	1684	97	17.36	7–20	2	–
1912	4792	241	1508	125	12.06	9–25	11	3
1913	2176	98	791	38	20.81	5–42	1	–

OVERALL CAREER RECORD – BATTING AND FIELDING

Team	M	I	NO	HS	Runs	Avge	100	50	Ct
Yorkshire	513	687	110	159	10993	19.05	4	44	277
Players	11	14	3	51	195	17.72	–	1	5
England	11	18	3	25	113	7.53	–	–	8
Lord Hawke's XI	3	3	–	15	27	9.00	–	–	2
C.I.Thornton's XI	3	4	1	30*	84	28.00	–	–	–
Lancs & Yorks	3	1	–	9	9	9.00	–	–	–
North	6	8	1	21	69	9.85	–	–	3
MCC	7	10	1	61	167	18.55	–	1	4
The Rest	1	1	–	0	0	0.00	–	–	–
Lord Londesboro' XI	3	1	–	56	56	56.00	–	1	–
Overall	561	747	119	159	11713	18.65	4	47	299

OVERALL CAREER RECORD – BOWLING

Team	Balls	Mdns	Runs	Wkts	Avge	Best	5wI	10wM
Yorkshire	72791	3506	29289	1876	15.61	9–25	127	28
Players	1348	40	695	23	30.21	5–55	1	–
England	1294	61	622	24	25.91	6–11	1	–
Lord Hawke's XI	594	57	199	19	10.47	8–34	1	1

Team	Balls	Mdns	Runs	Wkts	Avge	Best	5wI	10wM
C.I.Thornton's XI	336	8	192	3	64.00	2-65	–	–
Lancs & Yorks	264	9	128	5	25.60	3-44	–	–
North	845	21	489	26	18.80	5-35	3	1
MCC	930	43	362	33	10.96	7-58	2	–
The Rest	84	2	53	1	53.00	1-53	–	–
Lord Londesboro' XI	144	4	62	2	31.00	1-12	–	–
Overall	**78810**	**3751**	**32091**	**2012**	**15.94**	**9-25**	**135**	**30**

Haigh became the tenth bowler in first-class history to take four wickets in four balls, for MCC v South Africa Army in Pretoria on 13 January 1906.

Haigh took five hat-tricks in his career, beaten only by D. V. P. Wright (seven) and T. W. J. Goddard and C. W. L. Parker (both six).

Haigh was the leading wicket-taker in the season in England on five occasions: 1902 (158 wickets), 1905 (129), 1906 (174), 1908 (103) and 1909 (122).

Haigh is one of just 33 bowlers to take 2000+ first-class wickets in their career.

GEORGE HIRST CAREER STATISTICS

George Herbert Hirst, born Kirkheaton, Yorkshire 7 September 1871; died Lindley, Huddersfield, Yorkshire 10 May 1954.

Right-hand bat; left arm medium-fast.

Wisden Cricketer of the Year 1901.

Yorkshire 1891-1929; benefit 1904 and 1921.

Also played for: C. I. Thornton's XI (1984 to 1920), XI of Yorkshire (1894), North (1895 to 1908), Players (1897 to 1921), A. E. Stoddart's XI (1897-98 to 1898), The Rest (1898 to 1914), Under 30 (1901), Lancashire & Yorkshire (1903 to 1909), MCC (1903-04), MCC Australian Touring (1904), Lord Londesborough's XI (1908 to 1912), P. F. Warner's XI (1911), Kent & Yorkshire (1913), Europeans (1921-22).

TEST MATCH CAREER RECORD

Batting	M	I	NO	HS	Runs	Avge	100	50	Ct
1897-98 to 1909	24	38	3	85	790	22.57	–	5	18

Bowling	Balls	Mdns	Runs	Wkts	Avge	Best	5wI	10wM
1897-98 to 1909	4010	146	1770	59	30.00	5-48	3	–

Match list

Opponent/Date	Venue	1st Inns	2nd Inns	1st Inns	2nd Inns	Result
Australia 13/12/97	Sydney	62 B	DNB	0-57	0-49	W
Australia 01/01/98	Melbourne	0 B	3 LBW	1-89	DNB	L
Australia 14/01/98	Adelaide	85 Ct	6 LBW	1-62	DNB	L
Australia 26/02/98	Sydney	44 B	7 Ct	0-14	0-33	L
Australia 01/06/99	Nottingham	6 B	DNB	1-42	0-20	D
Australia 29/05/02	Birmingham	48 Ct	DNB	3-15	0-10	D
Australia 12/06/02	Lord's	DNB	DNB	DNB	DNB	D
Australia 03/07/02	Sheffield	8 Ct	0 B	0-59	0-40	L
Australia 11/08/02	The Oval	43 Ct	58 NO	5-77	1- 7	W
Australia 11/12/03	Sydney	0 B	60 NO	2-47	0-79	W
Australia 01/01/04	Melbourne	7 Ct	4 Ct	1-33	2-38	W
Australia 15/01/04	Adelaide	58 Ct	44 B	2-58	1-36	L
Australia 26/02/04	Sydney	25 B	18 Ct	0-36	2-32	W
Australia 05/03/04	Melbourne	0 Ct	1 Ct	0-44	5-48	L
Australia 03/07/05	Leeds	35 Ct	40 NO	1-37	1-26	D
Australia 24/07/05	Manchester	25 Ct	DNB	0-12	0-19	W
Australia 14/08/05	The Oval	5 Ct	DNB	3-86	1-32	D
S Africa 01/07/07	Lord's	7 B	DNB	1-35	1-26	D
S Africa 29/07/07	Leeds	17 Ct	2 B	1-22	1-21	W
S Africa 19/08/07	The Oval	4 Ct	16 HW	3-39	3-42	D
Australia 27/05/09	Birmingham	15 LBW	DNB	4-28†	5-58	W
Australia 14/06/09	Lord's	31 B	1 B	3-83	0-28	L
Australia 01/07/09	Leeds	4 B	0 B	2-65	1-39	L
Australia 26/07/09	Manchester	1 Ct	DNB	0-15	1-32	D

† *Hirst and Colin Blythe bowled unchanged in the first innings to dismiss Australia for 74; the pair took all 20 Australian wickets in the match.*

FIRST-CLASS CAREER RECORD

YORKSHIRE – BATTING AND FIELDING

Debut v Somerset, at Taunton, on 23-5 July 1891, scoring 10 and 5, and taking 0-51 and 2-32.

Final game v MCC, at Scarborough, on 11-13 September 1929, scoring 1 and taking 0-4 and 0-35.

Year	M	I	NO	HS	Runs	Avge	100	50	Ct
1891	1	2	–	10	15	7.50	–	–	1
1892	13	18	5	43*	210	16.15	–	–	11
1893	23	35	10	43	376	15.04	–	–	16
1894	27	39	7	115*	549	17.15	1	–	16
1895	31	45	10	64	685	19.57	–	3	12
1896	30	42	4	107	1110	29.21	1	9	20
1897	27	42	4	134	1248	32.84	1	8	21
1898	27	35	6	130*	506	17.44	1	–	23
1899	32	47	6	186	1546	37.70	3	8	22
1900	32	49	6	155	1752	40.74	4	12	26
1901	33	46	2	214	1669	37.93	2	12	20
1902	28	37	4	134	1113	33.72	2	6	9
1903	26	38	4	153	1535	45.14	4	9	20
1904	32	44	3	157	2257	55.04	8	9	17
1905	29	43	8	341	1972	56.34	5	9	19
1906	32	53	6	169	2164	46.04	6	12	21
1907	30	43	6	91*	1167	31.54	–	8	16
1908	32	46	8	128*	1513	39.81	1	11	23
1909	27	42	6	140	1151	31.97	1	9	33
1910	31	50	1	158	1679	34.26	3	8	24
1911	30	51	3	218	1639	34.14	3	6	36
1912	32	43	–	109	1119	26.02	1	7	25
1913	30	48	9	166*	1431	36.69	3	9	31
1914	29	45	6	146	1655	42.43	3	8	22
1919	30	37	3	180*	1312	38.58	3	6	21
1920	15	20	2	81	449	24.94	–	4	10
1921	7	10	–	64	212	21.20	–	2	4
1929	1	1	–	1	1	1.00	–	–	1

YORKSHIRE – BOWLING

Year	Balls	Mdns	Runs	Wkts	Avge	Best	5wI	10wM
1891	170	11	83	2	41.50	2– 32	–	–
1892	1701	134	617	30	20.56	6– 16	1	–
1893	4146	349	1425	99	14.39	7– 38	6	1
1894	3835	308	1459	95	15.35	7– 25	7	2
1895	6312	426	2560	150	17.06	7– 16	12	2
1896	4930	335	2234	98	22.79	8– 59	5	–

Year	Balls	Mdns	Runs	Wkts	Avge	Best	5wI	10wM
1897	4906	363	2023	91	22.23	6- 46	5	2
1898	1609	105	794	31	25.61	4- 85	–	–
1899	3923	259	1776	76	23.36	8- 48	4	2
1900	3176	123	1479	52	28.44	6- 49	1	–
1901	6329	245	2788	171	16.30	7- 12	15	5
1902	3399	170	1278	73	17.50	7- 68	3	1
1903	4205	197	1637	121	13.52	7- 36	8	3
1904	5600	190	2538	114	22.26	6- 42	7	1
1905	4018	147	1823	100	18.23	7- 48	5	1
1906	7268	263	3089	201	15.36	7- 18	19	4
1907	6010	229	2442	169	14.44	9- 45	17	4
1908	6150	270	2240	164	13.65	7- 51	15	3
1909	4311	151	1807	89	20.30	7- 95	7	–
1910	5380	219	2142	138	15.52	9- 23	11	2
1911	5968	217	2418	130	18.60	9- 41	14	3
1912	5149	252	1911	111	17.21	9- 69	6	3
1913	4863	225	1959	100	19.59	7- 33	3	1
1914	2878	117	1244	42	29.61	6- 34	3	–
1919	894	29	441	13	33.92	3- 40	–	–
1920	795	37	308	15	20.53	3- 19	–	–
1921	252	11	70	2	35.00	1- 8	–	–
1929	138	10	39	0	–	–	–	–

OVERALL CAREER RECORD – BATTING AND FIELDING

Team	M	I	NO	HS	Runs	Avge	100	50	Ct
Yorkshire	717	1051	129	341	32035	34.74	56	175	520
C.I.Thornton's XI	8	14	1	38	184	14.15	–	–	3
XI of Yorkshire	1	1	–	15	15	15.00	–	–	1
North	11	17	2	117	508	33.86	2	2	7
Players	27	43	10	124*	1338	40.54	1	10	24
A.E.Stoddart's XI	8	12	1	41	157	14.27	–	–	8
England	24	38	3	85	790	22.57	–	5	18
The Rest	9	15	3	76	418	34.83	–	3	10
Under 30	1	1	1	163*	163	–	1	–	2
Lancs & Yorks	2	2	–	26	32	16.00	–	–	–
MCC	7	8	–	92	352	44.00	–	3	3
MCC Aus Touring	1	1	–	51	51	51.00	–	1	1
Lord Londesboro' XI	6	8	2	77	207	34.50	–	2	7

Team	M	I	NO	HS	Runs	Avge	100	50	Ct
P.F. Warner's XI	1	2	–	19	26	13.00	–	–	1
Kent & Yorkshire	1	2	–	9	9	4.50	–	–	–
Europeans	2	2	–	62	71	35.50	–	1	–
Overall	**826**	**1217**	**152**	**341**	**36356**	**34.13**	**60**	**202**	**605**

OVERALL CAREER RECORD – BOWLING

Team	Balls	Mdns	Runs	Wkts	Avge	Best	5wI	10wM
Yorkshire	108315	5392	44624	2477	18.01	9-23	174	40
C.I.Thornton's XI	1085	54	525	19	27.63	4-48	–	–
XI of Yorkshire	200	16	66	2	33.00	2-38	–	–
North	1303	49	610	24	25.41	7-21	2	–
Players	2845	94	1335	54	24.72	8-35	1	–
A.E.Stoddart's XI	901	45	491	12	40.91	4-66	–	–
England	4010	146	1770	59	30.00	5-48	3	–
The Rest	1457	65	679	26	26.11	4-32	–	–
Under 30	133	8	40	5	8.00	4-30	–	–
Lancs & Yorks	312	15	97	4	24.25	2-32	–	–
MCC	1169	59	431	21	20.52	5-37	1	–
MCC Aus Touring	108	5	37	1	37.00	1-37	–	–
Lord Londesboro' XI	896	34	376	22	17.09	7-28	2	–
P.F.Warner's XI	226	8	145	5	29.00	4-74	–	–
Kent & Yorks	60	2	32	1	32.00	1-32	–	–
Europeans	367	23	113	10	11.30	6-33	1	–
Overall	**123387**	**6015**	**51371**	**2742**	**18.73**	**9-23**	**184**	**40**

Hirst's 2742 wickets puts him 12th on the list of all-time leading wicket-takers.

Hirst is the only player ever to score a century in each innings and take five wickets twice in a match, achieving the feat for Yorkshire v Somerset in Bath, 27-9 August 1906, when he scored 111 and 117* and took 6-70 and 5-45.

Hirst is the only player ever to score 2000 runs and take 200 wickets in a season (1906), when he scored 2385 runs and took 208 wickets.

Hirst scored 2000 runs and took 100 wickets in a season on two occasions: 1904 (2501 runs and 132 wickets) and 1905 (2266 runs and 110 wickets). This feat has been achieved just 21 times in history.

Hirst completed the fastest-ever Double of 1000 runs and 100 wickets, taking just 16 games to reach the landmark in 1906, by 28 June.

Hirst holds the record for most consecutive Doubles, achieving the feat 11 times from 1903 to 1913.

With 14 Doubles, Hirst has the second most by any player in history.

Hirst's first-class career spanned 38 years and 52 days, the eighth longest career; he was 58 years and 6 days old at the end of his final match.

WILFRED RHODES CAREER STATISTICS

Wilfred Rhodes, born North Moor, Kirkheaton, Yorkshire 29 October 1877; died Branksome Park, Poole, Dorset 8 July 1973.

Right-hand bat; slow left arm orthodox.

Wisden Cricketer of the Year 1899.

Yorkshire 1898-1930; benefit 1911 and 1927.

Also played for: Players (1898 to 1927), The Rest (1898 to 1926), C. I. Thornton's XI (1899 to 1928), North (1900 to 1922), Under 30 (1901), Lancashire & Yorkshire (1903 to 1909), MCC (1903-04 to 1929-30), MCC Australian Touring (1904 to 1920), Lord Londesborough's XI (1909 to 1913), MCC South African Touring (1910 to 1914), C. B. Fry's XI (1912), Kent & Yorkshire (1913), Europeans (1921-22 to 1922-23), Hindus & Muslims (1922-23), H. D. G. Leveson-Gower's XI (1923 to 1930), Capped (1923), Patiala (1926-27), Lord Hawke's XI (1929 to 1930).

TEST MATCH CAREER RECORD

Batting	M	I	NO	HS	Runs	Avge	100	50	Ct
1899 to 1929-30	58	98	21	179	2325	30.19	2	11	60

Bowling	Balls	Mdns	Runs	Wkts	Avge	Best	5wI	10wM
1899 to 1929-30	8225	365	3425	127	26.96	8-68	6	1

Match list

Opponent/Date	Venue	1st Inns	2nd Inns	1st Inns	2nd Inns	Result
Australia 01/06/99	Nottingham	6 Ct	DNB	4- 58	3- 60	D
Australia 15/06/99	Lord's	2 B	2 Ct	3-108	0- 9	L
Australia 14/08/99	The Oval	8 NO	DNB	0- 79	3- 27	D
Australia 29/05/02	Birmingham	38 NO	DNB	7- 17	1- 9	D

Opponent/Date	Venue	1st Inns	2nd Inns	1st Inns	2nd Inns	Result
Australia 12/06/02	Lord's	DNB	DNB	DNB	DNB	D
Australia 03/07/02	Sheffield	7 NO	7 NO	1- 33	5- 63	L
Australia 24/07/02	Manchester	5 Ct	4 NO	4-104	3- 26	L
Australia 11/08/02	The Oval	0 NO	6 NO	0- 46	1- 38	W
Australia 11/12/03	Sydney	40 NO†	DNB	2- 41	5- 94	W
Australia 01/01/04	Melbourne	2 LBW	9 LBW	7- 56	8- 68	W
Australia 15/01/04	Adelaide	9 Ct	8 RO	1- 45	1- 46	L
Australia 26/02/04	Sydney	10 St	29 Ct	4- 33	0- 12	W
Australia 05/03/04	Melbourne	3 Ct	16 NO	1- 41	2- 52	L
Australia 29/05/05	Nottingham	29 Ct	39 NO	1- 37	1- 58	W
Australia 15/06/05	Lord's	15 B	DNB	3- 70	DNB	D
Australia 24/07/05	Manchester	27 NO	DNB	2- 25	3- 36	W
Australia 14/08/05	The Oval	36 B	DNB	0- 59	0- 29	D
Australia 13/12/07	Sydney	1 RO	29 Ct	1- 13	0- 13	L
Australia 01/01/08	Melbourne	32 B	15 RO	1- 37	0- 38	W
Australia 10/01/08	Adelaide	38 Ct	9 Ct	0- 35	0- 81	L
Australia 07/02/08	Melbourne	0 Ct	2 Ct	0- 21	1- 66	L
Australia 21/02/08	Sydney	10 Ct	69 B	0- 15	4-102	L
Australia 27/05/09	Birmingham	15 NO	DNB	DNB	0- 8	W
Australia 01/07/09	Leeds	12 Ct	16 Ct	4- 38	2- 44	L
Australia 26/07/09	Manchester	5 Ct	0 NO	DNB	5- 83	D
Australia 09/08/09	The Oval	66 Ct	54 St	0- 34	0- 35	D
S Africa 01/01/10	Johannesburg	66 B	2 Ct	1- 34	0- 25	L
S Africa 21/01/10	Durban	44 Ct	17 Ct	0- 11	0- 43	L
S Africa 26/02/10	Johannesburg	14 Ct	1 Ct	1- 4	0- 6	W
S Africa 07/03/10	Cape Town	0 Ct	5 B	DNB	0- 2	L
S Africa 11/03/10	Cape Town	77 B	0 NO	DNB	0- 22	W
Australia 15/12/11	Sydney	41 Ct	0 Ct	0- 26	0- 4	L
Australia 30/12/11	Melbourne	61 Ct	28 Ct	DNB	0- 3	W
Australia 12/01/12	Adelaide	59 LBW	57 NO	DNB	0- 6	W
Australia 09/02/12	Melbourne	179 Ct	DNB	0- 1	DNB	W
Australia 23/02/12	Sydney	8 B	30 LBW	DNB	0- 17	W
S Africa 10/06/12	Lord's	36 B	DNB	DNB	DNB	W
Australia 24/06/12	Lord's	59 Ct	DNB	3- 59	DNB	D
S Africa 08/07/12	Leeds	7 Ct	10 B	DNB	0- 14	W
Australia 29/07/12	Manchester	92 B	DNB	DNB	DNB	D
S Africa 12/08/12	The Oval	0 B	DNB	DNB	DNB	W
Australia 19/08/12	The Oval	49 B	4 B	DNB	0- 1	W
S Africa 13/12/13	Durban	18 Ct	DNB	0- 26	DNB	W

Opponent/Date	Venue	1st Inns	2nd Inns	1st Inns	2nd Inns	Result
S Africa 26/12/13	Johannesburg	152 Ct	DNB	1- 23	0- 20	W
S Africa 01/01/14	Johannesburg	35 LBW	0 Ct	1- 9	0- 17	W
S Africa 14/02/14	Durban	22 LBW	35 LBW	3- 33	1- 53	D
S Africa 27/02/14	Port Elizabeth	27 B	0 NO	DNB	0- 14	W
Australia 17/12/20	Sydney	3 Ct	45 Ct	DNB	0- 67	L
Australia 31/12/20	Melbourne	7 B	28 Ct	1- 26	DNB	L
Australia 14/01/21	Adelaide	16 RO	4 LBW	0- 23	3- 61	L
Australia 11/02/21	Melbourne	11 Ct	73 Ct	DNB	0- 25	L
Australia 25/02/21	Sydney	26 Ct	25 RO	0- 23	0- 20	L
Australia 28/05/21	Nottingham	19 Ct	10 Ct	2- 33	DNB	L
Australia 14/08/26	The Oval	28 Ct	14 LBW	2- 35	4- 44	W
W Indies 11/01/30	Bridgetown	14 NO	DNB	0- 44	3-110	D
W Indies 01/02/30	Port of Spain	2 LBW	6 NO	1- 40	0- 31	W
W Indies 21/02/30	Georgetown	0 B	10 NO	2- 96	2- 93	L
W Indies 03/04/30	Kingston	8 NO	11 NO	1- 17	1- 22	D

† *Record tenth-wicket partnership of 130 with R. E. Foster for England v Australia.*

15 OR MORE WICKETS IN A TEST FOR ENGLAND

19-90	J.C.Laker	v Australia	Manchester	1956
17-159	S.F.Barnes	v South Africa	Johannesburg	1913-14
15-28	J.Briggs	v South Africa	Cape Town	1888-89
15-45	G.A.Lohmann	v South Africa	Port Elizabeth	1895-96
15-99	C.Blythe	v South Africa	Leeds	1907
15-104	H.Verity	v Australia	Lord's	1934
15-124	**W.Rhodes**	**v Australia**	**Melbourne**	**1903-04**

OLDEST TEST MATCH PLAYERS

Years/Days		Player	Match	Venue	Season
52	**165**	**W.Rhodes**	**E v WI**	**Kingston**	**1929-30**
50	327	H.Ironmonger	A v E	Sydney	1932-33
50	320	W.G.Grace	E v A	Nottingham	1899
50	303	G.Gunn	E v WI	Kingston	1929-30
49	139	J.Southerton	E v A	Melbourne	1876-77

LONGEST TEST MATCH CAREERS

Years/Days		Player	Team	From	To
30	315	W.Rhodes	England	Nottingham 1899	Kingston 1929-30
26	355	D.B.Close	England	Manchester 1949	Manchester 1976
25	13	F.E.Woolley	England	The Oval 1909	The Oval 1934
24	10	G.A.Headley	West Indies	Bridgetown 1929-30	Kingston 1953-54
24	1	S.R.Tendulkar	India	Karachi 1989-90	Mumbai 2013-14

FIRST-CLASS CAREER RECORD

YORKSHIRE – BATTING AND FIELDING

Debut v MCC, at Lord's, on 12-14 May 1898, scoring 4 and 16, and taking 2-39 and 4-24, bowling unchanged with F. S. Jackson to dismiss MCC for 69.

Final game v MCC, at Scarborough, on 3-5 September 1930, scoring 41 and taking 2-58 and 3-48.

Year	M	I	NO	HS	Runs	Avge	100	50	Ct
1898	30	36	–	78	515	18.39	–	3	17
1899	28	41	10	81*	375	12.09	–	1	18
1900	30	35	8	79	561	20.77	–	3	6
1901	34	42	10	105	841	26.28	1	1	23
1902	28	33	5	92*	335	11.96	–	1	11
1903	31	45	8	98*	947	25.59	–	6	13
1904	31	40	3	196	1251	33.81	2	5	19
1905	30	44	6	201	1353	35.60	2	10	38
1906	33	55	3	119	1618	31.11	3	12	36
1907	30	42	1	112	954	23.26	1	5	18
1908	32	50	1	146	1574	32.12	3	5	8
1909	27	45	2	199	1663	38.67	5	5	19
1910	30	52	4	111	1355	28.22	1	7	11
1911	30	54	3	128	1961	38.45	4	8	23
1912	24	39	5	176	1030	30.29	2	3	21
1913	32	56	4	152	1805	34.71	4	9	28
1914	30	47	2	113	1325	29.44	2	8	36
1919	31	43	9	135	1138	33.47	1	8	28
1920	29	39	3	167*	983	27.30	1	7	31
1921	27	38	7	267*	1329	42.87	3	5	22
1922	33	40	6	110	1368	40.23	4	5	27
1923	34	42	7	126	1168	33.37	2	5	30

Year	M	I	NO	HS	Runs	Avge	100	50	Ct
1924	35	46	7	100	1030	26.41	1	6	20
1925	36	41	9	157	1356	42.37	2	10	17
1926	30	32	3	132	1071	36.93	1	7	15
1927	33	35	6	73	558	19.24	–	1	8
1928	32	27	5	100*	565	25.68	1	4	21
1929	29	31	9	79	614	27.90	–	4	14
1930	24	26	7	80*	455	23.94	–	1	9

YORKSHIRE – BOWLING

Year	Balls	Mdns	Runs	Wkts	Avge	Best	5wI	10wM
1898	5625	446	1982	142	13.95	7- 24	12	3
1899	6264	470	2473	153	16.16	9- 28	11	3
1900	8182	411	3054	240	12.72	8- 23	23	7
1901	8733	475	3497	233	15.00	8- 53	23	8
1902	6153	336	2118	174	12.17	8- 26	15	5
1903	7257	383	2420	169	14.31	8- 61	14	3
1904	6547	326	2526	118	21.40	6- 27	8	3
1905	6144	267	2478	158	15.68	8- 90	14	4
1906	5253	164	2579	113	22.82	6- 90	7	1
1907	6088	223	2587	164	15.77	6- 22	12	2
1908	4186	213	1582	100	15.82	6- 17	5	–
1909	4355	187	1793	115	15.59	7- 68	11	2
1910	3540	133	1589	87	18.26	6- 38	6	1
1911	5002	154	2527	105	24.06	8- 92	7	2
1912	2041	64	1001	46	21.76	6-102	2	–
1913	4228	199	1818	81	22.44	7- 45	4	1
1914	4949	209	2120	117	18.11	7- 19	5	1
1919	5879	279	2233	155	14.40	8- 44	11	4
1920	5896	292	2008	156	12.87	8- 39	12	5
1921	5144	288	1672	128	13.06	7- 80	8	–
1922	4188	272	1232	100	12.32	6- 13	5	–
1923	5298	333	1460	127	11.49	7- 15	9	1
1924	3965	219	1420	96	14.79	6- 22	5	–

Year	Balls	Mdns	Runs	Wkts	Avge	Best	5wI	10wM
1925	3802	240	1131	57	19.84	4- 40	-	-
1926	4834	282	1530	102	15.00	8- 48	5	1
1927	5103	287	1635	82	19.93	6- 20	2	-
1928	6764	399	2104	111	18.95	7- 39	9	1
1929	6039	388	1803	100	18.03	9- 39	6	2
1930	4440	279	1262	68	18.55	7- 35	1	1

OVERALL CAREER RECORD – BATTING AND FIELDING

Team	M	I	NO	HS	Runs	Avge	100	50	Ct
Yorkshire	883	1196	161	267*	31098	30.04	46	155	587
Players	40	61	13	82	1307	27.22	-	5	26
The Rest	13	17	5	78	330	27.50	-	1	12
England†	60	100	21	179	2458	31.11	3	11	62
C.I.Thornton's XI	12	16	4	81	310	25.83	-	2	5
North	8	12	2	93	329	32.90	-	3	5
Under 30	1	1	1	5*	5	-	-	-	1
Lancs & Yorks	3	3	2	75*	110	110.00	-	1	2
MCC	62	81	20	210	2757	45.19	7	11	47
MCC Aus Touring	7	11	4	85	295	42.14	-	3	5
Lord Londesboro' XI	4	7	-	51	117	16.71	-	1	3
MCC S Af Tour	2	4	-	52	62	15.50	-	1	1
C.B.Fry's XI	1	2	-	12	21	10.50	-	-	-
Kent & Yorkshire	1	2	-	17	26	13.00	-	-	-
Europeans	5	8	1	183	478	68.28	2	1	5
Hindus & Muslims	1	2	-	79	108	54.00	-	1	-
Leveson Gower's	3	6	1	16*	36	7.20	-	-	3
Capped	1	2	1	79*	102	102.00	-	1	1
Patiala	1	1	1	13*	13	-	-	-	-
Lord Hawke's XI	2	2	-	4	7	3.50	-	-	-
Overall	**1110**	**1534**	**237**	**267***	**39969**	**30.81**	**58**	**197**	**765**

OVERALL CAREER RECORD – BOWLING

Team	Balls	Mdns	Runs	Wkts	Avge	Best	5wI	10wM
Yorkshire	155899	8218	57634	3597	16.02	9-28	252	61
Players	5007	209	2201	108	20.37	6-27	5	1
The Rest	1846	99	779	40	19.47	6-27	1	-
England†	8321	367	3485	128	27.22	8-68	6	1
C.I.Thornton's XI	1935	79	856	38	22.52	9-24	2	1
North	1292	47	673	38	17.71	6-19	4	-
Under 30	218	9	90	6	15.00	3-38	-	-
Lancs & Yorks	432	18	179	16	11.18	7-46	2	1
MCC	7335	319	2975	145	20.51	6-39	9	1
MCC Aus Touring	887	37	389	18	21.61	5-78	1	-
Lord Londesboro' XI	250	5	129	10	12.90	4-29	-	-
MCC S Af Tour	108	5	49	1	49.00	1-37	-	-
C.B.Fry's XI	-	-	-	-	-	-	-	-
Kent & Yorkshire	42	0	26	0	-	-	-	-
Europeans	937	68	276	31	8.90	7-26	3	1
Hindus & Muslims	294	8	156	5	31.20	3-99	-	-
Leveson Gower's	687	24	247	20	12.35	6-56	2	1
Capped	-	-	-	-	-	-	-	-
Patiala	144	4	73	3	24.33	3-73	-	-
Lord Hawke's XI	108	2	105	0	-	-	-	-
Overall	**185742**	**9518**	**70322**	**4204**	**16.72**	**9-24**	**287**	**68**

† Includes two first-class matches for England v The Rest.

Rhodes scored 1000 runs in a season on 21 occasions, the joint 14th most by any batsman (the record is 28 times).

In 1900, Rhodes took 261 wickets – the ninth most by any bowler in a season; he also took 251 wickets in 1901 – the 12th highest total.

Rhodes was the leading wicket-taker in the season in England on eight occasions: 1900 (261 wickets), 1901 (251), 1919 (164), 1920 (161), 1921 (141), 1922 (119), 1923 (134), 1926 (115). No other bowler has been the leading wicket-taker for five consecutive seasons.

Rhodes holds the record for most wickets in a debut season (154); only 11 bowlers have ever taken 100 wickets in their debut season.

Rhodes took 100 wickets in a season 23 times; D. Shackleton (20) and A. P. Freeman (17) are next on the list.

With 4204 wickets in his career, Rhodes is the most successful bowler of all time; A. P. Freeman (3776), C. W. L. Parker (3278) and J. T. Hearne (3061) are the only other bowlers to take 3000 or more first-class wickets.

Rhodes scored 2000 runs and took 100 wickets in a season on two occasions: 1909 (2094 runs and 141 wickets) and 1911 (2261 runs and 117 wickets). This feat has been achieved just 21 times in history.

Rhodes holds the record for most Doubles of 1000 runs and 100 wickets in a season, with 16; Hirst is second. He twice achieved the feat in seven consecutive seasons, from 1903–09 and 1914–24.

With 765 catches in his career, Rhodes has the seventh most of any fielder.

Rhodes holds the record for most first-class appearances (1110); F. E. Woolley (978), W. G. Grace (870), J. B. Hobbs (834), E. H. Hendren (833), G. H. Hirst (826) and C. P. Mead (814) are the only other players to have made 800 or more appearances.

NB: During the period of Haigh, Hirst and Rhodes's careers, the number of balls per over varied, so for the bowling figures I have used balls bowled, rather than overs bowled.

INDEX

Abel, Bobby 79, 118
Aberdeenshire Cricket Club 36–44
Accrington Cricket Club 58
Ackroyd, Jim 61
Aird, Ronnie 285
Akram, Wasim 106
Albury XV 227
Ali, Wazir 280
Allan, Frank 37
Allen, Gubby 285
All India XI 187, 229
Anderson, Jimmy 61
Arbroath United 63, 291, 292
Archer, A. G. 83
Arlott, John 195, 260
Armitage Bridge Cricket Club 38, 39,
    40, 48, 49, 87, 197, 214, 227, 296
Armstrong, Warwick 116, 121, 122,
    145, 147, 148, 247
Arnold, Ted 127, 130, 148, 208, 209
Ashes 4, 26, 92, 112, 114, 129, 148–9,
    206, 208, 222, 230, 237, 267, 268,
    271, 282, 292. *See also* Australia
    (national cricket team)
Ashton, Claude 226
Astill, Ewart 271, 280
Athletic News 46–7
Atkinson, George 52–3
Australia (national cricket team) 9, 10,
    16, 37, 49–50, 138, 168, 194–6,
    226, 238–9, 272–3

England, tour of (1882) 26
England, tour of (1896) 105
England, tour of (1899) 89–90
England, tour of (1902) 9, 114–23
England, tour of (1905) 144–9
England, tour of (1909) 173–6
England, tour of (1921) 238–9, 247–8
England, tour of (1926) 265–8
England tour of Australia (1894–5)
    and 76, 105, 132
England tour of Australia (1897–8)
    and 9, 69, 76–9, 92, 105, 112
England tour of Australia (1901–2)
    and 111–12
MCC/England tour of Australia
    (1903–4) and 129–37, 206, 207,
    208
MCC/England tour of Australia
    (1907–8) and 164–6, 206
MCC/England tour of Australia
    (1911–12) and 189–93
MCC/England tour of Australia
    (1920–1) and 224–6, 230,
    237–8
MCC/England tour of Australia
    (1924–5) and 231
MCC/England tour of Australia
    (1928–9) and 231
MCC/England tour of Australia
    (1932–3) and 282
Australian Imperial Forces 216, 218

Bahadur, Sir Jagatjit Singh Sahib 275
Bairstow, Arthur 96
Baldwin, Harry 54, 79
Bardsley, Warren 176, 265, 267
Barnes, Sydney 59, 83, 105, 116, 125,
    127, 164, 165–6, 175, 184, 189, 190,
    191, 192, 195, 204, 205, 234, 293
Bates, Billy 21, 164
Bates, Ederick 164, 181, 239
Batley Cricket Club 37, 38
Beaumont, John 40
Bedi, Bishan 278
Berry Brow 6, 29, 38–9, 50
Berry, John 19
Birley, Sir Derek 237
Birtles, Tommy 216
Bisset, Murray 85
Blake Lee House 11–13
Blythe, Colin 146, 152, 163, 164,
    167–8, 175, 180, 182, 201
Board of Control for Test Matches 112
Board, Jack 54, 83, 152, 158
Bodyline 102
Booth, Major 185–6, 194, 200, 212, 215
Border League 62
Bosanquet, Bernard 9, 75, 102, 130,
    134, 138, 144, 170, 207, 208, 209
Boswell, James 33, 62
Bowes, Bill 93, 236–7, 241, 269, 270,
    273, 284, 294, 295
Boyce, Keith 8
Boycott, Geoffrey 5, 37
Boyle, Harry 26, 37
Bradley, Bill 90
Bradley, Charley 223
Bradman, Don 272
Braund, Len 110, 118, 123, 130, 132,
    157, 164
Brearley, Walter 147, 150, 154, 155,
    168, 170, 182, 186
Briggs, Johnny 33, 42, 46, 76, 89
British Fascists 231–2
British Union of Fascists 231
Brockwell, Bill 79, 276
Bromley-Davenport, Hugh 83
Brown, Jack 28–9, 30, 34, 38, 52, 55,
    65, 66, 71, 80, 83, 84, 113, 124,
    137, 162, 164, 168, 184, 207, 245,
    290

Browne, Cyril 289
Bruce, Clarence 256
Burton, Cecil 216, 219, 221, 222, 236,
    245
Burton, D. C. F. 226
Byrom, J. L. 62
Bystander, The 289

Caledonian Cricket Club 42
Calthorpe, Freddie 271
Cambridge University 25, 27, 33, 49,
    75, 86, 149, 193, 216, 226, 236,
    248, 272, 275, 289
Cameron Highlanders 208
Cape Colony 85
Cardus, Neville 15, 249–50, 259, 260
Carr, J. L. 6
Castleford District 52
Catton, James 235
Central Lancashire League 234, 284
Chandrasekhar, B. S. 8
Charlesworth, Crowther 40
Cheshire County Cricket Club 22, 23
Chickenley Cricket Club 213
Chund, General Tara 275
Cliffe End Cricket Club 22
Close, Brian 4, 29
Cochrane, Stanley 169
Collins, Herbie 267
Conan Doyle, Sir Arthur 186
Constantine, Learie 250, 271
Cordingley, Albert 69, 70, 71, 72, 73
Cotter, Tibby 135, 144, 148, 154,
    225
County Championship:
    (1889) 24–5, 27
    (1890) 23
    (1891) 23
    (1892) 23–4, 29
    (1894) 30–2
    (1895) 33–4
    (1896) 48–52, 54
    (1897) 53, 54–8
    (1898) 71–5, 76, 79–81
    (1899) 86–7, 88–9, 90–1
    (1900) 94–100
    (1901) 102–4, 108–11
    (1902) 112–13, 125
    (1903) 123–9

(1904) 136–42
(1905) 149–52
(1906) 153–60
(1907) 161–4
(1908) 166–71
(1909) 171–3
(1910) 176–8, 180–3
(1911) 186–9
(1912) 193–5
(1913) 200–1
(1914) 206, 210–12
(1919) 215–24
(1920) 235–7, 252–3
(1921) 247
(1922) 249–52, 263
(1923) 263–4
(1924) 254–60, 264
(1925) 260, 264–5
(1926) 260, 264–5
(1927) 260
(1928) 242
(1929) 269
(1930) 272–3
(1931) 273
Crane, Charles 242
Cricket – A Weekly Record of the Game 44
Crieff Nondescripts 43
Curran, Sam 106
Cuttell, Willie 126

Dales, Horace 256
Darling, Joe 89, 118, 145–6, 147, 148
Darnley, Countess of 208
Dawson, Eddie 285
Denton, David 33–4, 35, 48, 50, 70, 71,
    96, 115, 136, 151, 152, 180, 184,
    185, 188, 194, 196, 209, 215–16,
    224, 227, 245
Derbyshire County Cricket Club 46,
    50, 55, 80, 95, 98, 109, 125, 139,
    146, 147, 149, 155, 161, 168, 172,
    181, 187, 211, 223, 264, 295
Dewar, John 44
District XVIII 53
Dolphin, Arthur 185, 212, 224, 255,
    257, 260–1, 268, 269, 280
Douglas, James 170
Douglas, Johnny 151–2, 189–90, 192,
    224, 225, 227, 237, 238, 282

Drake, Alonzo 186, 215, 290
Drumpellier 43, 45
Duff, Reggie 145, 148
Dundee Advertiser 45
Durham 49, 169

Earle, Guy 280
Eden Lacey, Francis 230–1
Edison, Thomas 59, 65, 130
Edward VII, King 182
Emmett, Tom 23, 155, 193, 281, 284
England (national cricket team) 10, 15,
    16, 26
  Australia, tour of (1894–5) 76, 105,
      132
  Australia, tour of (1897–8) 9, 76–9,
      92, 105, 112
  Australia, tour of (1901–2) 111–12
  Australia tour of England (1882) and
      26
  Australia tour of England (1896) and
      105
  Australia tour of England (1899) and
      89–90
  Australia tour of England (1902) and
      9, 114–23
  Australia tour of England (1905) and
      144–9
  Australia tour of England (1909) and
      173–6
  Australia tour of England (1921) and
      238–9, 247–8
  Australia tour of England (1926) and
      265–8
  Haigh career see Haigh, Schofield
  Hirst career see Hirst, George
      Herbert
  India tour of England (1911) and 16
  Lord Hawke's XI South Africa tour
      (1898–9) 82–5
  MCC/England tour of Australia
      (1903–4) 129–37, 206, 207, 208
  MCC/England tour of Australia
      (1907–8) 164–6, 206
  MCC/England tour of Australia
      (1911–12) 189–93
  MCC/England tour of Australia
      (1920–1) 224–6, 230, 237–8
  MCC/England tour of Australia

England (national cricket team) *continued*
(1924–5) 231
MCC/England tour of Australia
(1928–9) 271
MCC/England tour of Australia
(1932–3) 282
MCC/England tour of India (1933–
4) 278
MCC/England tour of South Africa
(1905–6) 152–3, 164, 206, 208,
209 MCC/England tour of
South Africa (1910–11) 178–80,
206
MCC/England tour of South Africa
(1913–14) 204–6
MCC/England tour of South Africa
(1927–8) 242
New Zealand, tour of (1929–30) 271
Rest of the World v (1970) 3
Rhodes career *see* Rhodes, Wilfred
South Africa tour of England (1907)
163
South Africa tour of England (1912)
and 83
South Africa tour of England (1929)
and 174
threaten strike action over match
payments (1896) 82
Triangular Tournament (1912) 195–7
Essex County Cricket Club 23, 24, 29,
55, 75, 86, 95–6, 108, 126, 127,
138, 149, 151–2, 155, 162, 163,
176, 187, 210, 218, 223, 229, 237,
256, 263, 265, 269, 270
Eton College 25, 26, 44, 213, 223, 224,
226, 237, 245, 281–90, 294

Faulkner, Aubrey 92, 153, 179, 204
Fender, Percy 224, 237
Fielder, Arthur 130, 186, 201
First World War (1914–18) 13, 164,
185–6, 211–14, 215, 225, 241, 261,
285
Firth, Dick 13
Fleetwood-Smith, Chuck 292
Flowers, Wilf 42
Forfarshire 43–4
Foster, Frank 190, 191, 192
Foster, Henry 156, 157

Foster, Tip 130, 132–3
Fry, C. B. 13, 75, 88, 89, 114, 115, 116,
129, 129, 148, 154, 184, 196, 277

Galashiels Cricket Club 62–3, 64,
66–8, 291
Geary, George 267, 268
Gehrs, Algy 148
Gentlemen of England 17, 46, 47, 52,
80, 88, 97, 104, 129, 149, 222, 245,
246
Gentlemen of Philadelphia 103
Gentleman v Players 17, 46, 47, 80,
88–9, 97, 149, 222, 245–6
Gibson, Alfred 32, 159
Gilligan, Arthur 231, 232, 280
Gilmour, Gus 106
Gloucestershire County Cricket Club
30, 49, 51, 54, 60, 74, 86, 95, 109,
111, 112, 126, 140, 142, 149, 158,
162, 174, 194, 200–1, 212, 218,
264, 295
Golcar 61, 64
googly 9, 75, 102, 135, 138, 180
Gordon, Sir Home 237
Goulder, George 62
GR Volunteers 214
Grace, W. G. 13, 26, 30, 31, 42, 51, 60,
71, 72, 74, 77, 80, 84, 86, 88, 89,
95, 103, 142, 150, 155, 159, 229,
272
Grange Cricket Club 40–1, 63, 68
Grant-Asher, Augustus 68
Greenwood, Andrew 20
Greenwood, Frank 270
Gregory, Jack 216, 225, 225, 247
Gregory, Syd 118, 119
Grimmett, Clarrie 265
Grimshaw, Irwin 27
Grimshaw, Sid 243
Gunn, Billy 89
Gunn, George 164, 165, 166, 271
Gunn, John 126

Hadlee, Richard 295
Haigh, John 85, 214
Haigh, Lillian (née Beaumont) 12–13,
80, 85, 94, 153, 163, 177, 197, 198,
239

Haigh, Schofield 6–7, 12, 38, 36–51,
  70, 74
  Aberdeenshire Cricket Club career
    36–8, 40–3, 63
  anxiety 91–3, 101, 171
  Armitage Bridge Cricket Club career
    38, 39–40, 48, 49, 87
  birth 38–9
  bowling action 54, 93
  bowling averages 7, 13, 47, 151, 202
  character 5, 14, 91–3, 101, 128, 188
  childhood 38–40
  County Championship (1896) 48–51,
    52, 54
  County Championship (1897) 54,
    55–8
  County Championship (1898) 79–80
  County Championship (1899) 88,
    90–1
  County Championship (1900) 96,
    97–9
  County Championship (1901) 108–9,
    111
  County Championship (1902) 112
  County Championship (1903) 126,
    128
  County Championship (1904) 136–7,
    139, 140
  County Championship (1905) 151,
    152
  County Championship (1906) 153–4
  County Championship (1907) 163
  County Championship (1908) 168,
    170, 171
  County Championship (1909) 176–7,
    178
  County Championship (1910) 182,
    183
  County Championship (1911) 187,
    188
  County Championship (1912) 193–4
  County Championship (1913) 201–3
  death 226–7, 245
  doubles 14
  England career 82–3, 86, 111–12,
    116–19, 144–7, 152–3, 164, 196,
    207, 208, 209, 210
  Hawke and 14, 91, 93, 99, 109, 112,
    113, 117, 183, 227
  Herbert and 91, 93, 108–9, 128–9
  injuries 124, 126
  Jessop and 87
  marries 80
  Perthshire Cricket Club career 43–7
  run-up 54, 93
  Silsden 213
  Test debut (1899) 86
  winter breaks 197–9
  Yorkshire Colts 48
  Yorkshire trial 43, 45–6
Haig, Nigel 271
Haileybury 83
Hall, Louis 26, 36–8, 40, 42, 195,
  281
Hampshire County Cricket Club 13,
  79, 83, 88, 95, 138, 139, 152, 182,
  183, 193, 218, 222, 223, 226, 244,
  269, 285, 295, 295
Hampshire Rovers 226
Hardisty, Charles 168–9
Hardstaff, Joe 166
Harris of Kent, Lord 25
Harrow School 223, 248, 284, 285,
  286, 287, 288, 289, 290, 292, 298
Harrow Town 290
Hartley, Jock 153
Haslingden 233–5
Haslingden Gazette 235
Hassett, Lindsay 292
Hastings Festival 74
Haw-Haw, Lord (William Joyce) 232
Hawke, Lord 52, 55, 56, 196, 260
  background 25, 143
  Barnes and 165
  benefit matches and 177–8, 188
  captaincy of Yorkshire, assumes
    (1883) 25
  changes to Yorkshire team/clear-out
    of old guard 27–8, 29, 198, 258
  greatest all-rounder in the history of
    cricket, opinion on 2
  Haigh and 14, 91, 93, 99, 109, 112,
    113, 117, 183, 227
  Hall and 37
  Hirst and 10, 24, 31, 91, 93, 108, 142,
    152, 159, 183
  Hunter and 167
  Jessop and 110

Hawke, Lord *continued*
  Macaulay and 258, 260
  MacLaren and 111–12, 117
  Moorhouse and 87–8
  Peate and 26, 27, 198, 258
  Peel and 56, 57, 58, 258
  president of Yorkshire County
    Cricket Club 25, 183
  Radcliffe and 184–5
  resigns as Yorkshire player 183
  Rhodes and 70, 71, 72, 75, 86, 95–6,
    109, 123, 124, 138, 149, 168,
    169, 184, 188 South Africa tour
    (1898–9) and 82–5
  Sutcliffe and 243
  The Shed and 200
  Toone and 231, 235, 241, 242
  25th year as Yorkshire captain 166,
    170–1
  Yorkshire pros, ensures good
    conditions for 80–2
  Yorkshire pros, enjoys company of
    82
Hawkins, Neil Francis 232
Hayes, Ernie 152, 170
Hayward, Tom 54, 88, 130, 133, 148,
  179, 208
Haywood, Stan 286
Hearne, Jack 73, 76, 77, 89, 90, 191,
  211, 256, 276
Heckmondwike Cricket Club 22, 213,
  286
Hendren, Patsy 256, 271
Herbert, Emma Kilner 51
Herbert, Mary 18–19
Higgins, Peter 43
Hill, Allen 20, 22
Hill, Clem 13, 61, 89, 116, 118, 145,
  190
Hirst, James 18
Hirst, George Herbert 2, 4–5, 8–9, 10,
  60, 64, 78–9, 88, 90, 91, 93, 96–7
  birth 5–6, 17, 18, 21
  character 5, 14–15, 32–3, 101, 188,
    246
  childhood 18–19, 20
  County Championship (1889) 22–5
  County Championship (1890) 23
  County Championship (1891) 23

County Championship (1892) 23–4,
  29–30
County Championship (1894) 30–2
County Championship (1895) 33–5
County Championship (1896) 49, 50,
  51–2, 53, 54
County Championship (1897) 54–8
County Championship (1898) 78–9,
  80
County Championship (1899) 88
County Championship (1900) 99–100
County Championship (1901) 102,
  103, 108, 109, 110, 111
County Championship (1902) 112,
  114
County Championship (1903) 124,
  125, 126–9
County Championship (1904) 136–7,
  139, 140, 141
County Championship (1905) 149,
  150, 151, 152
County Championship (1906)
  154–60
County Championship (1907) 161,
  162
County Championship (1908) 167,
  168, 169
County Championship (1909) 172
County Championship (1910) 181,
  182–3, 212
County Championship (1911) 186,
  187, 188
County Championship (1912) 193
County Championship (1913) 200–1
County Championship (1914) 211
death 294–5
double doubles 10, 17, 159–60, 162
England career 10, 76–9, 90, 114–23,
  130, 131–2, 133, 134, 135, 136,
  144, 146, 147, 148, 149, 163,
  173–4
Eton College, cricket coach at 223,
  226, 281–90
fame 156
first proper cricket match (1885) 21
First World War and 214
Haigh and 6, 54, 93, 108–9, 222, 227
Hawke and 10, 24, 31, 91, 93, 108,
  142, 152, 159, 183

health scares 293–4
in-swinger/swerve 8–10, 14, 101–2,
    105–6
India, visits to 16, 274, 276–7, 278,
    279, 280
Kirkheaton Cricket Club 21–3, 294
marries 51
name 19
Otley player 213
Phosferine Tonic Wine, advertises
    159–60
retires 224, 245
Rhodes and 68–9, 198
rugby and 22
runs and wickets record 10, 13, 14
run-up 106, 161
Scarborough Festival farewell 245–6
stamina 54
Sutcliffe and 220–1
toffee factory investment 141
touring and 207, 208, 210
winter breaks 197–9
Yorkshire coach 101–2
Yorkshire, final appearance for 224
Hirst, Molly 154, 157, 197
Hobbs, Jack 3, 13, 32, 59, 114–15,
    164, 169, 173, 179, 180, 189, 190,
    191–2, 195, 196, 205, 225, 237,
    258, 265, 267
Hodgson, Derek 253
Holmes, Percy 80, 216, 217, 219, 220,
    221, 227, 242, 250–1
Holmes, Reverend 24, 99–100, 116–17
Hopkins, Bert 116, 134, 146
Hordern, 'Ranji' 190
Horsforth Hall Park 213
Huddersfield and District League 8, 38,
    62, 64, 68, 214, 294
Huddersfield Chronicle 43, 44
Huddersfield Liberal Club 199
Huddersfield Weekly Examiner 189, 202
Hull Daily Mail 47
Hunter, David 27, 28, 30–1, 50, 51, 55,
    58, 82, 88, 102, 106, 107, 110, 113,
    125, 159, 167, 173, 184, 185, 188,
    202, 219, 245
Hutton, Len 191

Illingworth, Ray 4, 5

Illustrated Sporting and Dramatic News 188
Indian Premier League 275

Jackson, F. S. 34, 46, 48, 49, 50, 52, 55,
    71, 72, 86, 87, 100, 104, 110, 113,
    114, 115, 116, 117, 119, 137, 143–4,
    145, 146, 147, 148, 149, 151, 164,
    175, 285, 287
Jagatjit Palace 275
Jameson Raid 84
Jardine, Douglas 282
Jayes, Thomas 176
Jessop, Gilbert 13, 86–90, 95, 110, 111,
    117, 119, 124, 129, 142, 144, 146,
    158, 175, 284
Jones, Arthur 164, 174, 226

Keighley 226
Kelleway, Charlie 225
Kelly, James 146
Kent County Cricket Club 25, 104,
    110, 112, 125, 126, 130, 139, 146,
    149, 154, 155, 158–9, 162, 163,
    168, 173, 174, 200–1, 219, 221,
    222, 223
Kermode, Alex 150
Kilburn, J. M. 15, 25, 256
Kilner, Roy 194–5, 212, 215–16, 217,
    227, 239–40, 250–1, 252, 255,
    256, 257, 268, 279, 290
King, Bart 104
Kinnaird, Lord Alfred 44–5
Kinneir, Septimus 190
Kirkheaton 2, 5–6, 7, 18, 19, 20, 21,
    22, 23, 29, 51, 59, 60, 76, 94, 103,
    111, 122, 127, 154, 155, 164, 189,
    198, 284
Kirkheaton Cricket Club 21, 61, 64, 66,
    68, 69, 197, 239, 286, 294
Kirkheaton Seconds 21, 61
Kirkstall Cricket Club 70
Kortright, Charles 29
Kruger, Paul 84
Kumble, Anil 278

Lahore Tournament 279
Laisterdyke Cricket Club 221
Lancashire County Cricket Club 33,
    34, 42, 46, 47, 52, 56, 58, 78,

81, 88, 95, 100, 108, 125, 127,
137, 140–1, 149, 150, 151, 154,
155, 162, 168, 170, 172–3, 176–7,
182–3, 186–8, 194, 195–6, 224,
234, 235, 251, 252, 254–5
Lancashire League 58, 165, 169, 191,
233, 234, 244, 250, 258, 294
Lancaster, Willie 46
Lascelles Hall Cricket Club 21, 22, 40,
60, 160, 296
Last of the Summer Wine 6
Laver, Frank 133, 148, 175
Leach, Jack 122
Lee, Fred 27
Leeds Cricket Club 47, 49
Leeds District 52
Leeds Grammar School 285
Leeds Mercury 189, 240, 274, 275, 279,
284
Lees, Walter 54, 152
Leese, Arnold 232
Leicestershire County Cricket Club 75,
109, 125, 126, 137, 149, 154, 161,
162, 168, 169, 176, 187, 200, 229,
239, 256, 285
Leverhulme, Lord 81
Leveson Gower, H. D. G., 'Shrimp' 29,
54, 152, 157, 178, 201, 206, 265,
272
Leyland, Maurice 257, 259, 260, 280
Lilley, Dick 114, 118, 119–20, 121, 144,
147, 175
Llewellyn, Charlie 85
Lockwood, Abe 39
Lockwood, Bill 119
Lockwood, Dickie 22
Lockwood, Ephraim 21, 40
Lohmann, George 32, 82, 83
London Opinion 32, 159
Lord Londesborough's XI 17
Lord Sheffield's XI 48
Lumb Cup 22
Lupton, Major Arthur William 240,
244, 260–1

Macartney, Charlie 175, 265, 267
Macaulay, George 93, 249, 250, 252,
256, 257–9, 261, 284
MacLaren, Archie 76, 78, 88, 111, 112,
114, 116, 117, 140–1, 148, 156,
176, 183, 287
MacLeod, Ken 188
Mailey, Arthur 225–6, 265, 267, 268
Makepeace, Harry 255
Manchester Guardian 250
Mann, Frank 254
Marsden Moor Tragedy 12
Marshall, Howard 289
Marylebone Cricket Club (MCC) 68,
81, 94, 105, 112, 140, 144, 183,
196–7, 207, 230, 236, 257, 260,
285
Australia tour (1903–4) 206
Australia tour (1907–8) 164–6, 206
Australia tour (1911–12) 189–93
Australia tour (1920–1) 224–6, 230,
237–8
Australia tour (1924–5) 231
Australia tour (1928–9) 271
Caribbean tour (1929–30) 270–2
India tour (1926–7) 280
South Africa tour (1898–9) 82–5
South Africa tour (1905–6) 152–3,
164, 206, 208, 209
South Africa tour (1910–11) 178–80,
206
South Africa tour (1913–14) 204–6
South Africa tour (1927–8) 242
Yorkshire, games against 23–4, 27,
71–2, 75, 109, 123, 156–7, 173,
187, 201, 210, 217, 270, 294
McCabe, Stan 292
McCleish, William 47
McDonald, Ted 225, 247, 250
Mercer, John 280
Micklefield Disaster Fund 52
Middlesbrough Cricket Club 45–6,
113, 169
Middlesex County Cricket Club 26,
33, 56, 76, 77, 80, 87, 98, 105, 109,
125, 130, 135, 137, 138, 139, 141,
153–4, 161, 167, 168, 173, 182,
191, 209, 211, 218, 222, 224, 252,
254–60, 263, 276
Milligan, Frank 50, 55, 70, 83, 85, 100,
112–13
Mold, Arthur 33
Moon, Leonard 152

Moorhouse, Bobby 39, 40, 49, 87–8, 281, 290
Moorhouse, Robert 29
Morton, Arthur 211
Mosey, Don 10
Mosley, Oswald 231
Mounsey, Joe 281
Murdoch, W. L. 72–3
Myers, Hubert 140, 152

Narayan, Sir Nripendra 276
Nayudu, C. K. 277–8
Newnham, Captain A. H. 30, 31
New South Wales 134, 192, 209, 227
Newstead, Jack 169, 170
New Zealand 271
Noble, Monty 4, 89, 104, 105, 116, 121, 122, 132, 145, 147, 148, 173, 174, 175
North Eastern Counties 42
Northamptonshire County Cricket Club 168, 171, 172, 182, 210, 218, 220–1, 249
North of England 42
Norwood, Dr Cyril 285
Nottinghamshire County Cricket Club 13, 28, 42, 81, 88, 90, 103–4, 109, 125, 126, 151, 163–4, 169, 174, 186, 195, 196, 224, 263, 267, 269, 290, 295
Nottinghamshire Colts 28, 48, 71
Nourse, Dave 153

O'Connor, Jack 271
Old Brown Cow Inn 18, 19, 21
Oldroyd, Edgar 195, 233, 251
Otley Cricket Club 213

Palairet, Lionel 110
Pardon, Sydney 158, 178, 258, 259, 260
Parker, Charlie 174
Parkin, Cec 234, 255
Parsees 278
Parsons, Jack 274, 277, 280
Patiala, India 16, 275–80
Peate, Ted 26–7, 56, 58, 80, 198, 258
Peel, Bobby 27, 30, 33, 46, 50, 51, 52, 53, 56–8, 69, 70, 73, 76, 83, 89, 198, 258

People's Journal 44
Perthshire Cricket Club 37–8, 43–7, 290–2
Plimpton, George 32–3
Poidevin, Les 141
Ponsonby-Fane, Sir Spencer 81–2
Press Association 242
Preston, Joe 27
Procter, Mike 295
Pudsey Britannia 28, 49
Pullin, A. W. 202–3, 229, 296

Quadrangular Tournament 277–8, 279
Queensland Cricket Club 190, 296

Radcliffe, Everard 182, 184, 185, 193
Ramprakash, Mark 174
Ramsbottom Cricket Club 250
Ranjitsinhji, Prince 13, 73–4, 76, 77, 78, 89, 96, 114, 126, 129, 154, 163, 275
Rastrick Seconds 21
Red Rum 246
Reeves, Bill 256
Relf, Albert 92, 130, 132, 152
Rhode, Alfred 176
Rhodes, Cecil 84
Rhodes, Hollin 59–60, 93–4
Rhodes, Muriel 123, 197, 198, 266, 295
Rhodes, Sarah 12, 18, 94, 136, 189, 214, 234, 240–1, 266, 295
Rhodes, Wilfred 1, 2, 3–4, 5
    anxiety 92
    Barn legend (development of bowling style through winter practice in) 7, 8, 65–6, 73
    batting, enjoyment of 123–4
    batting stance, adopts two-eyed 245, 247–8, 288
    batting, studies psychology of 219
    birth 6, 59–60
    bowling action 7, 8, 60–1, 65–6, 73, 219
    character 15, 63, 101, 175, 188–9, 198–9
    Chickenley, plays for 213
    childhood 59–60
    County Championship (1898) 71–5, 76, 79, 80, 86

Rhodes, Wilfred *continued*
County Championship (1899) 86–9, 90
County Championship (1900) 95–9
County Championship (1901) 109–13
County Championship (1902) 112, 113
County Championship (1903) 123, 125–7, 129
County Championship (1904) 136–8, 139, 140
County Championship (1905) 149, 150, 151–2
County Championship (1906) 157–8
County Championship (1907) 161, 162–3
County Championship (1908) 167, 168–9, 170, 171
County Championship (1909) 171–2, 174, 176–7
County Championship (1910) 180–1, 184, 185
County Championship (1911) 187–9
County Championship (1912) 196
County Championship (1913) 200
County Championship (1914) 211–13
County Championship (1919) 215–16, 217, 218, 219–20, 222
County Championship (1920) 223, 224
County Championship (1921) 224
County Championship (1922) 249, 251–2, 263, 264
County Championship (1923) 264
County Championship (1924) 254–5, 264
County Championship (1925) 264
County Championship (1926) 264–5
County Championship (1929) 269
death 295
doubles 10, 14, 52, 129, 137, 181, 223, 264, 268
Edison, admiration for 59, 65, 130
England career 89–90, 111–12, 114–23, 129–31, 132, 133, 134, 135–6, 144–5, 146, 147, 148, 149, 163, 164–6, 174–5, 176, 178–81, 189–92, 193, 195, 196,
197, 204, 205, 206, 207, 208, 210, 224–5, 226, 247–9, 265–9, 270–3
eyesight deteriorates 3–4, 292–3
father's death 176, 187
Galashiels Cricket Club 62–4, 66–8
Haigh and 128, 227
Harrow coach 285–90
Haslingden player 233–4
Hawke and 70, 71, 72, 75, 86, 95–6, 109, 123, 124, 138, 149, 168, 169, 184, 188 Herbert and 69, 107, 108
Hollin death and 93–4
India, plays cricket in 16, 274–81
Kirkheaton player 61–2, 64, 294
Kirkheaton Seconds and 61
knowledge of the game 15, 269–70
last wicket in first-class cricket 272–3
marries 94
perfection of simple methods 75
Perthshire player 290–2
photography and 214
plate-laying gang job 64, 69, 76
popularity with ordinary supporters 188–9
Quadrangular Tournament 277–8
Slaithwaite trial 68
spin bowler, decides to become 64–5
stamina 54
Test debut (1899) 89–90
Toone and 178, 231, 232–3, 234–5, 236, 237, 238–9, 240–1, 242–3, 244
touring and 206, 207, 208, 210
Warwickshire, almost becomes player for 68
winter breaks 197–9
Yorkshire Colts, first game for 69
Yorkshire, first games for 71–3
Yorkshire Post, ghost-written column for 292
Yorkshire XI and Bedale and District XVIII trial match 71
Richards, Barry 295
Richardson, Arthur 267
Richardson, Tom 29, 30, 77
Ringrose, Billy 140, 158, 227

Robinson, Emmott 140, 222, 249–51, 256, 257, 259, 260, 268, 280
Root, Fred 264
Rossie Priory 44
Royal Air Force 214
Royal Flying Corps 214
Royal High School 67

Sahib, Jam 74, 96, 154
Sandham, Andy 271
Saunders, Jack 118–19
Scarborough Cricket Festival 17–18, 38, 90, 156, 178, 211–12, 222–3, 227, 245–6, 270
Scarborough Visitors 17
Schwarz, Reggie 153
Scottish County Championship 43
Scottish Referee 44, 45, 46
Scottish Roses Match 43
Selkirk Cricket Club 62, 63, 67
Sellers, Brian 5, 15, 185
Sewell, Edward 229
Shaw, Arthur 62
Shaw, Fred 279
Shaw, James 53
Sheffield Daily Telegraph 69, 256–7
Sheffield Evening Telegraph 46
Sheffield United Cricket Club 69
Sherwell, Percy 153
Shrewsbury, Arthur 92
Simpson-Hayward, George 179
Sinclair, Jimmy 85
Singh, Bhupinder 16
Singh, Harbhajan 278
Singh, Maharajah of Patiala, Rajendra 16, 275–6
six-ball over 95
Slaithwaite 68
Smith, Ernest 33, 88, 96, 152, 156
Smith, Razor 172, 181, 182
Smith, Sydney 182
Sobers, Garry 1, 3, 295
Somerset County Cricket Club 9, 23, 32, 48–9, 55, 73, 74–5, 81, 86, 110, 113, 126, 149, 155, 156, 157, 162, 171, 193, 194, 201, 210, 212, 264, 265
South Africa (national cricket team) 16, 113, 157, 163, 210, 291–2

MCC/England tour of South Africa (1898–9) and 82–5
MCC/England tour of South Africa (1905–6) and 152–3, 164, 206, 208, 209
MCC/England tour of South Africa (1910–11) and 178–80, 190, 206
MCC/England tour of South Africa (1913–14) and 204–7
MCC/England tour of South Africa (1927–8) and 242, 243
tour of England (1907) 163
tour of England/Triangular Tournament (1912) 83, 113, 195–7
tour of England (1929) and 174
Spofforth, Frederick 37
Spooner, Reggie 141, 148, 150, 156–7
Sporting Times 26
Staffordshire County Cricket Club 23
Stanyforth, Ronald 271
Starc, Mitchell 106
Steel, Allan 75
Steele, David 79
Stephenson, Franklyn 295
Stevens, Greville 252–3, 256
Stirlingshire Cricket Club 43, 45
Stoddart, A. E. 137
Stoddart, Andrew 76, 77, 92
Stokes, Ben 122
Strand Magazine 75, 156
Strathmore Cricket Club 45
Stubbins, Jim 65
Studd, Charles 26
Sugg, Frank 42
Sunday Chronicle 43
Surrey County Cricket Club 27, 29, 32, 40, 54, 74–5, 77, 79–80, 88, 98, 126–7, 130, 138, 149–50, 168, 169, 170, 172, 181, 196, 211, 224, 255
Sussex County Cricket Club 24, 95, 96, 103, 117, 125, 154, 173, 186, 187, 201, 211–12, 231, 263, 289
Sutcliffe, Herbert 80, 101–2, 216, 217, 219, 220–1, 227, 241, 242–4, 249, 250–1, 259, 267, 269
Swanton, E. W. 121
swing bowling ('swerve') 8–10, 14, 101–13, 115, 116, 124, 126,

127, 130, 135, 172–3, 182, 190, 195, 220, 221, 222, 249, 261, 264, 294

Tarrant, Frank 276, 280
Tate, Fred 83, 117–19, 158, 271
Tate, Maurice 280
Taylor, Herbie 204–5
Taylor, Tom 137
Tennyson, Lord and Lady 208
Tetlow, John 62
Thewlis, John 21
Thoms, Bob 73
Thornton, C. I. 90
Thornton, Charles 'Bun' 17–18
Toone, Frederick 178, 228–44, 259, 262
Townsend, Charlie 142
Transvaal 83–5
Trescothick, Marcus 92
Trollope, Arthur 216
Trott, Albert 72, 73, 83, 85, 87, 92, 104, 105, 131
Trott, Jonathan 92
Trueman, Fred 5, 15, 246
Trumble, Hugh 118, 121, 122, 135
Trumper, Victor 13, 89, 115, 116, 121, 133, 135–6, 145, 147, 148, 190, 192
Tunnicliffe, John 28, 29, 30, 33, 34, 42, 51, 52, 55, 80, 82, 111, 113, 125, 127, 152, 163, 164, 168, 184, 188, 219, 227, 245, 281
Turner, Charles 'the Terror' 202
Tyldesley, Dick 255
Tyldesley, Johnny 85, 114, 115, 130, 141, 146, 148, 150, 208

Uddingston Cricket Club 43
Ulyett, George 34, 37
United Services 226

Verity, Hedley 7, 93, 101, 234, 269, 284
Victoria Cricket Club 131, 190
Voce, Bill 271
Vogler, Bert 153, 157, 204

Waddington, Abe 217, 221, 222, 224, 238, 249, 250, 252–3, 256, 257, 258–60

Wade, Saul 27
Wainwright, Ted 24, 30, 31, 33, 50, 76, 77, 78, 79, 88, 92, 97, 104, 130, 290
Wall, Tim 272
Ward, Fred 123
Wardall, Tom 29
Wardle, Johnny 5
Warner, Sir Pelham 6, 15, 32, 81, 83, 87, 94, 103, 106–7, 129, 132, 133, 134–5, 152, 167, 189–90, 206, 207, 208, 218, 249, 257–8
Warren, Arnold 146, 147
Warwickshire County Cricket Club 34, 39, 40, 48, 50–1, 68, 125, 138, 151, 163, 182, 190, 218, 223, 249, 263, 269, 271, 274
Washbrook, Cyril 191
Washington, Irving 116, 125, 137, 194–5
Wass, Tom 109
Watsonians 63
Wells, William 182
Western Province 84, 152
West of Scotland 45
West, Peter 4
West Riding Regiment 214
White, Sir Archibald 193, 194
White, Gordon 153
Whitley Beaumont estate 18
Wilson, Benny 169, 195, 233, 288
Wilson, Clem 83
Wilson, Geoffrey 245, 248–9, 251–5, 257, 258, 260
Wilson, Rockley 87, 224, 227, 281–2
Wisden 9, 42, 108, 126, 146, 158, 169, 173, 178, 258, 260
Woodfull, Bill 265, 267
Woods, Sammy 9, 48–9, 99, 110
Woolley, Frank 13, 192, 196, 201, 219, 237, 267
Worcestershire County Cricket Club 95, 97–8, 110, 125, 127, 130, 138, 144, 148, 149, 151, 162, 163, 179, 182, 186, 193
Wormald, Alex 70–1
Worrall, Jack 89
Worsley, Captain William 244
Wostinholm, Joseph 24, 228, 239

Wright, Walter 103–4
Wyatt, Bob 272
Wynyard, Teddy 152, 157, 179

Yeadon Cricket Club 213
Yorkshire and Lancashire Association
209
Yorkshire Colts 28, 46, 48, 69, 71
Yorkshire County Cricket Club:
County Championship (1883) 26–7
County Championship (1887) 27
County Championship (1889) 22–3,
24–5, 27
County Championship (1890) 23
County Championship (1891) 23
County Championship (1892) 23–4,
29
County Championship (1894) 30–2
County Championship (1895) 33–4
County Championship (1896)
48–52, 54
County Championship (1897) 53,
54–8
County Championship (1898) 71–5,
76, 78–81, 86
County Championship (1899) 86–7,
88–9, 90–1
County Championship (1900)
94–100
County Championship (1901) 102–4,
108–11
County Championship (1902) 112–
13, 125
County Championship (1903) 123–9
County Championship (1904)
136–42
County Championship (1905)
149–52
County Championship (1906)
153–60
County Championship (1907) 161–4

County Championship (1908) 166–71
County Championship (1909) 171–3
County Championship (1910) 176–8,
180–3
County Championship (1911) 186–9
County Championship (1912) 193–5
County Championship (1913) 200–1
County Championship (1914) 206,
210–12
County Championship (1919)
215–24
County Championship (1920) 235–7,
252–3
County Championship (1921) 247
County Championship (1922) 249–
52, 263
County Championship (1923) 263–4
County Championship (1924) 254–
60, 264
County Championship (1925) 260,
264–5
County Championship (1926) 260,
264–5
County Championship (1927) 260
County Championship (1928) 242
County Championship (1929) 269
County Championship (1930) 272–3
County Championship (1931) 273
dour, surly, cautious team,
transformation into 15, 245–62
Hawke and see Hawke, Lord
membership numbers 226, 229
opponents/special matches see
individual opponent name
players see individual player name
Toone and administration of 228–44
winter pay 81–2, 197, 234
Yorkshire Evening Post 67, 120, 170, 187,
191, 203, 257, 292

Zulch, Billy 92